Baltic Socialism Remembered

What does it mean to tell a life story?

How is one's memory of communism shaped by family, profession, generation, and religion?

Do post-communist Baltic states embrace similar memories?

The Baltic states represent not only a geographical but also a mnemonic region. The mental maps of people who live on this territory are shaped by memories of Soviet socialism. Baltic Socialism Remembered captures the workings of the memory of diverse groups of people who inhabit the region: teachers, officials, young people, women, and believers. It comes as no surprise that their memories do not overlap, but often contradict to other groups and to official narratives. Baltic Socialism Remembered is a rare attempt to engage with the mnemonic worlds of social groups and individuals rather than with memory politics and monumental history. The contributors try to chart unpredictable ways in which public and national memory affect individual memory, and vice versa. Understanding complexity and diversity of memory workings in such compact region as the Baltic states will enable a more nuanced policy-making.

This book was originally published as a special issue of *Journal of Baltic Studies*.

Ene Kõresaar is an Associate Professor of Ethnology at the University of Tartu, Estonia. Her main research fields are memory of World War II and socialism, oral history, and life writing; she has also published on commemorative journalism and museums. She has edited and co-authored several books on cultural memory and life stories with a particular focus on post-communist developments.

T0347384

Baltic Socialism Remembered

Memory and Life Story Since 1989

Edited by
Ene Kõresaar

Routledge
Taylor & Francis Group

LONDON AND NEW YORK

First published 2018 by Routledge

2 Park Square, Milton Park, Abingdon, Oxfordshire OX14 4RN
52 Vanderbilt Avenue, New York, NY 10017

Routledge is an imprint of the Taylor & Francis Group, an informa business

First issued in paperback 2019

British Library Cataloguing in Publication Data
A catalogue record for this book is available from the British Library

ISBN13: 978-1-138-56005-5 (hbk)
ISBN13: 978-0-367-89217-3 (pbk)

Typeset in Myriad pro
by diacriTech, Chennai

Publisher's Note
The publisher accepts responsibility for any inconsistencies that may have arisen during the conversion of this book from journal articles to book chapters, namely the possible inclusion of journal terminology.

Disclaimer
Every effort has been made to contact copyright holders for their permission to reprint material in this book. The publishers would be grateful to hear from any copyright holder who is not here acknowledged and will undertake to rectify any errors or omissions in future editions of this book.

Contents

CONTENTS

Citation Information

The chapters in this book were originally published in the *Journal of Baltic Studies*, volume 47, issue 4 (December 2016). When citing this material, please use the original page numbering for each article, as follows:

Chapter 1
Life story as cultural memory: making and mediating Baltic socialism since 1989.
In memoriam: Aili Aarelaid-Tart
Ene Kõresaar
Journal of Baltic Studies, volume 47, issue 4 (December 2016) pp. 431–450

Chapter 2
Re-educating teachers: ways and consequences of Sovietization in Estonia and Latvia (1940–1960) from the biographical perspective
Aigi Rahi-Tamm and Irēna Saleniece
Journal of Baltic Studies, volume 47, issue 4 (December 2016) pp. 451–472

Chapter 3
Points of memory in the narrative of a 'Mnemonic Warrior': gender, displacement, and the anti-Soviet war of resistance in Lithuania
Dovilė Budrytė
Journal of Baltic Studies, volume 47, issue 4 (December 2016) pp. 473–496

Chapter 4
Memory of socialism and the Russian Orthodox believers in Estonia
Irina Paert
Journal of Baltic Studies, volume 47, issue 4 (December 2016) pp. 497–512

Chapter 5
The construction of continuous self in the life stories of former Soviet officials in Lithuania
Irēna Šutinienė
Journal of Baltic Studies, volume 47, issue 4 (December 2016) pp. 513–536

Chapter 6

Between improvisation and inevitability: former Latvian officials' memoirs of the Soviet era
Mārtiņš Kaprāns
Journal of Baltic Studies, volume 47, issue 4 (December 2016) pp. 537–556

Chapter 7

We were the children of a romantic era: nostalgia and the nonideological everyday through the perspective of a 'Silent Generation'
Kirsti Jõesalu
Journal of Baltic Studies, volume 47, issue 4 (December 2016) pp. 557–578

For any permission-related enquiries please visit:
http://www.tandfonline.com/page/help/permissions

Notes on Contributors

Dovilė Budrytė is a Professor of Political Science at Georgia Gwinnett College, USA. Her areas of interest are historical memory, gender studies, and nationalism. Her areas of interest include gender studies, trauma and memory in international relations and nationalism.

Kirsti Jõesalu is a researcher at the University of Tartu, Estonia. Her main fields of research are the social memory of socialism, study of socialist everyday life, and oral history. Her PhD thesis was on remembering 'mature socialism' in post–Soviet Estonia. She has published in several journals on remembering socialism and on oral history.

Mārtiņš Kaprāns is a researcher at the Institute of Philosophy and Sociology, University of Latvia, Latvia. His current research interests are focused on transnational remembering, historical politics in postcommunist countries, and representation of the past in social networking sites.

Ene Kõresaar is an Associate Professor of Ethnology at the University of Tartu, Estonia. Her main research fields are memory of World War II and socialism, oral history, and life writing; she has also published on commemorative journalism and museums. She has edited and co-authored several books on cultural memory and life stories with a particular focus on postcommunist developments.

Irina Paert is a Senior Researcher in the Department of Theology at the University of Tartu, Estonia. She specializes in Russian religious studies, focusing particularly on the history and culture of Old Believers and the Russian Orthodox Church.

Aigi Rahi-Tamm is an Associate Professor and Head of Archival Studies at the University of Tartu, Estonia. Her main field of research is twentieth-century Estonian history and Soviet history with particular emphasis on the history of mass violence under Soviet and Nazi Germany regimes.

Irēna Saleniece is a Professor of History and Head of Oral History Centre at Daugavpils University, Latvia. Her main research interests include schools policy in Latvia, Sovietization and Stalinism, identity of the people of the Eastern Latvia, and oral history as historical source. She has published two monographs and about sixty research articles on the topics.

NOTES ON CONTRIBUTORS

Irēna Šutinienė works as a researcher in the Institute of Sociology at the Lithuanian Social Research Centre. Her areas of interest include social memory, national and ethnic identity, and biographical research.

Life story as cultural memory: making and mediating Baltic socialism since 1989
In memoriam: Aili Aarelaid-Tart

Ene Kõresaar

Institute of Cultural Research and Arts, University of Tartu, Tartu, Estonia

ABSTRACT
This article creates a conceptual and methodological framework for reading case studies. First, it conceptualizes life story and oral history as medium of memory of the twentieth century. Second, it demonstrates how individual, social, and political formats and dimensions of memory intersect in remembering the Baltic socialism. Third, it shows how in a common attempt to remember the socialist past, groups and individuals encounter considerable differences of temporal horizon as well as differences in attributing importance to experiences and events.

Introduction

Cultural researchers characterize the mutual relationships of the Baltic states and cultures as those of 'distant relatives' (Undusk 2007, 12). Starting in the 2000s, more research has focused on the phenomenon of the Baltic memory (Mihkelev and Kalnačs 2007; Baliutytė and Mitaitė 2011). The Baltic memory is understood as the shared phenomenon of Estonian, Latvian, and Lithuanian memories and includes the common historical colonial experience of the nineteenth and twentieth centuries, especially the Soviet period (Jurgutienė 2007, 20, 31). Researchers emphasize that despite different patterns of development until the eighteenth century, incorporation into Tsarist Russia and especially the Soviet occupation and annexation of the Baltic states in 1940 has made these countries much more similar (27). Indeed, Estonian literary scholar Jaan Undusk even goes so far as to view the Molotov–Ribbentrop Pact and the later incorporation of the Baltic states into the USSR as the decisive factor in the birth of the Baltic memory (Undusk 2007, 16). Another anchoring moment for Baltic memory is the revolutionary movements of the late 1980s and early 1990s, symbolized by the Baltic Way in 1989 (Jurgutienė 2007, 28). The central question of the Baltic memory has now become how remembering in the post-1989 Baltic states compares with the remembered experience of the post-1940 Soviet era states. In other words, the new question is one of the Baltics as a mnemonic region (Wawrzyniak and Pakier 2013, 258) as related to the memory of Soviet socialism.

The problem related with the research of regional mnemonic cultures is to find '"usable" research traditions applicable to studying regional memories' (Wawrzyniak and Pakier 2013, 257). The response of this thematic volume to this problem concerning usable research traditions is to bring together Baltic life stories and oral history researchers to reflect on memory work articulated in life stories, memoires, and oral history interviews as mediums of memory. Luca and Kurvet-Käosaar (2013) observe that little attention has been paid to life writing and the way post-1989 changes are reflected in memoires, diaries, auto/biographies from or about the countries belonging to the Soviet Union and the former Eastern bloc countries. In a recent special issue on post-1989 life writing in eastern Europe, Luca and Kurvet-Käosaar agitate 'to open up a dialogue on the critical implications of life writing published or written after 1989 in the former eastern European countries' (3). This special volume contributes to it in two ways. First, it conceptualizes more closely the relationship between life story, oral history, and memory research. Second, it analyzes the dynamics of the post-1989 autobiographic interpretations from the socialist period, asking about the characteristics of the culture of autobiographical remembering in the Baltic countries and its ethnic, social, and cultural differences.

Life story as a medium of memory

The contributions published in this volume are concerned with the relationship of autobiographical and cultural aspects of memory while posing the question how life lived under socialism is remembered in the post-communist world. Life story treatments vary from the realistic (Rahi-Tamm & Saleniece) and sociological and social–psychological (Kaprāns, Šutinienė) to a more cultural approach (Budrytė, Jõesalu, Paert). The question of the 'individual and collective formats' (Assmann 2010, 40–44) of remembering, that is, the question what the study of life stories could contribute to collective memory research is implicitly included in every case study, although only a few authors refer explicitly to the relationship between life stories and memory studies. Thus, the relationship between memory studies and the study of life stories and oral history needs to be reconsidered.

The discrepancy between those who study 'individual' and 'collective' memories has posed an epistemological challenge to memory studies from the outset (Olick 1999, 2007, 9–11). Jeffrey Olick, when inspecting the field of memory studies in 1990s, saw in this challenge a conflict of different perceptions of culture: the individualistic 'collected memory,' as a category of meanings contained in human minds, versus the holistic 'collective memory,' understood as patterns of publicly available symbols (Olick 1999, 336). Indeed, until very recently, the relationships between memory studies and the study of life story and oral history were rather irreciprocal. From an oral history perspective, Hamilton and Shopes (2008, vii–x) recently observed that the interdisciplinary scholarship on (historical) memory rarely engage with oral history or examine how oral history reflects and molds collective memory. Like Olick, they view memory studies as differentiated from oral history by their more abstract approach, which asks how broader cultural memory is created, circulated, mediated, and received, while oral history concentrates on how individuals produce meaning from their memoirs. While one may agree that the work on autobiographical remembering in oral history is rarely included in studies on cultural and collective memory, the research on oral history and life stories has been increasingly engaged with questions how individual memory coincides with or rebuts shared or collective memory, how people use memory stories to position themselves in the present, and how present experiences shape interpretations of the past (Abrams 2010, 2014). In this process, oral historians and life story researchers have made use of concepts established in cultural memory studies (Heimo 2011) as well as developed their own concepts to identify links between the individual and the collective in oral history interviews (Abrams 2014). At the same time, debates among historians place increasing importance on the way historical remembrance is embedded in individual minds (Crane 1997; Fulbrook 2014). Trauma studies and eyewitness-related studies are among the areas in which the complementary understanding of individual and collective remembering has gained ground, where collective memory is perceived as the social articulation of individual experience and vice versa (Fulbrook 2014, 73; Rüsen 2006, 68). Nevertheless, the question about the contribution of the individual occasionally arises in collective memory studies (Crane 1997; Kansteiner 2010). Furthermore, the first attempts have been made within Baltic studies to address the issues of pluralism in collective memory in a complementary fashion (Pettai 2011) without falling into the trap of the collective vs. collected memory in this area of study (Wawrzyniak and Pakier 2013, 271). Another fruitful way to avoid this trap is to more closely connect the practice of oral history and life stories research with contemporary ideas of how memory works as social and cultural phenomenon (Hamilton and Shopes 2008). The mediation perspective has proved to be useful in the observation of connections and points of contact for the different treatments of memory (Võsu, Kõresaar, and Kuutma 2008; Erll and Rigney 2009).

An abundance of literature exists in an attempt to define the genre of life stories or oral history. It is not the aim of this introduction to summarize this literature. To create a firmer link between life story research and memory studies, however, it is crucial to focus on the role of a life story in collective remembering: the role of life story on the construction and circulation of knowledge and versions of a common past in socio-cultural contexts. Astrid Erll suggests media and mediation can be understood 'as a kind of switchboard at work between the individual and collective dimensions of remembering' (Erll 2011a, 113). As Erll points out, the actual transition from a 'media phenomenon' to a 'medium of memory'

> Often rests on forms of institutionalization and always on the use, the functionalization of a medium as a medium of memory, by individuals, social groups and societies. Because media must be used as media of memory, the memory-making role must be attributed to them by specific people, at a specific time and place. (Erll 2011a, 124)

Writing down one's life story or telling it to an interviewer during an oral history interview are ways for an eyewitness to do memory work. When renowned Latvian anthropologist Vieda Skultans started her medical anthropological fieldwork on neurasthenia in Latvia in 1990, she had to quickly abandon the academic area she found familiar. She began to find herself carried away by people's memories of the past: 'Eventually I let myself be carried by the narrative flow. In this way I found myself listening to accounts of events central to Latvian and, indeed, Soviet history' (Skultans 1998, xi). By this time, the process now referred to as the 'life story boom' had already begun. Stories of former deported persons and Gulag prisoners, which were closely connected with people's personal memories of the post-war partisan resistance, the Soviet and Nazi occupation, and the dissident movement in the Soviet period, encouraged the publication of an increasing number of similar stories. At the same time, the institutionalized collection of oral history and life stories began. In 1988, civic organi-zations in Lithuania started collecting memories (Šutinienė 2009, 153–155). In 1989, the Estonian Cultural–Historical Archives announced the first life story writing cam-paign – a method that became immensely popular over the following 20 years (Hinrikus and Kõresaar 2004). In 1992, the Institute of Philosophy and Sociology of the Latvian Academy of Sciences launched the Latvian National Oral History Project (http://www.dzivesstasts.lv; Bela 2009). These three national campaigns, their popu-larity, and the enormous success of published life stories with readers highlighted the increasing significance of autobiographical genres in post-communist societies for their presumed ability to transmit the 'true memory' of the past. Indeed, for some time, the life story was viewed in the same light as historiography (Kõresaar 2005, 20–25). To this day, life stories remain a popular genre, in which memories of the Soviet period are presented in several different mnemonic discourses (Aarelaid-Tart 2012).

Heinze (2011) argues that autobiography in the twentieth century has gained an instrumentalist role in the public sphere more than ever. It is unique to the twentieth century that social–political conditions change rapidly; the individual experience is increasingly related to the political sphere and one's life becomes an object of justification, legitimation, and debate. Legitimation and justification, Heinze maintains, is something that defines autobiographies that focus on the twentieth century experi-ence (5–8). As the articles in this volume argue, in post-1989 memory work to date, autobiographical storytelling can be understood as an act of internalization and externalization of memory regimes. Understanding life story and oral history as media of memory stresses the importance of life story as social-communicative self-expression in the framework of mnemocultural and historical political debates. A life story format is chosen consciously by autobiographers to argue socially, culturally, and politically and to take a stand on historical issues (18). One of the motives of life story telling as a sociocommunicative activity is to establish a common ground in cultural remembering – a shared memory. Moreover, the structure of autobiographical story-telling is rooted in politics as it is framed by social ideas and perceptions, historical remembering, and presentation of the past.

Life story as cultural memory

What kind of medium of memory is a life story? How does a life story mediate between individual and collective levels of memory? Most importantly – how is mediation of collective forms of memory visible in an autobiographical text?

Autobiographical memory is a dynamic process constructed 'on the basis of knowl-edge drawn from different memory structures' (Conway 1992, 169). The theory of cultural memory studies, from Halbwachs ([1925] 1952), Assmann (1988) to the more recent theorization of collective (Olick 1999) and cultural (Erll 2011a) memory, distin-guishes between collective or cultural memory of individual people operating within concrete sociocultural frameworks and collective/cultural memory which comes into being through interaction, communication, mediation, and institutionalization. In order to reestablish a link between the theories of cultural memory and early biogra-phical research, it is appropriate to refer to the German sociologist Peter Alheit's model of social memory, which is developed on the basis of the biographical method

(Alheit 1989). Alheit's model aims to illuminate how collective and individual remembering function in autobiographical narrating.[1]

Alheit's social memory model[2] combines both individual and collective levels of memory and has two interrelated dimensions: the proximate sphere of events and activities, which is close to experience, and the sphere of normative orientations and ideologies. Accordingly, autobiographically articulated social memory is differentiated between a remembering-schema and an interpretation-schema.

The remembering-schema is formed by individual and collective modes of knowledge, which organize themselves around the level of events and experience. On the lowest level are 'spontaneous biographical narratives,' the temporal dynamics of which are organized by activities and events. This lowest level is of particular importance to autobiographical memory. Those stories that are already beginning to organize themselves into a tradition are also structured according to remembering-schema. These are stories which are no longer close to the event and which already have an interpretive accretion (*lebensweltliches Deutungswissen*). Stable traditions, such as esthetic stylizations and genres, also belong to the remembering-schema. These various levels are integrated by the so-called strategic knowledge, the individual's ability to relate personal memories and stories to the collective.

By contrast, the interpretation schema is formed by relatively autonomous modes of processing social reality, which are no longer dependent on concrete events and experiences. Situated closest to the orientation of an individual's concrete activities is the practice of interpreting everyday life, that is, 'the theories of the everyday,' class- and stratum-specific orientations, interpretive patterns specific to a subculture or a milieu, which in turn influence the public sphere (mass media, political life). Institutionalized interpretation systems such as legal and educational systems, science, and religion, belong in the interpretation schema of 'social memory.'

According to Alheit, dominant knowledge and social counter-knowledge differ in respect to their relative degree of success, and in extent to which the two sides of social memory are related to one another. Specifically, dominant knowledge has a broad interpretative layer and relatively weak relationship to the level of action and experience. However, social counter-knowledge is closer to experience and action: it can have well-developed narrative cultures and everyday interpretation practices (e.g. social thematics), whereas organized or institutional interpretation systems are underdeveloped or even completely absent. To the extent that dominant knowledge is always available in the media and elsewhere in the public sphere, the interpretive layer of dominant knowledge influences not only what is remembered but also the practices by which it is interpreted. On the other hand, the differing epistemological profiles of social memory can be regrouped in society so that the experiential layer of counter-knowledge achieves the position of organized interpretation[3] (Alheit 1989, 145).

Of course, such a model is an ideal construct. According to Alheit, the various layers of social memory can be 'more porous, thicker or thinner' (Alheit 1989), but they all exert an influence on autobiographical remembering and shape the process by which biographical experience is formulated.

Alheit's social memory model presents a synchronistic view on one of the most central problems of memory researchers, that is, how individual memory becomes a part of a cultural memory and vice versa. In Alheit's model, different levels of collective memory operate simultaneously; individuals and group members have accepted cognitive and interpretative frames, which exert continuous influence on an individual's perception of reality and their actions.

In her recent works, Aleida Assmann has written extensively about differentiation between the collective formats of memory and their relation to individual memory. Relying on Halbwachs' classical concept of collective memory, and replying to the skeptics of collective memory, Assmann writes:

> Our personal memories include much more than what we, as individuals, have ourselves experienced. We have our share in the larger and more encompassing memory of the family, the neighborhood, the generation, the society, the state, and the culture we live in. These dimensions of memory, differing in scope and range, overlap and intersect within the individual who shares and incorporates those memories in various ways. Humans acquire these memories not only via lived experience, but also via interacting, communicating, identifying, learning, and participating. [–] It is often not easy to clearly determine where one memory format ends and another begins as they cross over, overlap, interact, and even jar within the individual person. (Assmann 2010, 40)

Intersections of individual and collective memories

What is apparent in the study of memory, as emphasized within oral history and life stories research, is that collective versions of the past, official or informal, are interrelated with individual memories in complex ways.[4] The articles gathered in this thematic volume offer a complementary view on how the different formats or levels of collective memory act and interact in and with autobiographical remembering.

Generational memory

According to the authors, one of the key formats of collective memory in the post-1989 Baltic states was – and continues to be – generational memory. Following Mannheim's (1928) notion of the specificity and uniqueness of each generation's experience resulting in the different character of their respective collective memories, each generation differentiates itself between pre- and post-war cohorts thereby stressing the dependence of generational memory of social change.[5] Rahi-Tamm and Saleniece, Kaprāns, Šutinienė, and Paert (implicitly) focus on the stories of people born in the 1920s and 1930s whose memories have played a major part in establishing the image of socialism in post-1989 Baltic countries (Jõesalu and Kõresaar 2013). Rahi-Tamm and Saleniece characterize life trajectory as follows:

> Their life experience included the change in political regimes, World War II (WWII), the occupation of their native land, terror, etc. During their socialization they needed to revise their intellectual, moral and psychological 'baggage' to adapt to very different rules. Often, in order to build up their identity they had to ask themselves 'who we are,' 'who we were,' 'how we should do things in this community.' (in Rahi-Tamm & Saleniece)

Within this generational group, Kaprāns – in turn – differentiates between birth decades. Kaprāns considers that people born in the 1920s consciously experienced WWII and Stalinist repressions, while those born in the 1930s 'formed a generational core in the 1960s and more actively experienced the liberations of the Soviet regime' (in Kaprāns). Jõesalu juxtaposes the life stories of people born in the 1940s who were born and socialized in Soviet society and spent the greater part of their working lives there with the generations born in the 1920s and 1930s. Hence, Jõesalu concludes, the time of late socialism 'was a time of self-realization and family building. In society in general, it was also a time of economic prosperity (in 1960s), and the working and living environment of individuals improved as a result' (in Jõesalu). In comparison to older generations, who reached retirement age before or during the 1990s, the autobiographers born in the 1940s had to adapt to the new economic and working conditions as well as to the (sometimes radical) devaluation of the Soviet-era work experiences.

Gendered memory

Jõesalu's explicit focus on the experience of everyday life while analyzing the articulation of generational consciousness in life stories also questions the political, male-centered definition of generation and searches for gendered memories of a generation. According to Jõesalu, 'the silenced dimensions of experiences could create connectivity within a generation, in the same way as participation in demonstrations.' Indeed, taking into consideration that males have written the majority of Latvian post-Soviet autobiographies, as Kaprāns maintains, Jõesalu's argument on the public and the private generation is valid. Memory and gender are intertwined in multiple ways (Paletschek and Schraut 2008).

In addition to generation and gender, Jõesalu points to the inter-relatedness of gender and nationalism in the Baltic memory, most notably in terms of deportation and survival. Dovilė Budrytė, while drawing on the feminist practice of memory studies, emphasizes that the introduction of gender analysis implies sensitivity to social relations and thereby helps to understand better the power structures as rooted in everyday life. Budrytė's analysis of Aldona Vilutienė's life narrative and activity as a 'memory entrepreneur' sheds light on the hierarchies in post-Soviet Lithuanian narrative about the post-war partisan resistance.

Professional memory

Another important mnemonic dimension in Baltic life stories and oral histories is that of the professional community. Rahi-Tamm and Saleniece focus on the Sovietization of teachers and argue that being a teacher is the overarching theme underlying the understanding of the whole life story. Šutinienė, as well as Kaprāns, focuses on the stories of former Soviet officials and demonstrate how their status during the socialist times helps them in making sense of their life stories.

Family memory

Interestingly enough, the family is not highlighted in recent Baltic memory narratives, even if family is one of the fundamental sites of remembrance and a source of identity and experience (Erll 2011b). Families 'must be considered as archives where memories are made, re-made, transmitted between and among members, experiences take place, and identities are moulded and rooted' (Srigley and Zembrzycki 2009a, 10). Oral history and life stories research have added significant research on families as vehicles where family members link individual, familial, and collective narratives to tell their stories. Oral history and life stories also allow family members to rationalize complicated family memories, deal with myths, and address silenced topics in history (see an overview in Srigley and Zembrzycki 2009b). Drawing on the examples of

Estonian life stories, Jõesalu shows that the family in the life stories of the beginning of the twenty-first century is weakly portrayed and fails to form a separate topic for the writer. This portrayal of the family is distinct from life stories written in early 1990s soon after the restitution of independence in Estonia; the life stories of this era are distinguished for their long and detailed family memory. The first major distinction is that there is a trend of more general individualization in autobiographical remembrances in the twenty-first century. If in the 1990s, it was important for the autobiographers to manifest their relationship with a collective (ethnic group, generation), then in the new millennium the first person singular (I) of the story is brought to the fore.[6] The second major distinction is the generational differences in how and to what extent the family line is thematized in memories. Finally, Budrytė's discussion of the visibility and invisibility of memory and experience is also a significant distinction. This distinction is expecially significant considering Jõesalu's findings that the topic of family in life stories is predominantly revealed through political memory. According to Jõesalu, life story writers raise the topic of the life of previous generations and older family members in terms of Stalinist repressions and deportations, which make up the core of the Estonian post-1989 political memory. Therefore, it is the dominant political memory that actualizes the topic of ancestors in the stories, which are otherwise focused on work and everyday life.

Šutinienė refers to opposite processes than discussed by Jõesalu. She shows that blame and guilt, associated with family experience, may form a basis for a counter-memory. Narrating stigmatized family experiences, Šutinienė argues, results in many contradictions and contrasting arguments, both explicit and implicit in nature, toward the public mnemonic discourse. These narratives of stigmatized family experiences effectuated the marginalization of these experiences, while simultaneously trying to adjust to the public discourse.

Political memory

Both in Baltic societies immediate after the events of 1989 and today, autobiographical remembering, especially in the public space, is in close and inevitable dialogue with the political memory carried by the state and public institutions. As Šutinienė points out, alongside the versions of the past that were once dominant and the only versions reported, new versions of the past emerge that contest the dominant narrative. Even then, political memory preserves its tendency toward homogeneous unity and self-contained closure conveying a coherent message anchored in material and visual sites and performative actions (Assmann 2010, 43). As such, political memory reactivates individual memories and – in a life story – intermingles with other, more volatile formats of memory. On the other hand, political memory may be contradicted, challenged, and contested by the other forms of memory. The case studies in this volume offer examples for both by demonstrating how individual, social, and political formats and dimensions of memory intersect and form complex constellations in remembering socialism.

Cultural memory

Last but not least, individuals employ cultural narratives to maintain and insert themselves into collective myths (Passerini 2009; Portelli 1990). Aleida Assmann describes this as making use of the active memory of the canon – a dimension of cultural memory embodied in performances, readings, citations, and references:

> The active memory of the canon perpetuates what a society has consciously selected and maintains as salient and vital for a common orientation and a shared remembering; its institutions are the literary and visual canon, the school curricula, the museum, and the stage, along with holidays, shared customs, and remembrance days. (Assmann 2010, 43)

Cultural remembering – like any collective remembering – is a mediated activity (Wertsch 2002). James Wertsch maintains that a group has a common representation of the past because its members have knowledge of certain texts. The result of using common texts may be homogeneous, complementary, or competing ways of remembering. Through participation in the textual community, the individual has experience of the collection of texts even without having directly read them (25–27). According to Irina Paert, religion provides coherent narratives that allow individuals to assemble meaningful structures for their lives, both in the past and in the present. Religious traditions can serve as mnemotechnics; the cultural memory of a religious group may include tradition and rites, but it also includes history, historiography, memoirs, literary texts, and Mass. Paert also demonstrates that, in the case of Russian Orthodox believers in Estonia, religion provides specific religious mechanisms to cope with traumatic memories.

Like several other authors in this special volume, Paert shows how different formats of remembering intermingle and manifest simultaneously in a life story and oral history. In the example of Russian Orthodox believers, the religious memory is further supplemented by the Russian diaspora's cultural memory in the Baltics, which is defined not only by the language and shared culture, but also by a sense of social and cultural marginalization. Paert concludes that the relationship between the autobiographical and the institutional is complex; even if the two levels overlap they never coincide completely:

> The autobiographical memory often operates with the narrative schemes that can be found in religious teaching, while the individual experience of suffering and violent death can be incorporated into the 'institutional' memory as martyrdom. (in Paert)

All in all, the authors of this special issue share the theoretical premise that collective memory provides material, social, and mental structures within which the experience is embedded, constructed, interpreted, and mediated. Based on their specific case studies from all three Baltic countries, the authors show that complex relationships between the individual, social, national-political, and cultural remembering, indicating disruptions and continuities, are revealed at the level of autobiographical narration.

The Baltic memory of socialism

Mnemonic regions can be defined in many ways. A prominent, recent differentiation of European mnemonic communities defines eastern Europe as a separate political category referring to 'the half of the continent that in the twentieth century experienced double totalitarianism, wars, and the decades of communism and Soviet dependency' (Wawrzyniak and Pakier 2013, 258).

Within eastern and central Europe, multiple mnemonic 'meso-regions' have been identified. The Baltic states are found to be different than other post-socialist countries due to their 'unconditioned denial of their socialist past' while other countries remain more ambivalent (Troebst 2007, 24–25). Jurgutiené has been able to differentiate even more cultural profiles such as genetic linguistics, folklore, and (historical) cultural space expanded by cultural contacts (Jurgutiené 2007, 31–32). The aim of such differentiations has been to point out the intrinsic heterogeneity of regional memory cultures, their controversies, relationships of power, and identity articulated at the local level. Focusing on cultural remembering through the autobiographical prism will lend us additional 'mnemonic' lenses to demonstrate that in a common attempt to remember the socialist past, groups and individuals encounter considerable differences of temporal horizon, as well as differences in attributing importance to experiences and events.

'Baltic memory' does not refer to a region as a predefined, geographical category. Rather, 'region' is understood as a set of discursive mechanisms with their own history beyond national borders, resulting in regionally intelligible representations (Wawrzyniak and Pakier 2013, 271). A question about a mnemonic region is a question about discourses that mold the experience prospectively and the interpretation of the experience retrospectively.

Rahi-Tamm and Saleniece open this thematic issue with an article, which uses complementary analysis of institutional documents and the life stories of teachers to show how the Soviet model was applied to the Baltic education system since 1940 and how teachers as key actors were socialized into this system. The authors maintain that despite being forced to experiment with various approaches and seek compromises, the Soviet authorities' actions remained very similar across the country. The authors also argue that teachers' retrospective accounts from the post-Soviet era correspond with the patterns of experiences introduced by the Soviet authorities. On one hand, the unstable social norms caused by the changing times of 1940s and early 1950s are mirrored in autobiographical depictions of inconsistency and irregularity of personal actions. On the other hand, introducing a degree of stability beginning in the early 1950s is reflected retrospectively with subjective awareness of the educational system's working mechanisms. Thus, Rahi-Tamm and Saleniece's comparative case study effectively demonstrates that the social patterns of experience formed since 1940 in the Baltic countries directly relate to the narrative patterns of experience articulated in the post-1989 life stories and oral histories.

Another important aspect framing the Soviet experience, besides radical social transformations, is forced mass deportation and repression by the Soviet regime. In two major events in 1941 and 1949 alone, approximately 140,000 people were deported, as well as the number of sporadically deported people during the postwar Stalinist period (Rahi-Tamm 2009). Within the Soviet Baltic republics, the deportation experiences constituted a taboo topic. Furthermore, returning deportees were generally stigmatized by their own societies (Anepaio 2003).

The testimonies and memoires written by those who survived deportation to the gulag were instrumental in the construction of a new national memory and post-Soviet identity in these societies (Davoliūtė and Balkelis 2012, 10). They had a crucial role in dealing with cultural trauma (Aarelaid-Tart and Bennich-Björkman 2011, 13–15). However, several researchers note that although the genuine concern about the deported among public quickly gave way to the economic reform and development agenda (Anepaio 2002, 54–55), the stories of former deportees were eagerly adopted as national martyrologies (Davoliūtė and Balkelis 2012, 10, 23). Several commissions and special investigations were launched in late 1980s and early 1990s in the Baltic states (Pettai 2015, footnote 5) to compile the names of the deported, record evidence of repressive policies, and much more. A public discourse on 'Soviet genocide' emerged in all three countries and was institutionalized through state holidays, museums, and remembrance policies (Tamm 2013).

Budrytė's article deals with another, related discourse of the past that began at the end of the 1980s, namely the 'fighting and suffering' paradigm of remembering the post-war armed resistance to the Soviet regime. Together, they form a discourse of 'rupture' (Kõresaar 2004) or 'displacement' (Davoliūtė 2013 in Budrytė), which played a major role in the shaping of a narrative time and the comprehension of past and present reality in post-Soviet Baltic societies.[7]

'Suffering and resistance' as the official narrative of the past, elaborated upon during the 1990s, forms a point of reference and an object of discussion for the authors of this volume when analyzing the dynamics of continuity and discontinuity in autobiographical memory work. First, the authors draw out the dynamics from the turn of the millennium, which consists in the symbolic differentiation of everyday life experience as an alternative parallel to the public memory culture. Second, the authors show how, and in what aspects, interaction with the public discourse takes place; in which cases it enables remembering and agency, and in which it is a limiting factor. Third, the authors inquire about the boundaries and possibilities of group-specific remembering.

Using the example of the memory projects of the Russian diaspora in Estonia, Irina Paert shows that in the making of the 'Russian memory in the Baltic,' three significant periods – the Imperial era, the pre-WWII Republic of Estonia, and the post-Soviet era – are linked. Most of the semipublic mnemonic efforts explicitly exclude the Soviet past, thus adapting to the Estonian public discourse. Comparing the institutionalized cultural remembering among the Russian diaspora in Estonia with the autobiographical narratives of Russian Orthodox believers, Paert shows that, distinct from the life stories of Estonians, 'the annexation of Estonia by the Soviet Union was a landmark, but not a watershed' (in Paert). This observation corresponds to the earlier observations of life story researchers.

When comparing the life stories of Estonians and Estonian Russians from early 1990s, Tiiu Jaago has found that the biographical schema and assessments of different periods of their lives made by these two groups are contradictory. In the life stories of Estonians, the dominant features are positive childhoods in the 1930s, the horrible post-war period (rupture), negation of the late Soviet period, and a positive assessment of the restoration of national independence. In the life stories of Estonian Russians, childhood in the 1930s is viewed negatively (Stalinist repressions in Russia), followed by a positive period of finding work and home after the war, a positive description of 'mature socialism,' followed by a negative period of rupture with Estonian independence at the beginning of 1990s (Jaago 2004). In more recent research, 'an intense dissonance between the "bad" Estonian present and the "good" Soviet past' is identified as one of the major leitmotifs in the biographical narratives with Russian-speakers in Estonia (Aarelaid-Tart 2011, 93). Paert's study enables a detailed description of how Orthodox Russians remember the Soviet past. It offers a complementary case to Rahi-Tamm and Saleniece by showing that the memory offered by the Soviet public and institutional spaces was not necessarily conflictual with the religious memory of the Orthodox Church. Paert also discusses the Russian

Orthodox oral historical responses to the Estonian dominant narrative about Stalinist modes of violence as means of ethnic genocide. Additionally, Paert discusses more private discourses of remembering that are similar to those of Estonians (and Lithuanians and Latvians). According to Paert, biographical accounts of Estonian Orthodox Russians of their Soviet experience are comprised of multiple fragmented discourses, some more and others less positive, which also integrate meta-narratives of the mnemonic culture of the Russian diaspora.

Another intriguing aspect of the memory of socialism – which is significantly underrepresented in the academic literature – is that of one's (or one's family member's) participation in Stalinist repressions. Two cases are dealt with in this volume. Paert's analysis demonstrates that the participation in the Stalinist repressions remained a well-kept secret for people involved (where keeping the secret was possible). She argues that the memory of individuals participating in Soviet deportations is dualistic. On one hand, it involves the awareness of one's own experience of deportation. On the other hand, it is marked by one's inability to feel collective responsibility, as there were no such attempts at the state level or in terms of public memory during the Soviet era. Šutinienė, in turn, ascribes the inability to take a reflective stance to perpetrator experiences to one's unconditionally stigmatizing status in a national mnemonic community. The dualistic memory of taking part in Soviet deportations, Šutinienė argues, results in missing the opportunities to build up a more coherent *self*. Analyzing the story of a daughter of a man who participated in the execution of post-war Stalinist repressions, Šutinienė demonstrates that there is no other discursive space to maintain a positive image of her family than directly opposing the dominant anti-Soviet discourse and criticizing present society. Thus, Šutinienė forms a counter-narrative organized around the stigma of the narrator's father's experience. Šutinienė also argues that the lack of intention to reflect critically on the perpetrator experience in Soviet society can be seen as an effect of transitional justice applied in post-communist societies in general.

Budrytė discusses the inability of simplified public discourses to incorporate the many roles women had to fulfill during the post-war resistance war. Her analysis demonstrates that in these discourses women rarely emerge 'as complex historical figures influencing history and creating memory paradigms.' Focusing on oral testimonies, the gray areas of behavior, such as betrayal, can be revealed.

The hegemonic nature of the post-1989 public discourses about the Soviet past is criticized in the arguments of Šutinienė, Kaprāns, and Jõesalu in that the negative evaluation of the Soviet era experience provided limited options for a positive identification for an individual. Former Soviet officials are clearly a group publicly stigmatized after the post-communist turn in the Baltic societies. Šutinienė's and Kaprāns' focuses are based on Lithuanian and Latvian materials, respectively, on the memories of Soviet officials' life in the Soviet society and ask how positive identity can be achieved and expressed in their memoires. Jõesalu, however, concentrates on life stories written by women born in the 1940s, which she treats as a group that is discarded from public memory work because no public significance is attributed to them. All three authors contribute thoughts about how the memory of the late socialist everyday life becomes alternative knowledge, if not counter-knowledge, about the Soviet past in the Baltics, and whether or to what extent the memory regime that is dominant so far is compatible with this knowledge.

The authors of this thematic volume maintain that even in the 1990s, the experience of the later Soviet period was not a topic acknowledged frequently in the Baltic memory work. The Soviet era identity was felt as the takeover of the cultural 'other,' as something to be ashamed of. This identity was further facilitated by popular economic and sociopolitical discourses emphasizing the natural inability of a Soviet work experience and general mentality to adjust to the needs of the capitalist future. On the life story level, the late socialist experiences of withdrawal to the private sphere, as well as adjustment and gaining social competence, could neither fit to the acknowledged modes of narrative remembering with the 'people's story' in its focus, nor to the main ideology of remembrance culture focusing on the destruction of the national way of life and the invasion of foreign norms, rules, and habits (Kõresaar 2005, 212–213). The turn of the millennium seems to have brought gradual changes in social memory in all Baltic countries, with more stress on continuity of life and habitus, and with attempts to depoliticize everyday experience by presenting alternative, pragmatic, and nostalgic perspectives.

The retrospective de-ideologization (Jõesalu) is the most clearly exposed in memories when the ideologically significant 'other' is constructed to counterbalance one's own more ambivalent position. According to Kaprāns, a narrative strategy of constructing the communist elite as an alien group is a manner in which to establish positive identity in a life story. Kaprāns could identify this strategy not only in the memoires of Latvian ex-officials but also in those of intellectuals. The same strategy is also observed in life stories of other groups (Kõresaar 2001). Kaprāns concludes that '...a never-ending vertical of Soviet power provides everyone with an opportunity to relocate responsibility symbolically to imagined party, elite, or nomenklatura and present one's self as an executor rather than a decision maker' (in Kaprāns).

However, one's membership of the Communist Party was an unequivocally stigmatizing factor in a post-Soviet, post-socialist society and researchers' interest as to the ways of dealing with it retrospectively reaches back to the post-communist turn. Living with consciously cultivated double standards (Aarelaid-Tart 2003), or even as a person 'red outside and white inside' (Siemer 2002), serve as major leitmotifs in describing one's Soviet-era conformity. Kaprāns and Šutinienė list several arguments comprising the 'repertoire' of dealing with one's communist past: accepting privileges offered by the party (pragmatism), coercion (lacking agency), and entering the path of professionally successful people, among others. Šutinienė demonstrates that the connections between the political and professional sphere are complicated. The story of professionalism, for example, includes controversial images of dishonest noncommunists and highly skilled communist professionals. Kaprāns assumes that '[p]rofessionalism and personal achievement, as well as a realistic and self-confident approach to the system one has to live in, are virtues that might be accepted by a post-Soviet neoliberal society as fairly general characteristics of positive identity' (in Kaprāns). One might add, borrowing from the Estonian experience, that the tendency toward the narrative normalization of Communist Party membership coincides with the increase in the role of parties in local politics and as a result, indirectly with the system in which positions of local importance are appointed to supporters of political parties.[8] Hypothetically, we can see links between the changes in today's political culture and memory culture.

Highlighting professionalism, altruism, and solidarity by focusing on horizontal, predominantly work relationships is, as Šutinienė, Kaprāns, and Jõesalu demonstrate, a way to achieve positive identity in remembering socialism. The notion of 'working for the benefit of society' accompanied by a strong sense of professional identity, is a common theme not only in Baltic Soviet ex-officials' memoires, but also in teachers' stories analyzed by Rahi-Tamm and Saleniece and in oral histories of Orthodox Russians analyzed by Paert. Jõesalu, in turn, demonstrates that believing in a better world and dedication to professional working life may become cultural themes to form generational consciousness. Although not reduced to pride in one's Soviet origin, reminiscence of onetime ideals and belief in the future (cf. also Šutinienė) are characteristic of remembering socialism. Considering the importance of the professional sphere in shaping the socialist lifestyle (Roth 2004), it is only expected that work memory, which often takes the form of career biography on the individual level, is one of the dominant motifs of the social memory of socialism, at least in Eastern Europe.[9] Furthermore, Jõesalu points out that '[b]elieving in the future and making the world a better place is not only common for narrators from the eastern side of the Iron Curtain, but similar ideas can be found in the reminiscences of those who were active in the student movements of the 1960s in the West' (in Jõesalu). At the same time, Kaprāns reminds us that the existing subregional memory regimes still set limits for mnemonic patterns becoming the same. In the Latvian case (and this may be expanded to the Baltics in general), Kaprāns maintains that the anti-fascist ideas related to the memories of one's socialist-era political engagement, represented widely in east and central Europe (Mark 2010), would be interpreted as signs of support to the Soviet order, and would not be accepted as legitimate ideology.

Last but not least, this thematic issue contributes to researching the wave of nostalgia that has hit the former socialist bloc (Todorova and Cille 2010), by offering differentiated, detailed readings of articulations of nostalgia that sprouted in the second half of 1990s and became influential at the turn of the millennium. Paert distinguishes between the implicitly political, institution-centered nostalgia and the nonpolitical, age-specific nostalgia, and refers to the lack of the former among Orthodox Russians. Šutinienė and Jõesalu apply the critical concept of nostalgia, interpreting nostalgia as a counter-memory to the hegemonic discourse about the Soviet past. In particular, Šutinienė inserts nostalgia into the framework of post-Soviet marginalization and powerlessness. On the other hand, the authors emphasize the complicated and multifaceted nature of nostalgia, showing that one nostalgic practice may include several different nostalgias or even arguments opposing nostalgia. For example, according to Kaprāns, the nostalgia toward the 'good old Soviet times' simultaneously excludes such feelings: when searching support from the past to one's criticism of the present, Soviet legacy is interpreted as something impossible to get rid of. The case studies of this volume also demonstrate that the salience of particular nostalgic components as well as their mutual relationships is determined by the temporal horizons of particular groups (Giesen 2004) and their relationships to particular memory regimes.

Conclusion

This thematic volume focuses on the positions of different disciplines to the question how remembering in the post-1989 Baltic states relate to the remembered experience of the post-1940 socialist life-world. In more general terms, the authors of this volume contribute to the understanding of the Baltic states as a mnemonic region as related to the memory of Soviet socialism. The method in these approaches concentrates on life story and oral history as the medium of memory, following the social, cultural, and political function of autobiographical narrating in remembering the twentieth century, especially beginning at the end of the 1980s.

The case studies in this volume demonstrate how individual, social, and political formats and dimensions of memory intersect in remembering socialism. As this volume showed, one of the key formats of cultural memory in the post-1989 Baltic states was generational memory, which has played a major part in establishing the image of communism in post-1989 Baltic countries. There are critical references to the male-centric definition of the generation, and from this aspect, to the interrelatedness of gender and nationalism in the Baltic memory, most notably in terms of deportation and survival. The analysis also revealed that professional society is an important mnemonic dimension in the post-1989 Baltic memory, while the role of the family in memory narratives seems to be downplayed. On the other hand, family memory is a similar source of social counter-memory to the professional community or the dia-spora, which is defined not only by the language and shared culture but also by a sense of social and cultural marginalization. Religion – like the shared narrative of the national past – provides coherent structures for individual meaning making of the past and present.

The in-depth analyses presented in this volume enable a differentiated view on the Baltic memory and its post-1989 development as compared to a perspective from outside. The volume draws a heterogeneous picture of the post-1989 dynamics of remembering Baltic socialism by pointing out differences in unity, continuities in ruptures, and vice versa. The empirical research of remembering Baltic socialism through life stories demonstrates both the domination of the public national, social, and cultural discourses in the individual memory and the discrepancy between the individual and public levels of memory. In a common attempt to remember the socialist past, groups and individuals encounter considerable differences of temporal horizon as well as differences in attributing importance to experiences and events.

Notes

1. Alheit himself does not connect his model to Assmanns' and the cultural memory studies or to the German communicative and social memory studies developed by Harald Welzer.
2. Methodologically, Alheit's point of departure is phenomenological sociology, which considers culture to be a shared system of everyday knowledge and meanings, which allow an individual to organize his/her everyday experience, to live and cope in everyday life.
3. Here, however, Alheit differentiates between social memories in totalitarian and democratic societies: in a totalitarian system, dominant knowledge and social counter-knowledge are sealed off from each other, while in a democratic society they are contrasting, conflictual, or competing, maintaining nonetheless a reciprocal influence.
4. On various approaches on memory – autobiography relationship see Roberts (2002, 134–147).
5. In this context, see also the treatment by Aili Aarelaid-Tart on the entwinement of generational, historical, and political time in the context of the 1900–1999 Estonia (Aarelaid-Tart 2006, 24–29).
6. For instance, the popular life writing campaign dedicated to the celebration of the ninetieth anniversary of the Republic of Estonia in 2008 elicited highly individualistic stories, although the emphasis of the appeal was directed at the relationships of the writer with their relevant others (from a verbal discussion with Tiiu Jaago).
7. In this common trend of the meaning making of the past, the internal division has been more visible in Lithuanian memory culture and remembrance policy than in Estonia or Latvia. Accompanied with the peculiarities of law and related to political identities and power

arrangements, this has resulted in a more ambivalent and defensive evaluation of the Soviet past from the early 1990s onwards (in Šutinienė).

8. Estonian politologist Anu Toots (2003) confirms that due to several law amendments at the beginning of the 2000s, the role of political parties in local politics changed. The parties became stronger organizationally and more and more local elections and decision-making started to resemble that of the parliament, where all processes went through political parties. This in turn affected other local-level positions becoming indirectly related with the parties, which brought about the understanding that 'in this job you cannot do your work properly if you do not have some political party backing you.'

9. Another such mnemonic motif is informal relationships facilitated by blat (Ledeneva 1998). See Kaprāns and Paert in this volume.

Disclosure statement

No potential conflict of interest was reported by the author.

Funding

This research was supported by the Estonian Science Foundation: [Grant Number 8190], by the institutional research funding [Grant Number IUT34-32] of the Estonian Ministry of Education and Research, and by the European Regional Development Fund (Centre of Excellence in Cultural Theory).

References

Aarelaid-Tart, A. 2003. "Double Mental Standards in the Baltics during Two Afterwar Decades in Baltics." In *The Baltic Countries under Occupation. Soviet and German Rule 1940–1991*, edited by A. Kõll, 213–226. Stockholm: Stockholm University Proceedings.

Aarelaid-Tart, A. 2006. *Cultural Trauma and Life Stories*. Helsinki: Kikimora Publications.

Aarelaid-Tart, A. 2011. "Let Me Tell You a Sad Story – Soviet Russians Immigrants in Independent Estonia." In *Baltic Biographies at Historical Crossroads*, edited by A. Aarelaid-Tart, and L. Bennich-Bj§orkman, 86–106. London: Routledge.

Aarelaid-Tart, A. 2012. "Nõukogude aeg nähtuna erinevate mälukogukondade silmade läbi [Soviet Past through the Lenses of Different Communities of Memory]." *Acta Historica Tallinnensia* 18: 142–158. doi:10.3176/hist.2012.1.06.

Aarelaid-Tart, A., and L. Bennich-Björkman. 2011. "Introduction: On Living through the Twentieth Century in the Baltic States." In *Baltic Biographies at Historical Crossroads*, edited by A. Aarelaid-Tart, and L. Bennich-Björkman, 1–22. London: Routledge.

Abrams, L. 2010. *Oral History Theory*. London: Routledge.

Abrams, L. 2014. "Memory as both Source and Subject of Study: The Transformations of Oral History." In *Writing the History of Memory*, edited by S. Berger, and B. Niven, 89–110. London: Bloomsbury.

Alheit, P. 1989. "Erzählform und 'soziales Gedächtnis': Beispiel beginnender Traditionsbildung im autobiographischen Erinnerungsprozess [Narrative Form and 'Social Memory': Emerging of Tradition in the Process of Autobiographical Remembering]." In *Biographisches Wissen: Beiträge zu einer Theorie lebensgeschichtlicher Erfahrung* [Biographical Knowing: Contributions to a Theory of Autobiographical Experience], edited by P. Alheit, and E. M. Hoerning, 123–147. Frankfurt am Main: Campus.

Anepaio, T. 2002. "Reception of the Topic of Repressions in the Estonian Society." *Pro Ethnologia* 14: 47–65.

Anepaio, T. 2003. "Boundaries in the Soviet Society – The Case of the Repressed." In *Making and Breaking of Borders. Ethnological Interpretation, Presentation, Representation*, edited by T. Korhonen, H. Ruotsala, and E. Uusitalo, 67–78. Helsinki: Finnish Literature Society.

Assmann, A. 2010. "Re-Framing Memory. Between Individual and Collective Forms of Constructing the Past." In *Performing the Past Memory, History, and Identity in Modern Europe*, edited by K. Tilmans, F. van Vree, and J. M. Winter, 35–50. Amsterdam: Amsterdam University Press.

Assmann, J. 1988. "Kollektives Gedächtnis und kulturelle Identität [Collective Memory and Cultural Identity]." In *Kultur und Gedächtnis* [Culture and Memory], edited by J. Assmann, and T. Hölscher, 9–19. Frankfurt am Main: Suhrkamp.

Baliutytė, E., and D. Mitaitė, eds. 2011. *Baltic Memory: Processes of Modernisation in Lithuanian, Latvian and Estonian Literature of the Soviet Period*. Vilnius: Institute of Lithuanian Literature and Folklore.

Bela, B. 2009. "Elulood läti ühiskonna uurimise allikana [Life Stories in the Research of Latvian Society]." *Mäetagused* 43: 159–180. doi:10.7592/MT.

Conway, M. A. 1992. "A Structural Model of Autobiographical Memory." In *Theoretical Perspectives on Autobiographical Memory*, edited by M. A. Conway, D. C. Rubin, H. Spinnler, and W. A. Wagenaar, 167–194. Dordrecht: Kluwer Academic Publishers.

Crane, S. A. 1997. "Writing the Individual Back into Collective Memory." *The American Historical Review* 102 (5): 1372–1385. doi:10.2307/2171068.

Davoliūtė, V. 2013. *The Making and Breaking of Soviet Lithuania: Memory and Modernity in the Wake of War*. London: Routledge.

Davoliūtė, V., and T. Balkelis. 2012. "Introduction." In *Maps of Memory: Trauma, Identity and Exile in Deportation Memoirs from the Baltic States*, edited by V. Davoliūtė, and T. Balkelis, 10–25. Vilnius: Institute of Lithuanian Literature and Folklore.

Erll, A. 2011a. *Memory in Culture*. Basingstoke: Palgrave Macmillan.

Erll, A. 2011b. "Locating Family in Cultural Memory Studies." *Journal of Comparative Family Studies* 42 (3): 303–318.

Erll, A., and A. Rigney, eds. 2009. *Mediation, Remediation, and the Dynamics of Cultural Memory*. Berlin: Walter de Gruyter.

Fulbrook, M. 2014. "History Writing and Collective Memory." In *Writing the History of Memory*, edited by S. Berger, and B. Niven, 65–88. London: Bloomsbury.

Giesen, B. 2004. "Noncontemporaneity, Asynchronicity and Divided Memories." *Time & Society* 13 (1): 27–40. doi:10.1177/0961463X04040741.

Halbwachs, M. [1925] 1952. *Les cadres sociaux de la mémoire* [The Social Frameworks of Collective Memory]. Paris: Presses Universitaires de France [originally published in *Les Travaux de L'Année Sociologique*, Paris: F. Alcan, 1925].

Hamilton, P., and L. Shopes. 2008. "Introduction: Building Partnership between Oral History and Memory Studies." In *Oral History and Public Memories*, edited by P. Hamilton, and L. Shopes, vii–xvii. Philadelphia: Temple University Press.

Heimo, A. 2011. "Vuoden 1918 muistot Sammatissa ja historian yhteiskunnallinen rakentaminen [Memories of 1918 in Sammati and Public History]." *Kasvatus & Aika* 5 (3): 82–113.

Heinze, C. 2011. "'Das Private wird politisch' – interdisziplinäre Perspektiven auf autobiografisches Schreiben im Horizont von Erinnerungskulturen und Zeitgeschichte ['The Private Becomes Political' - Interdisciplinary Perspectives on Autobiographical Writing in Contexts of Memory Cultures and Recent History]." *Forum Qualitative Sozialforschung/Forum: Qualitative Social Research* 12 (2): Art. 9.

Hinrikus, R., and E. Kõresaar. 2004. "A Brief Overview of Life History Collection and Research in Estonia." In *She Who Remembers Survives: Interpreting Estonian Women's Post-Soviet Life Stories*, edited by T. Kirss, E. Kõresaar, and M. Lauristin, 19–34. Tartu: Tartu University Press.

Jaago, T. 2004. "Narrationen von Heimat und Abstammung. Esten und ethnische Minoritäten in Estland erzählen [Narratives of Home and Origin: on Storytelling of Estonians and Ethnic Minorities in Estonia]." In *Erzählen zwischen den Kulturen* [Narrating between Cultures], edited by S. Wienker-Piepho, and K. Roth, 173–185. Münster: Waxmann Verlag.

Jõesalu, K., and E. Kõresaar. 2013. "Continuity or Discontinuity: On the Dynamics of Remembering 'Mature Socialism' in Estonian Post-Soviet Remembrance Culture." *Journal of Baltic Studies* 44 (2): 177–203. doi:10.1080/01629778.2013.775849.

Jurgutienė, A. 2007. "Reception and History: Baltic Memory." In *We Have Something in Common: The Baltic Memory*, edited by A. Mihkelev, and B. Kalnačs, 19–34. Tallinn: Under and Tuglas Literature Centre; Institute of Literature, Folklore and Art of the University.

Kansteiner, W. 2010. "Memory, Media and Menschen: Where Is the Individual in Collective Memory Studies?" *Memory Studies* 3 (1): 3–4. doi:10.1177/1750698009348276.

Kõresaar, E. 2001. "A Time Ignored? About the Role of the Soviet Period in Biographies of Older Estonians." *Ethnologia Fennica. Finnish Studies in Ethnology* 29: 45–55.

Kõresaar, E. 2004. "The Notion of Rupture in Estonian Narrative Memory: On the Construction of Meaning in Autobiographical Texts on the Stalinist Experience." *Ab Imperio* 2004: 313–339. doi:10.1353/imp.2004.0088.

Kõresaar, E. 2005. *Elu ideoloogiad: Kollektiivne mälu ja autobiograafiline minevikutõlgendus eestlaste elulugudes* [Ideologies of Life: Collective Memory and Autobiographical Meaning-Making of the Past in Estonian Life Stories]. Tartu: Estonian National Museum.

Ledeneva, A. V. 1998. *Russia's Economy of Favours: Blat, Networking and Informal Exchange*. Cambridge: Cambridge University Press.

Luca, I., and L. Kurvet-Käosaar. 2013. "Life Writing Trajectories in Post-1989 Eastern Europe." *European Journal of Life Writing* 2: T1–9. doi:10.5463/ejlw.2.51.

Mannheim, K. 1928. "Das Problem der Generation [The Problem of Generations]." *Kölner Vierteljahreshefte für Soziologie* 7: 309–330.

Mark, J. 2010. *The Unfinished Revolution: Making Sense of the Communist Past in Central-Eastern Europe*. New Haven: Yale University Press.

Mihkelev, A., and B. Kalnačs, eds. 2007. *We Have Something in Common: The Baltic Memory*. Tallinn: Under and Tuglas Literature Centre – Institute of Literature, Folklore and Art of the University of Latvia.

Olick, J. 1999. "Collective Memory. The Two Cultures." *Sociological Theory* 17 (3): 333–348. doi:10.1111/0735-2751.00083.

Olick, J. 2007. *The Politics of Regret. On Collective Memory and Historical Responsibility*. New York: Routledge.

Paletschek, S., and S. Schraut. 2008. "Introduction. Gender and Memory Culture in Europe: Female Representations in Historical Perspective." In *The Gender of Memory: Cultures of Remembrance in Nineteenth- and Twentieth Century Europe*, edited by S. Paletschek, 7–28. Frankfurt: Campus.

Passerini, L. 2009. *Fascism in Popular Memory. The Cultural Experience of the Turin Working Class*. Cambridge: Cambridge University Press.

Pettai, E.-C., ed. 2011. *Memory and Pluralism in the Baltic States*. London: Routledge.

Pettai, E.-C. 2015. "Negotiating History for Reconciliation: A Comparative Evaluation of the Baltic Presidential Commissions." *Europe-Asia Studies* 67 (7): 1079–1101. doi:10.1080/09668136.2015.1064862.

Portelli, A. 1990. *The Death of Luigi Tastrulli: And Other Stories: Form and Meaning in Oral History*. New York: State University of New York Press.

Rahi-Tamm, A. 2009. "Küüditamine Nõukogude repressiivpoliitika komponendina. - Uuemaid aspekte märtsiküüditamise uurimisest [Deportation as a Component of the Soviet Repressive Politics. – New Aspects of the Historiography of the March Deportation]." In *Eesti Ajaloomuuseumi teaduskonverentsi materjale* Proceeding of the Estonian History Museum Conference], edited by O. Liivik, and H. Tammela, 12–32. Tallinn: Estonian History Museum.

Roberts, B. 2002. *Biographical Research*. Buckingham: Open University Press.

Roth, K., ed. 2004. *Arbeit im Sozialismus – Arbeit im Postsozialismus: Erkundungen zum Arbeitsleben im östlichen Europa* [Work in Socialism - Work in Postsocialism: Studies on Working Life in Eastern Europe]. Münster: LIT Verlag.

Rüsen, J. 2006. *Kultur macht Sinn: Orientierung zwischen Gestern und Morgen* [Culture has Meaning: an Orientation between the Past and the Future]. Köln: Böhlau.

Siemer, K. 2002. "'Who is Red Outside and White Inside?' The Topic of Soviet Rule in Estonian Life Stories." In *Lives, Histories and Identities*, edited by T. Jaago, 188–203. Tartu: University of Tartu, Estonian Literary Museum.

Skultans, V. 1998. *The Testimony of Lives: Narrative and Memory in Post-Soviet Latvia*. London: Routledge.

Srigley, K., and S. Zembrzycki. 2009a. "Remembering Family, Analyzing Home: Oral History and the Family." *Oral History Forum/d'histoire orale* 29. Special Issue *Remembering Family, Analyzing Home: Oral History and the Family*. Accessed November 15, 2013. http://www.oralhistoryforum.ca/index.php/ohf/issue/view/10.

Srigley, K., and S. Zembrzyck, eds. 2009b. *Remembering Family, Analyzing Home: Oral History and the Family*. A Special Issue of the *Oral History Forum/d'histoire orale*, 29.

Šutinienė, I. 2009. "Eluloo- ja suulise ajaloo uurimine Leedus [Biographical and Oral History Research in Lithuania]." *Mäetagused* 43: 145–158. doi:10.7592/MT.

Tamm, M. 2013. "In Search of Lost Time: Memory Politics in Estonia, 1991–2011." *Nationalities Papers* 41 (4): 651–674. doi:10.1080/00905992.2012.747504.

Todorova, M., and Z. Cille, eds. 2010. *Post-Communist Nostalgia*. New York: Berghahn Books.

Toots, A. 2003. "Kohaliku esindusvõimu erakonnastumine [Politicization of the Local Municipalities]." *Riigikogu Toimetised* 7: 140–146.

Troebst, S. 2007. "'Budapest' oder, 'Batak'? Varietäten südosteuropäischer Erinnerungskulturen ['Budapest' or 'Batak'? Variations of South-East European Memory Cultures]." In *Zwischen Amnesie und Nostalgie. Die Erinnerung an den Kommunismus in Südosteuropa* [Between Amnesia and Nostalgia. The Memory of Communism in South-East Europe], edited by U. Brunnbauer, and S. Troebst, 15–26. Köln: Böhlau.

Undusk, J. 2007. "The Problem of Baltic Unity: Opening Address." In *We Have Something in Common: The Baltic Memory*, edited by A. Mihkelev, and B. Kalnačs, 11–18. Tallinn: Under and Tuglas Literature Centre; Institute of Literature, Folklore and Art of the University.

Võsu, E., E. Kõresaar, and K. Kuutma. 2008. "Mediation of Memory: Towards Transdisciplinary Perspectives in Current Memory Studies." *Trames: Journal of the Humanities and Social Sciences* 12 (3): 243–262. doi:10.3176/tr.2008.3.01.

Wawrzyniak, J., and M. Pakier. 2013. "Memory Studies in Eastern Europe: Key Issues and Future Perspectives." *Polish Sociological Review* 3 (183): 257–279.

Wertsch, J. V. 2002. *Voices of Collective Remembering*. Cambridge: Cambridge University Press.

Re-educating teachers: ways and consequences of Sovietization in Estonia and Latvia (1940–1960) from the biographical perspective

Aigi Rahi-Tamm[a] and Irēna Saleniece[b]

[a]Institute of History and Archaeology, University of Tartu, Tartu, Estonia; [b]Centre of Oral History, Daugavpils University, Daugavpils, Latvia

ABSTRACT

This article is based on a comparative analysis, juxtaposing archival and oral historical sources, to identify changes that took place in the teaching profession in the annexed Baltic States. Attention is paid to the generation of Estonian and Latvian teachers, born in the 1920s–1930s and trained as Soviet teachers in the 1940s–1950s. Their transformation into 'Soviet people' included acceptance of Soviet values and rejecting the inherent ones. Therefore, the research focuses on the course and outcomes of reeducation of teachers pursued by the Soviet authorities up to the early 1960's.

Introduction

Research on, and the interpretation of, the Soviet period, coupled with the activities of individuals under a dictatorship, have not lost relevance to the present and continue to be subjects of discussion. Our research encompasses a number of questions: how the new concepts forced on people by the regime were accepted or rejected, what their life strategies were like, and which measures were taken by the state for influencing people.

The profession of teacher is undoubtedly one of the most demanding and responsible occupations; preparing young people for life requires special knowledge and skills. Teachers are expected to set a personal example, and thus, higher demands are made of them than the general public. Each era imposes its specific demands on teachers (Eacute and Esteve 2000; Grosvenor, Lawn, and Rousmaniere 1999).

The teachers of the Baltic states found themselves needing to meet new demands in the summer of 1940. The political situation had unexpectedly changed overnight and forced the teachers to make a decision about whether or not to comply with the new demands from the Soviet authorities. The teachers encountered problems that caused not only personal dilemmas but also problematic interactions with their students. Responsibility attributed to teachers made them constant objects of supervision, subjecting them to politically correct patterns of behavior. If these patterns of behavior were ignored, punishment usually followed (Ewing 2002; Fitzpatrick 1999; Gross 2002; Livschiz 2008; Pilve 2013).

This study is concerned with the young teachers who were born in independent states in the 1920s and 1930s, and the processes they went through to become Soviet teachers. Currently, these teachers represent the oldest generation of teachers alive; their memories have been gathered and recorded beginning at the end of the 1980s. This was the first generation of Estonian and Latvian teachers trained as Soviet teacher and their life experiences included the change in political regimes, World War II, the occupation of their native land, terror, and much more. The scope of this study is confined to Estonia and Latvia due to the lack of material on a similar group of Lithuanian teachers. During their reeducation, teachers needed to adapt their previous experience and values systems to a set of very different norms. Often, in order to build up their identity they had to ask themselves 'who we are,' 'who we were,' 'how we should do things in this community' (Bennich-Björkman 2007, 116).

The aim of this research is to concentrate on teachers' strategies measures introduced by the regime during the first decades of Sovietization, when the process of reformation of the society in accordance with the Soviet patterns was taking place. First, this study examines how the generation of teachers born in the 1920s and 1930s described or interpreted the changes in society. Second, this study investigates how both the state and teachers interpreted the control that was established over situations, whether more active or passive strategies were applied, and what compromises were made. The themes dealt with in the research are three interrelated relationships between the state, teachers, and students (Ewing 2002, xi). The students' point of view is used selectively as far as their assessments of teachers' behavior in certain situations is concerned. We combine the research on memories with the analysis of different practices in the institutions that characterized Soviet society (Bassin and Kelly 2012, 8).

Sources and methods

This study is based on several sources. The largest source is the collection of auto-biographies of teachers born in the 1920s and 1930s gathered by the association 'Estonian Life Histories' and kept in the culture-historical archives of the Estonian Literary Museum (EKLA). A selection of life stories also appeared in several publications (Hinrikus 2000; Paklar 2009; Hinrikus and Kirss 2009). The Estonian Life Histories' Association was founded in 1996 to collect biographical material. In order to do so, a number of life stories competitions on several topics were organized, for example, 'Women's life stories' (1995), 'Life stories of the 20th century' (1998), and 'My life in the Estonian Soviet Socialist Republic (ESSR) and the Republic of Estonia' (2000) (Hinrikus and Kõresaar 2004, 19–34; Hinrikus 2003, 191–205). Teachers have always been willing to write their life stories; in 1998 a special collection of teachers' stories was issued within the framework of the project 'The Biographies of Teachers of the Baltic States' and was analyzed by Kõresaar (2004). The most recent campaign for gathering teachers' stories in Estonia took place in the spring of 2013 under the title 'Teacher, do you remember what your life was like?' The EKLA has gathered about 200 stories by teachers, and approximately a quarter of these are used in this research.

Another source of memories are the teachers from East Latvia, some of which are published (Vaivods 2009; Paukšte 2011), while others are found in the collection of the

Oral History Centre at Daugavpils University. The Centre has undertaken ten annual (2003–12) oral history expeditions in South-eastern Latvia (Latgale region and South Sēlija) to gather the historical experience of residents of this area who vary both by their ethnic and religious backgrounds.[1] As a result, more than 1000 life histories have been compiled, including about 200 stories of local teachers. These oral narratives are free, unregulated narrations by individuals about themselves, recorded on a voice-operated recorder and transcribed afterwards. Depending on the individual style of the narrators, these were either in the form of a monologue of several hours, or a shorter dialogue between the narrator and the interviewer. In many cases, the inter-viewers asked the narrators to tell more about the historical events in which they had participated or witnessed.

In addition to the collections described above, we also made use of smaller collec-tions. To more thoroughly evaluate the processes that took place in schools, we asked Tallinn's Gustav Adolf Gymnasium to be allowed to use their archives of life stories that they had gathered from teachers born in the 1920s and 1930s. With their permission, we used the memories of 11 teachers. To broaden our viewpoint, we also used students' memories from the former Tartu 5th Secondary School and Viljandi 2nd Secondary School (Kurs 2009; Mikelsaar 2009; Renno, Jüri, and Arno 2010). Memories of senior students about their teachers were published in school almanacs and as contributions to collections on the students' resistance movement (Josia 2004; Kaska 2008).

Since the teachers did not write their life stories about their development or recall events in their interviews in the form of successive temporal strategies, the material appears as completed narrative biographical texts that do not follow any particular guidelines and are often multilayered (Hinrikus 2003, 171–183). This is why certain events, and their impact on the life stories, emerge through comparisons of different periods. For instance, a number of features of the Stalinist period appeared in the descriptions of more recent times, when the situation became more stable and the years 1940–1950 were looked upon as part of a longer process. As a rule, the period from 1940 to the mid-1950s was characterized by simply trying to survive. By 1960, new standards had become generally established and patterns of behavior had been set.

The period under observation is not homogeneous, therefore the assessments given to those years cannot follow a uniform pattern. The period under investigation can be divided into three stages: pre-war (1940–1941), post-war late-Stalinism (1944–1953), and an era of weakening terror and occasional liberalization (1953–1960). The following period in the Baltics lasted until the end of the 1960s; the time frame of 1960 in this article conditionally denotes the period when Soviet education policy started following the guidelines of the new school reform, thus marking changes in ideolo-gical work.

In some life stories, Soviet school was compared to a military-like institution, subjected to totalitarian Communist ideology, where teachers, as representatives of the state, exerted mental terror, and brainwashing on students, and pupils were forbidden any initiative or freedom of thought (Kõresaar 2004, 296). Alternatively, others had a much different perspective on school under the Soviet regime: 'I have good memories about the school life of that time. I have no idea where the myth started that school was like a prison where one could not laugh or study, have no fun or go in for no sports. All this was done, no matter how' (KM EKLA, f 350, Sirje Rätsep). Thus, when speaking about schools in the

Soviet time today, we can find quite different views or stereotypes that signal plurality of personal opinions, circumstantial situations, and relationships between Soviet theory and practice.

Although teachers have always been active in producing memories, they often do not focus on their reeducation or only make periodic references to what requires an appropriate historical context to recognize the details of the reeducation process itself. The lack of information about teacher's reeducation made us look for archival materials that would provide a framework for the fragments of teachers' memories. First, we created an overview of the strategies that the Soviet state has used to influence teachers. Creating an events-based framework made it possible to bring forth reactions by the teachers or their families to the actions planned by the state, and to distinguish certain campaigns (e.g. periods when ideological pressure became stronger or weaker). The events-based framework enables researchers to identify strategies, dilemmas, factors, and motives that had influenced individual choices. We agree with Ene Kõresaar and the researcher on religious biographies, Lea Altnurme, who admit that memories about the late Soviet period tend to gradually disappear from biographies, or that the period of the ESSR is described in a simple impersonal style, as if the memorizing took place 'in a public debate-room' (Kõresaar 2001, 130; Altnurme 2006, 106–111).

For a comparative analysis we contrast the biographical material with state-designed strategies for reeducating the teaching profession, using various materials from the Estonian National Archives (ERA) and the State Archives of Latvia (LNA LVA).[2] We mainly use materials from the Central Committee of the Communist Party of Latvia (LNA LVA stock R101) and the ESSR Ministry of Education (ERA stock R14) that consisted of reports at both regional and republican levels, which also describe educational policy more broadly than just pointing to problems with schools, teachers, or students.

The following interpretation is based on the method of reconstructive cross-analysis in oral history proposed by Thompson (2000, 268–282). The application of the reconstructive cross-analysis is rooted in the idea that the individual life is the actual vehicle of historical experience, but to make generalizations possible, the evidence extracted from different oral history interviews and written memoirs is compared with data from other types of historical sources. In this way, the overall shape of the reconstruction of the past is not predetermined by life stories, but emerges from the inner logic of argumentation designed by a historian. The reconstructive model of analysis also sets limits on the length of the presentation of life histories within the text.

Contrasting teachers' experiences to state-planned strategies drawn from the materials stored in various institutions discloses situations brought about by a variety of factors. The folklore researcher Tiiu Jaago analyzed individual choices on the basis of the life stories and explained that individuals sharing the same historical–political framework do not perceive the space identically. In addition, depending on personality traits, an individual can be influenced by numerous other factors, including interpretations and meanings ascribed to events (Jaago 2006, 83–100). Using various sources and contrasting individual memories with materials at the state level enables us to broaden the view of society and learn more about the era under observation, its richness, nuances, and contradictions. From broader view, the distinctive features of the local area can be identified, which are important for an in-depth analysis of the functioning of socialist society.

In order to analyze the various strategies adopted between individuals and the state, we present an overview of the characteristic features of the period, repressions, and mental pressure and, following this, the 'Thaw era.' Against this background, different practices and dilemmas are outlined at the individual and state levels, and key factors for understanding the historical-cultural process of this very controversial era can be presented.

The reorganization of education policy

The Sovietization of the Baltic education sector began with institutional changes, which primarily entailed simply implementing the Soviet model (Tannberg 2007; 2010; Zubkova 2008). Education policy management in the Baltic republics, put into practice through the Ministries of Education, was regulated by the school departments of the Communist Party Central Committee (CP CC), and delegated to the party propaganda secretary. As CP reports indicate, the main task for the Ministries of Education until 1953 was to discharge ineligible teachers. The duties of the party school departments ranged from reviewing school programs to ideological supervision. Through these functions, the schools' ideological-educational work was carried out and inspected when development in the area was monitored (Tarvel 2002, 242–247). The reorganizations to be carried out originated from Moscow and were based on the resolutions and guidelines of the All-Union Communist (Bolshevist) Party Central Committee. Thus, school became one of the main battlefields for the enforcement of the new Soviet ideology. Similar Soviet-style models of education systems, with distinctive features for each country, were imposed throughout Eastern Europe, especially in East Germany, where Soviet officials felt direct responsibility for the introduction of a new cultural and educational system (Connelly 2000, 3–4, 40–42, 58–60).

Major changes were also introduced into programs of study, which were required to follow Soviet standards. Local history with significant patriotic content,[3] religious education, civic education, and ancient languages were removed from the curricula in favor of the Russian language, which began to enjoy a special place in education.[4] Beginning in1948, school programs gradually became more and more ideologically biased and the teaching of national history was cancelled in Baltic schools and replaced with the history of the Russian people, as had already been done in other union republics.[5]

However, the agents of Sovietization were teachers. Therefore, the question of 'cadres' became one of the most complicated problems for the introduction of the Soviet model of education. The role of the intelligentsia, including teachers (Manheim 1994, 466), was not unimportant in bringing up and educating 'new individuals' and society, thus the process had to begin with reforming the attitudes and mentality of the intellectuals themselves. Bringing up the 'New Man' for the communist society was the focal point of the Soviet education policy, which was based on the idea that human nature can be molded in any way that one would wish (Halfin 2003, 1–2; Sandle 2010, 214). For this purpose, a Soviet person had to develop a new type of socialist self-consciousness in accordance with ruling ideology; through coercive measures and education the Soviet regime hoped to produce 'purified' people, with all private and individual features suppressed (Pipes 2005, 170). People were enticed with lofty promises of possibilities for a new and better life for all. One of the policy pillars was the assertion that the role of intellectuals in small local minorities in the Baltic republics would become more important than ever due to the solidarity with the Russian people and 'positive' influence of the Russian culture. The sense of togetherness needed to be demonstrated and illustrated in every possible way (Sirk 2004, 52). However, catchy promises did not receive a unanimous, enthusiastic reception, or substantial sympathy from the majority of the people. Thus, the establishment of Soviet power in the Baltic countries turned out to be a long-term struggle between new and old values and principles, going through a number of stages. In the education arena, using a variety of measures, it aimed at reeducating teachers and students, as well as their families.

Landmarks of the first Soviet year, 1940–1941

Undoubtedly, physical pressure and fear made up the central power strategy which most influenced people's behavior and which supported the introduction of control mechanisms during the period under observation. This is the background against which people's activity was determined.

Those in power were motivated by lasting resistance and divided the population into 'us' and 'them,' and 'good' and 'bad' groups (Gross 2002, 114–122). The first clear division into supporters and opponents of the new regime began to appear in 1940. Local functionaries and employees of executive committees were assigned to control the local people's mentality and find out those 'among teachers willing to go along with the new regime and those not willing to do so' (Paavle 2009, 47). First, the atmosphere inside schools was controlled with the help of supporters of the new regime and newly established All-Union Leninist Young Communist League, (usually known as *Komsomol*: Комсомо́л, a syllabic abbreviation from the Russian *Kommunisticheskii Soyuz Molodyozhi*) organization. At the end of 1940, the pressure of the regime on teachers began to build up, and within 4 months, more than 300 secondary school teachers and headmasters were dismissed (Karjahärm and Sirk 2007, 304). Most were allowed to continue their work in other distant regions and headmasters for secondary schools began to be appointed by the party central committee personnel department, which closely scrutinized their *curriculum vitae* and mentality.

In such circumstances, the majority of teachers decided to distance themselves from ideology. 'In that period everybody tried to do their best. My Dad's sister, Dad himself, his cousins – all worked as teachers. And everybody worked with the only wish that Latgale would gain education,' remembers Silva Linarte (DU MV, 599). However, this strategy could not last long. Earlier, socially active teachers and their political contacts had belonged to some political party or military organization, such as Estonia's Defense League or Latvia's Aizsarg organization. This gave the regime sufficient reasons for introducing a more intense penal policy. The struggle against the people's 'past' continued, ever more forcibly. An individual's pronouncements or concrete acts under the new regime actually played a less decisive role than the data that the security organizations gathered about the mentality of that individual, their families, social status, and activity in the period of the independent republic (Rahi-Tamm 2009, 127–128).

At first, the teachers, and society as a whole, decided to use 'wait-and-see' tactics, being unaware of the hidden strategies of the state. A crucial change in their attitudes took place in June 1941 when a major deportation operation was simultaneously carried out in all three Baltic republics a few weeks before the war broke out. The deportation operation greatly affected teachers. Based on Centre for Registration and Retrieval of Deported and Mobilized Estonians (ZEV)[6] data, 127 secondary school teachers and 322 primary school teachers in Estonia were killed or deported to Siberia during the first year of the Soviet regime, amounting to more than 10% of all Estonian teachers (Karjahärm and Sirk 2007, 305). The deportation, which simultaneously struck thousands of families of all ages and backgrounds, instantly changed the overall mentality of the people (Rahi-Tamm 2005, 27). The deportations were a breaking point in the public's attitude to the Soviet regime and revealed the truth about the Soviet rulers and their promises.

The continuation of physical pressure

Soviet 'purges' continued after WWII. Although the war, German occupation, and the mass emigration to the West[7] reduced the numbers of both students and teachers, it did not bring a decrease in violence. On the contrary, the number of people punished increased as the Soviet regime created new categories of enemies related to one's activity under the German occupation. Teachers were hit particularly hard by a new wave of discharges, arrests, deportations, and other kinds of 'disclosures' between 1948 and 1951 when the struggle against the intelligentsia became fiercer.

The majority of Estonian teachers were not aware that the gravest danger of losing their job had threatened them in 1950, when Kelberg, secretary of propaganda and agitation work suggested to Käbin, the first CP CC secretary, that all the teachers with a 'smeared background' be dismissed from their posts. As was revealed by an Estonian Communist (Bolshevist) Party C(B)P report, 78% (5924 people) of teachers had stayed on in Nazi-occupied Estonia (ERA. R14-3-568, 29–35). Therefore, all of these teachers could be accused of living in the enemy's territory and ignoring the order to evacuate to the Soviet zone in the summer of 1941. However, Käbin, decided not to press for such a radical resolution as dismissals (Kuuli 2007, 105). There were hardly any appropriate professional teachers with 'pure CVs' left in the Baltic area. Had this plan of dismissing teachers in Estonia been carried out, the situation would have been similar to that in the Soviet occupation zone in East Germany, where the majority of teachers who had been working under the Nazi regime were removed by 1946; in total 75% of teachers (39,000 people) were deprived from their jobs in East Germany. Many teachers were so scared that they gave up hope of returning to teaching, preferring to take unskilled jobs in factories, on farms, or in industry (Rodden 2002, 30–31).

One must ask how extensively such 'purges' impacted the teaching profession in Estonia and Latvia and the atmosphere of terror was like in these two countries. By 1948, about a quarter, that is, about 1000 Estonian teachers of the 4405 who had commenced work in schools in the autumn of 1944, were removed for political reasons (Raudsepp 2005, 22). New actions followed immediately: between 1949 and 1951, 439 more teachers were removed in the Estonia SSR, and an additional 150 teachers were arrested or deported during the March 1949 deportation operation (ERA. R14-3-568, 186; Rahi-Tamm and Kahar, 2009). The number of the suppressed was growing. Proportionally, 'purges' were similar in the Latvian SSR. Between 1945 and 1949, approximately 1500 teachers were dismissed (LNA LVA. R.101-12-74, 59). Only in 1952 did such actions begin to slow. Only after the 6th Congress of the Estonian C (B) P in April 1951 it had been substantiated that 'bourgeois nationalists' had been given a crushing blow and cooperation between party organizations and the intelligentsia had improved. It was admitted that the time had come to develop more differentiated strategies for intellectuals, and also that the party should help intellectuals more (Sirk 2004, 66).

The total number of teachers who were removed for political reasons is unclear. It is known that the data about numerous dismissals in the reports of executive committees were not recorded accurately. Many highly qualified teachers found work as unskilled workers. Martha Marie Aabram, a talented and strict teacher, according to her former students, was forced to give up her professional work in 1950 because she had traveled to England in the 1930s to improve her English, which made her politically unreliable and ineligible to be a teacher. She began work as an unskilled worker at a fertilizer factory, and only in 1959 was she allowed to begin teaching again in a small country school (Renno, Jüri, and Arno 2010, 190).

As far as the 'purges' are concerned, it should be noted that their intensity varied considerably across regions, which can also be observed in the respective memories: while most of the stories strongly emphasized the background of terror, there are also stories where this environment is only mentioned in passing. The ferocity of political pressure directly affected both the composition of the teaching profession, which consisted of older teachers with considerable teaching experience and inexperienced new teachers. It also affected the quality of education, as well as general mentality in schools. For example, Daugavpils, historically a multiethnic region where many religions were practiced, underwent numerous political operations, and in 1945 lost more than 90% of its pre-war teachers (Saleniece 2003, 201–202). The region had considerable difficulty in finding new teachers.

One of the methods of 'purifying' the teaching staff was compulsory certification. In Latvia, teachers had to pass certification between October 1949 and July 1951 (LNA LVA. R101-12-18, 108–109; Bleiere 2012, 125). The process of certification made it possible to assess every individual teacher, not only with regard to their professional qualifications, but also to their moral position and family background. As Olga Spūle (born 1921) recalls,

it was probably the year 1950 when the teachers' certification took place. They thoroughly examined whether your parents or relatives appeared somewhere or not [for having been disloyal to the communist regime]. It had been checked before and laid in front of you. (DU MV, 28)

Although the post-war political course aimed at mass 'purification,' limits were set by the lack of human resources to develop such a society. Obviously, it was not possible to replace the whole teaching profession in one stroke and doing so would clearly not have solved all of the problems. The most direct consequence of the mass 'purification' policy was a considerable shortage of teachers and labor turnover. Various measures were taken to compensate for the lack of teachers, such as organizing crash courses for teachers-to-be, looking for teachers from outside the republic, and engaging demobilized soldiers straight from the army. The last two options failed dramatically:

For me the most unpleasant one was the Russian teacher Ivasjuk who had been sent to Estonia to 'foster culture', from somewhere in Russia or the Ukraine. Our lessons consisted in reading and translating from the all-union newspaper '*Pravda.*' Since he did not know any Estonian we could translate it whatever way we pleased. A few words he did know, though… As he was a heavy boozer, there was always the smell of booze and garlic on his breath. After he had stolen a female teacher's handbag and got caught with it in the fight on the Town Hall Square, he was sent to Narva to work as the director of a school. (KM EKLA, f 350, Sirje Rätsep)

The simplest way of getting rid of such problematic teachers was to re-appoint them to a new place of work which not only did not solve the problem in the schools, but also put these troublesome individuals off or left them to others to take care of.

The inability of the authorities to solve the problems according to the established principles can be seen very clearly in the way teaching staff was selected. There are several examples of 'worthless' teachers with the 'wrong political past,' who stayed on in schools until alternates were found. The CP had sufficient information pointing to the fact that former teachers did not adapt to the requirements of the new regime, and they were often stated to be 'hard to reform and mostly a backward part of the profession' (ERA. R14-1-258, 157). Thus, the state had to make compromises and be flexible in selecting its teachers. Such revision of the education policy sent a message to the people about the range of opportunities and the selective implementation of requirements.

It was typical of the post-war period of confusion that teachers were not able to work out definite behavioral strategies. The 'purification' message to the population was overwhelmingly threatening. The accusations made against people became more crafty and refined year by year, containing more and more details, not only from the last war, like service in the German army or occupation-related crimes, but also from earlier periods (Weiner and Rahi-Tamm 2012, 24–26). People could not guess what issues from their past would emerge as politically unacceptable and when they would be punished for them. Where could these people go to escape from their past? Many of the teachers who foresaw impending dangers of arrest or dismissal, moved from one place and post to another for years and eventually gave up their professional work altogether. Yet, the majority of former teachers kept working as teachers as long as they were allowed to. Some students' memories state 'in some subjects we had a new teacher every year.' This happened in country schools in particular, as it was easier to employ teachers for city schools.

A continuous sense of fear taught people to conform to circumstances and forced them to make more compromises (Mertelsmann and Rahi-Tamm 2009). To speed up the process of adaptation to the circumstances, the Soviet regime offered the teachers a solution – the option of ideological reeducation wherein they had to renounce their earlier life and past. Guidelines dictated by Stalin for the given situation in school were 'simple' – teachers could best protect themselves by modifying their own thinking, thus the Soviet authorities were coercing teachers into believing that their best hope for self-protection would be found in the new authoritarianism (Ewing 2002, 8–9). The Marxist–Leninist purgatory gave intellectuals the possibility of rebirth to become a Soviet person.

Ideological confrontation and the teaching of Soviet consciousness

Ideological educational work was always a topic in Soviet schools, both during periods of extreme tension and in more relaxed times. During the post-war period, ideological education was a powerful tool, along with 'purification,' to reeducate society. In the schools, teachers were put in a contradictory position – they were simultaneously both victims and instruments of power. In practice, this contradiction meant being caught in the cross fire when earlier conventions had to be forgotten and the Soviet facade put on.

Beliefs held during the period of independence were stigmatized, and all views expressed in the classroom had to be in line with the established CP directions and vocabulary. The entire period of independence was to be presented only in terms of negative comparisons: reactionary, backward, fascist, bourgeois, etc (Kreegipuu 2007, 65–68).

Wherever possible teachers attempted to spare both themselves and their students from excessive ideology. Such attempts could easily lead to the teacher being dismissed. Numerous regulations were fulfilled only ostensibly, just as numerous political circles for reeducating teachers were theoretical rather than practical. A 1947 report by the Ministry of Education admits that teachers knew the Marxist theory but this did not keep them from apolitical teaching at school. There were schools where 'teaching is connected with the present-day only when some stranger is visiting the class, where "cultural mornings" are not organized... or they are boring and formal, reminding one of onetime morning prayers... Teaching is not related to contemporary events and phenomena, students often know nothing or very little about what is going on around them' (ERA. R14-3-258, 162, 163).

Similar double-standard situations were more clearly illustrated by an event in the Tallinn 10th Secondary School. When a city party committee instructor appeared to inspect the school, a teacher shouted to her students across the corridor: 'Girls, quick! Take off the crosses from around your necks! A communist has come to the school!' (Veskimägi 1996, 145). Wearing crosses, rings, badges, and other adornments decorated with tricolor (blue, black, and white in Estonia and red, white, and red in Latvia) national symbols had always been strictly forbidden and wearing one was a punishable offense in schools during the Soviet era.[8] Despite the ban, the youth daringly wore forbidden symbolic decorations and teachers were in no hurry to veto this action. 'At that time there were numerous teachers among us [students who had organized resistance movement] who thought the same as us, we often recognized them by a hidden smile or wink when hearing some communist crap,' an active participant in the youth movement, Jaan Isotamm recalled (Isotamm 2004, 289, 290). While teachers did not pay attention to their students' 'silent' opposition to the regime, we cannot speak about the Soviet triumph in schools. Reeducation of teachers did not proceed at the pace expected by the regime.

During the early post-war years, ideological attacks were somewhat restrained and the party functionaries shared the opinion that intellectuals, including the old intelligentsia, could be reformed and reeducated, even if it took time. Later it became obvious that the 'wait-and-see' strategy did not show the expected results. The majority of teachers, as with the population as a whole, tried to live two lives simultaneously: the 'former times' continued to exist in their private lives and the 'Soviet times' existed when dealing with government offices (Aarelaid 2000, 765). The campaign, which began in 1947 and 1948, against 'bourgeois-nationalist remnants' had to put a stop to such a phenomenon.

One component of the teachers' reeducation process was related to performing duties for the state. To persuade the party of changes in their personal beliefs and thoughts, necessary to become a worthy Soviet person, teachers had to demonstrate their loyalty and persuasiveness as propagandists for the regime. Teachers were given a number of socio-political tasks, like organizing elections, taking part in local Soviet institutions, being closely connected with environmental issues, etc. (ERAF. 1-4-669, 62–66; LNA LVA. R.101-12-74, 60).

> My Mum was a country school teacher and had to obey not only the headmaster's orders but also those given by the village executive committee. In 1948 teachers were ordered to go into the villages and canvass farmers for joining into collective farms. My Mum had to explain advantages of collective farming to the people. She was quite unhappy and confused because she herself did not think it necessary to organize collective farms. But she did do it, although not believing in the tales she had to retell. She wasn't actually thrown out of any house because she was a teacher and the farmers' kids went to the same school where my Mum taught. (Tarto 2010, 60)

It was obvious that teachers could not fulfill all the tasks successfully. These duties caused shame and embarrassment, particularly in rural areas, where people mixed more closely with one another and so being 'the tool of the regime' caused negative feelings and distrust of teachers.

Another area of ideological struggle, where teachers had to demonstrate their eagerness that often resulting in embarrassment, was anti-religious activity, which became more intense at the end of the 1940s. As was stated at the 2nd Congress of the ESSR Intelligentsia, the 'teachers' task is to show how moral degrading and hypocritical religion practice and church activity had always been and still is and how it is directed to lulling the working people's consciousness' (Branch of Estonian State Archives ERAF. 1-4-669, 62–66). Atheist propaganda began to outline negative stereotypes of believers. They were described as deceived, uneducated, crazy people, disloyal to the state. In the Soviet concept, decent people did not go to church. The demolition of religion took place, together with establishing a so-called 'red religion,' creating new rituals and symbols and, thus, attempting to create an apology for religion (Altnurme 2006, 69). Both extracurricular and cultural-educational work building on from these goals became part of the teachers' duties.

As a result of this pressure, people began to withdraw from church. Today, numerous memories tell of the ways in which, in spite of the prohibition of religious rites, going to the church and other ceremonial activity were secretly practiced, and how religious holidays were celebrated in secret. Olga Spūle (born 1921) recalled:

> My children were also baptized, they had been born in 1952 and in 1954. Well then, that was how Luberts was. He brought for me a priest on a motorcycle from Ilūkste in the middle of the night. The windows were tightly covered, and so my kids were baptized. Anyway, I just asked the priest not to record this event in the parish register, for I am a teacher, and such things are not allowed. (DU MV, 28)

To have the courage of one's convictions required strength of mind, but the majority of people chose double standards and adaptation. Now, decades later, one hears more and more often bitterness about the spiritual retreat committed many years ago. Many blame themselves for not persevering with their faith, nor being able to communicate their religious beliefs to their children, or the values and thoughts acquired earlier in the pre-war society, which were replaced by Marxist dogmas under the pressure of Communist propaganda. The children and grandchildren of these people do not have a similar adherence to religious beliefs. This is partly a consequence of the efforts of atheist activity, but parents also take partial responsibility: 'When I worked as a teacher, I definitely worked under Soviet rule; I did not teach the children anything about God' (DU MV, 244).

Although teachers attempted to ignore or ostensibly fulfill instructions, they had to surrender to Soviet requirements designed for actual collaboration with the authorities. As the comparison of the various sources has indicated, the extensive resistance of society to Sovietization in the 1950s was gradually replaced by adaptation to the circumstances.

In 1952, when the campaign against 'bourgeois-nationalists' had abated somewhat and the party changed its political course by replacing the persecution strategy with more differentiated approaches toward intellectuals, ideological pressure, also partly slackened. The moves toward the liberalization of society after the death of Stalin in 1953 did not prove radical. Discussions about innovating education policy dealt primarily with the ideological education of the young, and in this light, the emphasis was shifted to the need to increase the significance of the humanities, like history, literature, and art, so as to teach Soviet patriotism and civic duty to students. At the same time, however, the youth's negative attitudes to Soviet ideology became more apparent.[9] The resistance of society toward Soviet ideology increased after the Hungarian uprising was suppressed in 1956, and pressure on the youth and schools was building up once again.

Use of ideological vocabulary became an everyday occurrence. When teachers today consider the past, they attach no special significance to this, regarding ideological vocabulary as a requirement they had to get used to. As Lehte Rein (born 1930), who worked as an Estonian language and literature teacher for over 30 years, recalls:

> Endless communist propaganda characterized the Soviet time – boring. But one gets used to anything. In general, politics was not talked about. [...] When some kind of a report had to be compiled – and teachers had to do it quite often – it was simple: you found a suitable paragraph in the works by Lenin or Stalin, later by Brezhnev, extended it with your own ideas and ended up with another wise thought by one of our political leaders. One got used to it. Reeducationalists did their work, and got paid for it, acting teachers tried to teach their subjects as well as possible and thus earned their bread. (Lehte Rein, private collection of Rahi-Tamm)

Making school serve the party

The most important indicator of the growth of teachers' political awareness was the rise in the number of CP members, 'candidate-members' of the CPSU (Communist Party Soviet Union), and *Komsomol* members. Success in political reeducation mainly depended on the number of communists in schools and their mentality; great emphasis was put on organizing primary party organizations in schools. Despite all of the efforts, the number of teachers who became communists remained low. In 1949 only 4% of Estonian and 4.8% of Latvian teachers were either members or candidate members of the CP; only 8% of Estonian teachers were *Komsomol* members and in Latvia less than 10% of teachers were *Komsomol* members (ERA. R14-3-568, 190; LNA LVA. R.101-12-74, 59, 62).

Since it was harder to persuade older teachers to join the CP, younger teachers were put under increasing pressure to do so until the end of the 1950s. Malle Purje (born 1939) recalls, 'School leaders were required to find as many people as possible to join the party... No one agreed to enroll. Then the director probably assumed that I as the youngest and unqualified teacher would not dare to resist' (KM EKLA, f 350, Malle Purje).

As public figures, the pressure on teachers to join the CP was quite intense throughout the Soviet period. This is referred to in all of the teachers' memoirs, whether they joined the CP or not. Gunnar Karu (born 1930) was skillful in avoiding the 'obligation':

> The first time I was proposed to join the party happened in Põltsamaa in the 1950s. There were only two party members at school, the headmaster and the history teacher who was the wife of the ideology secretary of the local party committee. The headmaster motivated his proposition by the fact that together with me there would be three members and so we could form a primary organization and the example of the deputy head would inspire colleagues to join the party as well. Our talk remained unfinished and luckily for me one of the teachers agreed to become a candidate member. [...] Some time later the headmaster returned to the question of my joining the party, saying, 'You will not get away with it,' however, I did get away with it. (KM EKLA, f 350, Gunnar Karu)

From the CP position, it was essential that each school had a primary party organization to show that the CP had gained control of the school. The CP had to be in control of everything, directly participating in local affairs as well as administering all social processes. In reality, the aim of reeducation was transformed by self-regulation in accordance with locally operating social contacts over the years and the level of control began to vary across different regions.

Despite the stiff opposition at the beginning, the number of CP members among teachers increased. By 1961, the number of teachers in the Estonian CP had grown to 17%, and to 36% by 1966. Particular pressure was exerted on history teachers, and by 1965, 55% of all Estonian history teachers were CP members (Raudsepp 2005, 36, 39). The figure was not as high in the population as a whole; by 1988 CP membership reached an all-time high in the Estonian SSR with only 10% of the population (Palumets and Titma 2001, 101). In the Latvian SSR it was even lower – the Latvian CP membership was about 6.5% of the whole population (http://www.letonika.lv/groups/?title=Latvijas%20kompartija/32445 (23 August 2013)).

How do the teachers explain their attitude toward joining the CP at that time? Economic considerations were the primary motivation to join the party. The teachers wished to improve their living standards and the promise of career and further study options or other welfare benefits were strong incentives of membership. When a decision was required about party membership, low living standards often pushed ideology-related questions to the background. The history teacher, Imbi-Sirje Torm (born 1940), explained her choice as follows:

> I did not fight back when the proposition to join the CP was made to me for I hoped to get more information, a wider circle of interaction, a possibility of working as a teacher of civic studies. At home my father (who had survived a Soviet prison camp) became quite serious at my message. There was not a single communist in my parents' families or their circle of friends. [...] My father had well informed me about Estonian history. In my lessons I followed the principle 'Better be quiet but do not lie. (KM EKLA, f 350, Imbi-Sirje Torm)

By way of generalization one could add that 'keeping quiet' became one of the main strategies of behavior under Soviet rule, which is also discussed in most of the teachers' stories.

Not many people explained that their choice was a result of coercion or pressure. Malle Purje (born 1939), who joined the party to get a suitable teacher's position (she was an organizer of extracurricular activities at the same time), is very frank in her statements:

I am writing on the topic because today one can come across a lot of tasteless chit-chat about how people joined the CP to undermine the position of the Russian [Soviet] state or how they were almost physically forced to join it. I for one cannot boast about any of it and I don't even want to. I could not even dream any longer about the re-establishment of the independent Republic of Estonia, even less could I imagine how to undermine the Soviet state and act in the name of it. I was not coerced to the CP, if I had resolutely opposed it, I could have gone to work somewhere else. At that moment I chose the most suitable variant because my elderly parents who had made it possible for me to go to the university deserved it that I was close to them when they passed away. (KM EKLA, f 350, Malle Purje)

It is important to mention that some teachers decided to join the party because they became convinced that the communist ideology was correct:

In 1956, a new headmaster, a youngish man Hillar Hanssoo came to our school. [...] The truth of the matter is, he was a genuine communist, among the communists whom I ever saw or met during my long life he was the only one who was of the kind as a communist was ideally described: unselfish, self-sacrificing, committed to his aim and steadfast, but condemning foolishness. Partly he had remained in the era where those ideals first originated from but in many ways his thinking was far advanced in comparison to others. (KM EKLA, f 350, Helgi Piir)

This is how Helgi Piir (born 1940) characterized her former teacher. Similarly, there were teachers who regarded communism as the best model, but nevertheless did not agree to join the CP. Latvian teacher, Raisa Žilinska (born 1934), recalls:

I was no pioneer, no *Komsomol*, nothing... I was a communist by my heart, even not having the party membership card. I strongly believed and thought that everything was happening in such a bad and wrong way (stealing, drinking, flinging away) because those in power [CP and Soviet government] did not know what in fact was going on. (DU MV, 54, Raisa Žilinska)

Focus on work

Because this article is based on the memories of teachers born in the 1920s and 1930s, it is interesting to note that the topic of work came up in all of the teachers' life stories. As Kõresaar points out, the teachers' life stories were distinguished by selective approach to the remembered events and strong professional identity. These elements were expressed in detailed descriptions of their careers and work; being a good teacher served as the focus in the autobiographies (Kõresaar 2004, 293–294). Work can be looked upon as mechanism of escape, where one does not even think of what they are doing, or why. Ninety-two-year-old Konstantin (born 1921) stated the essence of being a teacher as follows: 'The main problem in the teaching work is... whether it makes me happy, ...and whether I will be regarded as their "own teacher."... If I succeed in this then the political background does not play any significant role' (Konstantin Rein, private collection of Rahi-Tamm, 2013).

Although today it is important for us to know how people behaved in frightening situations, how they managed to cope with absurd orders, ideological brainwashing, and the many other horrors that took place between 1940 and 1960, the life stories individually do not provide sufficient support for an in-depth analysis of all of these topics. In retrospect, the stories[10] have mainly focused on self-realization and descriptions of the level of circumstantial difficulties within which all kinds of work coped.

All the things we Soviet teachers as we were called at that time, were supposed to do out of sense of mission and for meager wages too. Each one of us had to fulfill one certain socially beneficial task, sometimes more. I for one was a trade union organizer and bursar for years. For a number of years I chaired the primary school subject board... In springs a competition of inter-class amateur activities took place. It was a huge do... In springs I organized excursions to Estonian nature spots. During the study year, students had to collect immense amounts of waste paper and scrap metal. (Gustav Adolf Gymnasium, Tallinn, Aili Zōryanova)

It was possible to give meaning to everyday life through work as a concrete object of evaluation. Working was an attitude that was free from instruction from higher levels and it was also related to the transfer of the former generations' concepts of culture and the preservation of one's self-consciousness.

The logic of work for this generation of teachers, both the Estonians and Latvians, was supported by the work-related values originating from the attitudes developed when the states were independent, and were further related to teachers' childhood memories. Furthermore, values, like diligence, precision, honesty, a sense of duty, and obedience were closely connected to the work ethic (Altnurme 2006, 110). Excellence was the goal of all work and work was considered to be a source of individual or family welfare. Working hard was implicitly regarded as appropriate labor behavior, not only from the viewpoint of improving one's income and welfare, but also as a founder of social status and means of self-realization (Jõesalu 2004, 22). Anna Babre (born in 1928) recalls:

So I survived without the communist party, just with my work [thanks to] the strong family support and a striving for pedagogy and moral upbringing. And I was among the best anyway, although the appointment board after graduating from the institute sent me to distant Kurzeme. During the first year I worked as a teacher in the Raņķi seven-year school. I worked the best way I could and it was noticed by the district administration and the next year I was appointed headmistress in the Zirņi seven-year school of the same district. And so I was the small headmistress of a big school, there were 150 children in school (it was a boarding school), much work and I had to know many things. At first I refused, I didn't want to go, I was scared. But then they threatened me: if you were taught this kind of attitude towards work, then you can't even work as a teacher if you refuse the offer. I was scared but took the position and worked successfully. (DU MV, 131, Anna Babre)

At the same time, the subject of work and working people were keywords that were repeatedly emphasized in the Soviet lexicon (Hellbeck 2001). Similarly, the main part of the educational reform of 1958 and 1959 established the requirement for consolidating the communist education of a Soviet person so that students were better prepared for real life. This requirement emphasized four central keywords: internationalism, patriotism, atheism, and labor training (Raudsepp 2005, 36). Tasks and obligations drawn from introducing labor education did not seem to intimidate teachers, unlike the tasks of carrying out ideological-educational lessons like events dedicated to Soviet patriotism or atheist propaganda.

In spring and autumn we had to take children to work on collective farms. Sometimes the weather was rainy and it was cold, children got bored. Then all kinds of tricks had to be thought of to humor them. Thus I went to a household and asked to give the children a basketful of apples... keeping the children's spirits up we could work well and the team leaders were pleased with our work. My slogan for the children was 'Do your work and stay honest, then you can survive even in the hell.' Teachers themselves set a good example. (KM EKLA, f 350, Lehte Kets)

This slogan could also be seen as one of the teachers' central life strategies to which so many of them were clinging when facing various problems in their teaching careers. Thus, focusing on work became a model of control that outwardly fit in with the standards suggested by the regime and also helped teachers cope with the system. Only the individual, or the people very close to the individual, knew what the actual effect of this focus on work was. It is difficult to open up one's private sphere of life, even in memories, although in some of the memories, traces of the double-thinking which inevitably accompanied the adaptation process can be observed.

By 1960, the teaching profession realized that school and teaching in general were subordinated to and coordinated by all-union requirements, which were strongly tied to ideology. How and to what extent the requirements were observed depended not only on a teacher's personality and courage, but also on the school leadership and the school mentality, and on the mutual confidence and skills in finding appropriate compromises among the teaching staff.

Conclusion

A retrospective cross-analysis of personal strategies of activity manifested in teachers' biographies, on one hand, and state-designed strategies of activity issued in institutional documents, on the other, disclosed numerous processes that characterized the society from the 1940s to the 1960s. First of all, these were decades of major changes and confusion, concentrating on the reformation of the mentality and attitudes of the citizens of the former independent states to make them appropriate to those of Stalinism and the socialist era.

Although Moscow's policy envisaged the application of the Soviet model to the Baltic education system, it was not possible to realize this in its ideal form, which made the authorities experiment with various approaches and seek certain compromises. For reeducating teachers and reforming schools, various components were introduced by the state, from paralyzing the whole society through a sense of fear and ideological pressure, to enticing people to collaborate by offering them favored places in the ranks of power and better living and working conditions.

The main counter-strategy teachers used was to distance themselves from what was going on through passiveness, double thinking, and conservatism. At times, depending on the situation, these distance-producing strategies combined with somewhat more active strategies, such as looking for a more suitable environment, changing schools, hidden sympathy for students' anti-government activity, sparing them from excessive ideology, and so on.

The generation born in the 1920s and 1930s, who were reeducated after the state's failure to find suitable teaching staff, and who had to fill the gaps left by the teachers dislodged from schools, remained relatively vague in their biographical retrospect of the years from 1940 to 1960; they do not discuss clear-cut typical strategies of coping with Communism. It seems as if the confusion typical of those years is still partly characteristic of many individuals who were young at that time. The different phases of Sovietization were often not clearly perceived by the teachers who wrote about the years of terror (1940–1950). In their treatment of complicated situations, the authors referred to the contradictory nature of their profession – that they felt caught in the cross fire, but they mostly avoided in-depth analyses. Unstable social norms, caused by the changing times, made young teachers, like most other people, act in irregular ways.

36

None of the authors positioned themselves in extreme positions – being consciously resistant to Soviet rule, or following those who did so – rather, those strategies were in materials from institutions and students' memories. Their stories are, first of all, about the difficulties of adaptation.

After the 'major purification' (1948–1951), the party orientation was in favor of people who tended to steer a 'middle course'. Situations relating to embarrassment, humiliation, or severe criticism are hard to recall, therefore we very seldom came across such descriptions, although the phenomena listed were typical of a system that manipulated people. Investigating the manipulation mechanisms would be very useful for the post-conflict society as a whole (McCully 2011, 164), on one hand, and making comparisons with practices applied in different regions and the assessment of their consequences, on the other.

From the mid-1950s, when the situation became more stable, and people could take some control over their lives, there were things and phenomena which were regarded as inevitable and better left alone: it was sensible to avoid talks on political topics, to obey orders within reason, and live one's life without irritating anyone directly. Life taught people about 'keeping quiet' and focusing on work. Work became a sort of lifeboat. Such an approach suited the authorities very well. Many of the strategies in the stories were presented as individual solutions, thus pretending to be aware of the system and planning further movements in subsequent strategies, and showing their skills in manipulating the Soviet system. This becomes a clear issue in the strategies in the following decades.

Getting the situation under control was also confirmed in party reports from the beginning of the 1950s. The number of teachers who were CP members began growing gradually, and the political activities of teachers outside the classroom stepped up. They began organizing various events, including outings and extracurricular activities, which were evaluated very positively by both pupils and parents. Ideologically, these activities would lead people to collectivism and thus to the recognition of the value of a socialist society. Giving an active meaning to the life of the young meant keeping them away from bad influences (Applebaum 2012, 332–337). The social activity of the young had to be channeled through Pioneer and Komsomol organizations so that political and ideological aims were attributed to almost all of their undertakings.

Therefore, one could come to the conclusion that by 1960, the teachers' generation born in the 1920s and 1930s, being at the center of the authorities' attention, and consequently reeducated, had found a middle way through the turns of history. They tried to achieve their self-respect through their work; and this strategy of work corresponded to a widely-spread saying – work has not been banned in any society by any power. However, could it be that this conclusion was suggested by one of the most dominant social groups – the teachers who passed through the Soviet period unharmed? Were those teachers who did not adapt unhappy; were they leading a miserable life? They cannot or do not want to explain what happened, they are reserved and uncommunicative, lacking any motive to retell their stories and so they likely never will. What will become of the experience of those and many others who kept quiet? This article did not moderate the voices of the teachers who had experienced extreme situations, for example, those who had personal experience of imprisonment and therefore found it nearly impossible to find work as teachers.

Without knowing the strategies exercised by the state and referring to additional sources, the life stories alone cannot disclose all of the strategies characteristic of the era. Attention should also be drawn to a certain paradox – although the teachers' generation under observation had to live through various twists and turns, and even if they radically changed their views over the course of their lives, the teachers of the Soviet period remain somewhat dogmatic and are not particularly ready to acknowledge a point of view different from their own. In many ways, those teachers resemble the personalities who, during challenging times, would know what they expected from life, combining the difficulties of adaptation in their experience (and life stories) with the creation of new identities (Laanes 2009, 51–53).

The teachers' reeducation process could not be declared complete by 1960, although schools were under the control of the party. Behind the appearance of loyalty, reticence, and the development of a new society, a lot of legacy and values belonging to the old society were preserved. The legacy and values determined the characteristics of a region and its social relationships. In turn, characteristics and relationships provided the basis for quite different, often uncontrollable tendencies and these could be analyzed by comparing the interactions of the students' strategies and orientations with teachers of different generations, both older and younger.

Notes

1. South-eastern Latvia (Latgale and South Sēlija region) is historically a multiethnic community, where a number of religions are practiced. It has stable traditions of ethnic and religious tolerance and mutual cultural enrichment. For centuries it has been inhabited by Latvians, Lithuanians, Belo-Russians, Russians, Germans, Polish, and Jewish people, with the major religious groups being Roman Catholics, Lutherans, Russian Orthodox, Old-Believers and Judaic. Everyday life was marked by mutual interaction and the enrichment of various cultures that gave rise to a particular culture and conduct. Tolerant treatment of 'others' was considered polite and was understood.

2. Since 2011 the State Archives of Latvia has been a structural department of the Latvian National Archives.

3. The use of the proper names Republic of Estonia or Republic of Latvia were also forbidden, according to Soviet historical treatment the period was called the 'ruling of bourgeois dictatorship.'

4. After the war, 97% of the Estonian education system used Estonian as the study language; by 1956/57 there were only 77% of Estonian-based general-education schools left. The policy favoring immigration reduced the native population: At the beginning of the 1980s Russian-based education formed one-third of the entire educational sphere in Estonia. In the 1937/1938 study year, Latvian as the language of instruction was used in 78.7% of schools, but in 1993/1994 only 49.2% of school children attended Latvian schools and about 50% attended schools with Russian as the language of instruction. Russian-based schools used Russian Soviet Federated Socialist Republic study programs, so the contact with the native population and its culture remained weak, teaching the Estonian and Latvian languages was often formal, giving rise to two different language – and culture-barred communities (Karjahärm and Sirk 2007, 82–84; Saleniece and Kuznetsovs 1999, 244–246).

5. Local history began to be taught in Estonia again in the 1957/1958 study year when a new history textbook was issued, and Estonian history was also unofficially taught in some schools earlier than this. In 1957, a new program for the history of the CPSU was worked out (Raudsepp 2005, 71, 94).

6. In the autumn of 1941, an organization of ZEV – Zentralstelle zur Erfassung der Verschleppten Esten (Centre for Registration and Retrieval of Deported and Mobilized Estonians) – was setup in Nazi-occupied Estonia to register those deported, arrested or mobilized by the Red Army and killed for gathering information. No equivalent data has been found for Latvia.

7. About 90,000 citizens from Estonia and 130,000 from Latvia escaped to the West.
8. Stringent punishments were meted out for wearing national symbolic decorations from the first months of Soviet rule. For public use of the Estonian national flag and other symbols in the summer of 1940, a number of schoolboys were among the first arrested. It was absurd because the national flag was not officially banned at that time and so on many houses the Soviet red flag and Estonian tricolor were hanging side by side (Kaasik and Hiio 2006, 309).
9. As the activities of the forest brothers declined, underground youth organizations continued their resistance movement, primarily during the years 1955–1962. Numerous school and university students were participants in the resistance movement of that period and they assessed the struggle of the years 1940–1968 as one process. The death of Stalin and the following events changed the youth's aspirations and activity in quantity but the quality remained the same(disseminating anti-Soviet leaflets, raising national flags, destroying Soviet symbols of power, helping those in active resistance, collecting weapons to be used at the x-hour etc.) (Isotamm 2004, 287–294).
10. Ene Kõresaar has underlined the fact typical of teachers' memories, that the whole of a teacher's life story is actually the biography of their working life (Kõresaar 2004, 293).

Acknowledgments

Aigi Rahi-Tamm's research for this article was supported in the framework of the project 'Estonia in the Cold War' (SF0180050s09) and 'Practices of Memory: Continuities and Discontinuities of Remembering the 20th Century' (ETF8190).

Disclosure statement

No potential conflict of interest was reported by the authors.

Funding

This work was supported by target funding project no SF0180050s09 and ETF8190 of Estonian Ministry of Education and Science.

References

Aarelaid, A. 2000. "Topeltmõtlemise kujunemine kahel esimesel nõukogulikul aastakümnel." *Akadeemia* 4: 755–773.
Altnurme, L. 2006. *Kristlusest omausuni. Uurimus muutustest eestlaste religioossuses 20.saj.II poolel*. Tartu: University of Tartu Press.
Applebaum, A. 2012. *Iron Curtain. The Crushing of Eastern Europe 1955–56*. London: Penguin Books.
Bassin, M., and C. Kelly. 2012. "Introduction: National Subjects." In *Soviet and Post-Soviet Identities*, edited by M. Basin, and C. Kelly, 3–16. Cambridge: Cambridge University Press.

Bennich-Björkman, L. 2007. *Political Culture under Institutional Pressure. How Institutional Change Transforms Early Socialization*. New York: Palgrave Macmillan.

Bleiere, D. 2012. "Vispārējās izglītības sovetizācija Latvijā: vēsturiskais konteksts, institucionālās vadības sistēma un kadrupolitika (1944-1964)." *LatvijasVēstures Insturūta Žurnāls* 4: 105–137.

Connelly, J. 2000. *Captive University. The Sovietization of East German, Czech, and Polish Higher Education, 1945–1956*. Chapel Hill: University of North Carolina Press.

DU MV (Collection of the Oral History Centre at Daugavpils University, Latvia).

Eacute, J., and M. Esteve. 2000. "The Transformation of the Teachers' Role at the End of the Twentieth Century: New Challenges for the Future." *Educational Review* 52 (2): 197–207. doi:10.1080/713664040.

EKLA (Estonian Cultural History Archives of the Estonian Literary Museum).

ERA (Estonian National Archives).

ERAF (Branch of Estonian State Archives).

Ewing, T. E. 2002. *The Teachers of Stalinism. Policy, Practice, and Power in Soviet Schools of the 1930s*. New York: Peter Lang Publishing.

Fitzpatrick, S. 1999. *Everyday Stalinism. Ordinary Life in Extraordinary Times: Soviet Russia in the 1930s*. New York: Oxford University Press.

Gross, J. T. 2002. *Revolution from Abroad. Soviet Conquest of Poland's Western Ukraine and Western Belorussia*. Princeton: Princeton University Press.

Grosvenor, I., M. Lawn, and K. Rousmaniere, eds. 1999. *Silences and Images. The Social History of the Classroom*. New York: Peter Lang.

Halfin, I. 2003. *Terror in My Soul. Communist Autobiographies on Trial*. Cambridge, MA: Harvard University Press.

Hellbeck, J. 2001. "Working, Struggling, Becoming: Stalin-Era Autobiographical Texts." *The Russian Review* 60 (3): 340–359. doi:10.1111/russ.2001.60.issue-3.

Hinrikus, R., ed. 2000. *Eesti rahva elulood I*. Tallinn: Tänapäev.

Hinrikus, R. 2003. "Eesti elulugude kogu ja selle uurimise perspektiive." In *Võim ja kultuur*, edited by A. Krikmann, and S. Olesk, 171–213. Tartu: Eesti kultuuriloo ja folkloristika keskus.

Hinrikus, R., and T. Kirss, eds. 2009. *Estonian Life Stories*. Budapest: CEU Press.

Hinrikus, R., and E. Kõresaar. 2004. "A Brief Overview of Life History Collection and Research in Estonia." In *She Who Remembers, Survives. Interpreting Estonian Women's Post-Soviet Life Stories*, edited by T. Kirss, E. Kõresaar, and M. Lauristin, 19–34. Tartu: Tartu University Press.

Isotamm, J. 2004. "Kas me olime mässajad?" In *Saatusekaaslased: Eesti noored vabadusvõitluses 1944–1954*, edited by U. Josia, 287–294. Tartu: Endiste Õpilasvabadusvõitlejate Liit.

Jaago, T. 2006. "Individuaalsed valikud ja sotsialiseerumine eluloojutustuste põhjal." *Mäetagused* 33: 83–100.

Jõesalu, K. 2004. "Sotsiaalsed suhted nõukogude tööelus: biograafilisi uurimusi argielust ENSV-s." Unpublished MA-thesis, University of Tartu, Faculty of Philosophy.

Josia, U., ed. 2004. *Saatusekaaslased: Eesti noored vabadusvõitluses 1944–1954*. Tartu: Endiste Õpilasvabadusvõitlejate Liit.

Kaasik, P., and T. Hiio. 2006. "Political Repression from June to August 1940." In *Estonia 1940–1945. Reports of the Estonian International Commission for the Investigation of Crimes against Humanity*, edited by T. Hiio, M. Maripuu, and P. Indrek, 308–318. Tallinn: Estonian International Commission for Investigation of Crimes against Humanity.

Karjahärm, T., and V. Sirk. 2007. *Kohanemine ja vastupanu. Eesti haritlaskond 1940–1987*. Tallinn: Argo.

Kaska, V., ed. 2008. *Võrumaa kooliõpilaste vastupanuvõitlus 1944–1950*. Viljandi: Vali Press.

Kõresaar, E. 2001. *Nõukogude perioodi vanemate eestlaste elulugudes: probleeme ja tähelepanekuid*, 120–131. Edited by T. Jaago. Tartu: Tartu University Press.

Kõresaar, E. 2004. "Towards a Social Memory of Work. Politics and Being a Good Teacher in the Life-Stories of Soviet Teachers." In *Arbeit in Sozialismus – Arbeit in Postsozialismus. Erkundungenzum Arbeitsleben im östlichen Europa*, edited by K. Roth, 291–310. Münster: Lit-Verlag.

Kreegipuu, T. 2007. "Ajaloo rakendamine propagandarelvana ehk kuidas kujundati ajalookäsitlus Nõukogude võimu kehtestamisest 21. juunil 1940 Nõukogude Eesti ajakirjanduses aastatel 1945–1960." *Tuna* 3: 46–69.

Kurs, O., ed. 2009. *Tartu 5. Keskkool. Koolikaja. Killukesi kohalikust kultuuriloost*. Tartu: O. Kurs.

Kuuli, O. 2007. *Stalini-aja võimukaader ja kultuurijuhid Eesti NSV-s (1940–1954)*. Tallinn: Tallinna Raamatutrükikoda.

Laanes, E. 2009. *Lepitamatud dialoogid. Subjekt ja mälu nõukogude-järgses Eesti romaanis.* Tallinn: Underi ja Tuglase kirjanduskeskus.

Livschiz, A. 2008. "Pre-Revolutionary in Form, Soviet in Content? Wartime Educational Reforms and the postwar Quest for Normality." In *Sovetskaja sotsialnaja politika: stseny i deistvujutscie litsa, 1940–1985* [Soviet Social Policy: Scenes and Actors, 1940–1985], edited by Jelena Jarska-Smirnova and Pavel Romanov, 151–173. Moskva: Variant.

LNA LVA (State Archives of Latvia).

Manheim, K. 1994. *Diagnoz nashevo vremeni.* Moskva: Yurist.

McCully, A. 2011. "History Teaching, 'Truth Recovery' and Reconciliation." In *Memory and Pedagogy*, edited by C. Mitchell, T. Strong-Wilson, K. Pithous, and S. Allnutt, 161–176. London: Routledge.

Mertelsmann, O., and A. Rahi-Tamm. 2009. "Cleansing and Compromise: The Estonian SSR in 1944–1945." *Cahiers du monde russe* 49: 319–340.

Mikelsaar, R.-H., ed. 2009. *Tartu õpetajaid õpilase nägemuses.* Tartu: Greif.

Paavle, I. 2009. "Kohaliku halduse sovetiseerimine Eestis 1940–1950." PhD-thesis, Tartu University Press.

Paklar, V., ed. 2009. *Mu kodu on Eestis. Eestimaa rahvaste elulood.* Tallinn: Tänapäev.

Palumets, L., and M. Titma. 2001. "Kommunistlikku parteisse kuulumine: eeldused ja tagajärjed." In *Sõjajärgse põlvkonna elutee ja seda kujundanud faktorid*, edited by T. Mikk, 97–122. Tartu: Tartu University Press.

Paukšte, J. ed. 2011. *Dzimtāszemeselpa* [Breath of the native land]. Daugavpils: Daugavpils Universitātes akadēmiska isapgāds "Saule".

Pilve, E. 2013. "Nõukogude noore kasvatamisest paberil ja päriselt. Ideoloogiline ajupesu Eesti NSV kooli(tunni)s 1953–1991." *Tuna* 3: 82–100.

Pipes, R. 2005. *Kommunism. Lühiajalugu.* Tartu: Ilmamaa.

Rahi-Tamm, A. 2005. "Human Losses." In *The White Book on Estonian Population Losses in the Occupations from 1940 through 1991*, edited by V. Salo, Ü. Ennuste, E. Parmasto, E. Tarvel, and P. Varju, 25–46. Tallinn: Estonian State Commission on Examination of the Policies of Repression, Estonian Encyclopaedia Publishers.

Rahi-Tamm, A. 2009. "Arhiivid Nõukogude repressiivaparaadi teenistuses. 'Poliitvärvingute' kartoteek Eestis 1940–1956." *Ajalooline Ajakiri 127/128* (1/2): 123–154.

Rahi-Tamm, A., and A. Kahar. 2009. "The Deportation Operation 'Priboi' in 1949." In *Estonia since 1944: Report of the Estonian International Commission for the Investigation of Crimes against Humanity*, edited by T. Hiio, M. Maripuu, and P. Indrek, 429–460. Tallinn: Estonian International Commission for the Investigation of Crimes against Humanity.

Raudsepp, A. 2005. "Ajaloo õpetamise korraldus Eesti NSv eesti õppekeelega üldhariduskoolides 1944–1985." PhD-thesis, Tartu Tartu University Press.

Renno, O., S. Jüri, and S. Arno. 2010. "Mälestusi õpetajatest Viljandi II Keskkoolis aastail 1944–1950." *Viljandi Muuseumi toimetised* I: 185–199.

Rodden, J. 2002. *Repainting the Little Red Schoolhouse: A History of Eastern German Education, 1945–1995.* Oxford: Oxford University Press.

Saleniece, I. 2003. "Teachers as Object and Subject of Sovietization: Daugavpils (1944–1953)." In *The Sovietization of the Baltic States, 1940–1956*, edited by O. Mertelsmann, 197–206. Tartu: KLEIO.

Saleniece, I., and S. Kuznetsovs. 1999. "Nationality Policy, Education and the Russian Question in Latvia Since 1918." In *Ethnicity and Nationalism in Russia, The CIS and the Baltic States*, edited by C. Williams, and T. D. Sfikas, 236–264. Aldershot: Ashgate.

Sandle, M. 2010. *Kommunism.* Tallinn: Pegasus.

Sirk, V. 2004. "Haritlaskond osustus visaks vastaseks. Jooni stalinlikust intelligentsipoliitikast." *Tuna* 1: 51–69.

Tannberg, T. 2007. "Moskva institutsionaalsed ja nomenklatuursed kontrollimehhanismid Eesti NSVs sõjajärgsetel aastatel." *Eesti Ajalooarhiivi toimetised* 15 (22): 225–272. *Eesti NSV aastatel 1940–1953: sovetiseerimise mehhanismid ja tagajärjed Nõukogude Liidu ja Ida-Euroopa arengute kontekstis* (Tartu: Eesti Ajalooarhiiv).

Tannberg, T. 2010. *Politika Moskvy v respublikah Baltii v poslevoennye gody (1944–1956): issledovanija i dokumenty.* Moskva: ROSSPEN.

Tarto, H., ed. 2010. *Meie lugu. "Prillitoosi" kirjad.* Tallinn: Varrak.

Tarvel, E., ed. 2002. *Eestimaa Kommunistliku Partei Keskkomitee organisatsiooniline struktuur 1940–1991.* Tallinn: Kistler-Ritso Eesti Sihtasutus.

Thompson, P. 2000. *The Voice of the Past: Oral History.* Oxford: Oxford University Press.

Vaivods, A. ed. 2009. *Cilvēkadzīve*. Daugavpils: Daugavpils Universitātes akadēmiska isapgāds "Saule".

Veskimägi, K. 1996. *Nõukogude unelaadne elu. Tsensuur Eesti NSV-s ja tema peremehed*. Tallinn: Tallinna Raamatutrükikoda.

Weiner, A., and A. Rahi-Tamm. 2012. "Getting to Know You: The Soviet Surveillance System, 1939–1957." *Kritika: Explorations in Russian and Eurasian History* 13 (1): 5–45. doi:10.1353/kri.2012.0011.

Zubkova, J. 2008. *Pribaltika i Kreml 1940–1953*. Moskva: ROSSPEN.

Points of memory in the narrative of a 'Mnemonic Warrior': gender, displacement, and the anti-Soviet war of resistance in Lithuania

Dovilė Budrytė

School of Liberal Arts, Georgia Gwinnett College, Lawrenceville, Georgia

ABSTRACT

Drawing on feminist theories on memory and memory work, this article analyzes the biographical narrative of Aldona Vilutienė (neé Sabaitytė), a former partisan messenger and deportee, who created the first museum commemorating the anti-Soviet resistance and the deportations carried out under Stalin in post-Soviet Lithuania. The analysis is focused on points of memory, a theoretical concept developed by Marianne Hirsch who defined them as 'points of intersection between past and present, memory and post-memory, personal remembrance and cultural recall.' This approach helps us to better understand the complex processes of memory production and reconstruct the lived experiences associated with remembering war and displacement. In addition, it challenges the portrayal of partisan war and deportations as monumental national traumas.

Introduction

As astutely stated by Marianne Hirsch (2012), current debates among those who study memory in various fields include questions about 'the ethics and aesthetics of remembrance' in the aftermath of traumatic events (2012, 2). What are the proper ways to remember the pain and trauma experienced by others, without trivializing or appropriating their experiences? How do we ensure sure that various experiences are represented fairly? Which traumatic events are memorialized by governments and how? Additionally, there are questions related to the aesthetics of the remembrance of traumatic events, such as: which representations make it to the public sphere and which stories and images are likely to be marginalized or even silenced? What should be done with memories that are rarely voiced or shown and are considered to be too mundane, inappropriate, or even shameful, to be shared in public? These questions pertain to the construction and survival of memory regimes that consist of a set of visible, constructed memories that are institutionalized and attract at least some support from the public (Langenbacher 2008).

To gain insight into processes of memory production, this essay analyzes a biographical narrative of a memory entrepreneur; a political actor who, as theorized by

Elizabeth Jelin (2003) has actively sought 'social recognition and political legitimacy of *one* [her own] interpretation or narrative of the past' (33–34). Aldona Vilutienė could be described as a 'mnemonic warrior,' or someone who 'tends to draw a sharp line between themselves (the proprietors of the "true" vision of the past) and other actors who cultivate "wrong" or "false" versions of history' (Kubik and Bernard 2014, 13).

Attention to the ways in which memory entrepreneurs tell their stories, use iconic images, develop strategies to gain political legitimacy, and position themselves vis-à-vis the existing hegemonic narratives can be useful in understanding the origins of memory regimes and the development of norms supporting or contesting the legitimacy of agendas pursued by memory entrepreneurs.

Assessing the emotional power of memory regimes: discourses, visuals, and points of memory

There is a growing acknowledgement in memory studies that the visual elements of memory regimes, such as popular images in photographs, are social and political constructs that are, in the words of Linda Devereux, 'censored and mediated by dominant social discourses' (2010, 124). A study of these images and relevant discourses can help to reveal underlying power structures. Autobiographical narratives of those whose lives are linked to these images and those who are able to transfer these images into the public sphere become indispensable for understanding the processes related to the remembrance and transmission of memories.

Marianne Hirsch (2012) coined the term 'points of memory.' These points include photographs, artwork, or personal items from the places of suffering, are 'points of intersection between past and present, memory and post-memory, personal remembrance and cultural recall' (61). This concept is useful for the study of how memory transcends the individual level and enters the collective (or public) realm because it embraces both the geographical (spatial) dimension and the temporal dimension. Thus, the intersection of two important variables in the workings of memory (space and time) is captured, and this helps to understand the power with which these objects penetrate 'the levels of oblivion' (Hirsch 2012, 61). Points of memory are also 'arguments about memory, objects or images that have remained from the past,' and they emerge in encounters between people (Hirsch 2012, 62). Hirsch's theorization about the points of memory suggests that the study of the transmission of traumatic memory is inseparable from the study of powerful visuals and relevant narratives.

Many studies have analyzed the impact of photographs and other visuals, such as artifacts from ghettos, in the construction of the ethics and aesthetics surrounding the remembrance of the Holocaust (Lothe, Suleiman, and Phelan 2012). Similar approaches have been used to study other collective traumatic events (without erasing important historical differences and recognizing the enormity of the Holocaust). Certain objects – images of trains and camps in Siberia, rosaries made of bread, or photographs with the tortured bodies of partisans – have become parts of the memory aesthetic and related discourses associated with trauma and displacement in post-Soviet Lithuania. This memory regime, which can be described as *kovos ir kančių istorija* [history of fighting and suffering] was especially visible during the time of *Atgimimas* [the rebirth], the initial stage of democratization and nationalism in the late 1980s until the restoration of independence in 1991, when memoirs of the former deportees and objects related to their displacement were prominently positioned in the public space and served as an indictment of the previous regime.

As argued by Violeta Davoliūtė (2013), the emergence of a 'discourse of displacement' (part of the memory regime during *Atgimimas*) can be traced back to the Soviet Lithuanian culture that prepared the ground for the explosive reception of deportee memoirs and, by extension, the creation of the memory aesthetic commemorating displacement in the late 1980s. Davoliūtė's (2013) account of the emergence of this discourse highlighted the role of leading Lithuanian writers, all men, in constructing this discourse. As processes of democratic consolidation took place, memory pluralism followed. Various groups competed for recognition of their memories in the public space (Onken 2010). Some have argued (e.g. Rubavičius 2007) that in the mid-1990s, a narrative about the 'silent resistance' promoted in the memoirs of the former members of the Soviet establishment 'overshadowed' the narrative about displacement based on the memoirs of former deportees, thus reducing the political power of the latter.

Despite the visible decline of the emotional appeal of the narratives of the former victims and corresponding visuals associated with the former deportees and political prisoners, elements of these narratives were incorporated into official memory, which, in turn, has acquired an international dimension. Official memory can be conceptualized as consisting of various mechanisms, such as history education in public schools, state-supported commemorations, state-supported institutes, and state-sponsored museums. These mechanisms contribute to the shaping of public consciousness in a particular direction, and therefore are an important part of memory regimes in both transitional and established democracies.

In post-Soviet Lithuania, the mass deportations carried out by the Soviet Union and the anti-Soviet war of resistance have remained part of state-supported official memory. At the same time, there are strong counter-narratives, both in Lithuania and abroad, that resist this memory regime. In addition, the fact that some Lithuanians who later became anti-Soviet partisans also participated in the Holocaust has recently received more attention. For example, in 2015, the journalist Rimvydas Valatka published an article titled 'Ką pagerbė Lietuva – partizanų vadą Generolą Vėtrą ar žydų žudiką' [Who Has Lithuania Honored: The Partisan Commander General Vėtra or a Jew Killer?] (Valatka 2015). This article prompted a vigorous debate about who should be considered a 'national hero' and whether the anti-Soviet partisans who were commemorated as national heroes in the late 80s and early 90s should continue to be venerated. In 2016, Rūta Vanagaitė published the book *Mūsiškiai* [Ours], which discusses the participation of some Lithuanians who later became anti-Soviet partisans in the Holocaust (Vanagaitė 2016). This book, which became a bestseller, prompted more questions about the memory regime based on the veneration of the anti-Soviet resistance and deportations carried out under Stalin. Prior to 2016, as demonstrated by Maria Mälksoo (2014), elements of official memory regimes from the Baltic states have become part of what she calls 'transnational mnemopolitics' in Europe that includes a fight for the criminalization of Communist crimes. The Lithuanian diaspora in the United States has also been engaged in cultural work constructing and reconstructing the traumatic memory of the deportations and political repressions that were carried out under Stalin.[1]

The construction and reconstruction of the memory regime have included various actors, including the victims who were directly affected by traumatic events, the state, and social groups with political demands. Elizabeth Jelin (2003) has described such processes as 'memory negotiations.' Some actors, Jelin argues, have stronger voices than others, depending on their access to 'the microphones of power,' willingness to get engaged in self-censorship, and moral legitimacy in the eyes of the public (36). Memory entrepreneurs make traumatic memories based on the discourse of displacement politically relevant. These memories become part of political landscape, together with other institutionalized traumatic memories and counter-memories. There are social and political power structures contributing to the construction and survival of these traumatic memories, and gender-sensitive approaches to the study of memory help to gain a better understanding of these processes.

Gender-sensitive approaches to the study of traumatic memories

With several notable exceptions (Kirss, Kõresaar, and Lauristin 2004; Lazda 2006), the study of traumatic memory embedded in memory regimes in the Baltic states usually does not include a gender dimension. Indeed, what can gender perspectives add to the understanding of the construction of traumatic memories and related phenomena? As discussed by Myrna Goldenberg and Amy H. Shapiro (2013), gender analyses, focusing on individual lives and experiences, are complex and undermine the tendency of researchers (especially in the social sciences) to universalize experiences while constructing elegant theories (2013, 11). Furthermore, is asking a classical feminist question 'Where are the women?' simply immoral when writing about traumas that involve substantial human suffering that affected not only women but also men and children? Marianne Hirsch (2012) identifies several potential contributions of gender perspectives to the study of memory, such as the inclusion of perspectives that 'otherwise remain absent from the historical archive' (15), the opening of new spaces for the study of themes such as 'affect (feeling), embodiment, privacy, and intimacy as concerns of history,' and 'shift(ing) our attention to the minute events of daily life' (16). Hirsch argues that gender can 'fulfill a number of functions in the work of memory' (18) that include serving as 'a figure' regulating the circulation of images and narratives in the transmission of memory, a 'position through which memory can be transmitted within family or beyond it,' and 'a lens through which to read the domestic and the public scenes of memorial acts' (18). Hirsch's study of points of memory from a gendered perspective (a cook book and a book containing art from concentration camps) demonstrates the value of being sensitive to gender in the studies of traumatic memory (Hirsch 2012). The author is able to recover details of everyday life that are usually left out from mainstream historical accounts and gain insight into various channels and structures of memory transmission.

The article follows the methodological principles of feminist approaches to the study of memory that Jansson, Wendt, and Åse (2008) discuss. These principles include a belief that the study of experiences, women's experiences in particular, remains the most important feature of memory work. Admittedly, memory scholars embracing not only feminism but also various other schools of thought have recently welcomed foci on experiences of minorities, children, and other previously ignored groups. However, Ackerly and True (2010) explain that an important original contribution of feminist perspectives is to 'open new lines of inquiry versus simply "filling in the gaps" in already established disciplinary terrains' (2). Opening up new lines of inquiry implies sensitivity to power structures, dynamics of power, and social relationships that include a gender dimension. Furthermore, new lines of inquiry also imply an understanding that gender can shape historical experiences and the ways in which they are remembered.

As Jansson, Wendt, and Åse (2008) establish, it is necessary to make sure that women's experiences are not treated as given or objective, and is crucially important to explore the tensions between the lived experiences and the ways in which they are articulated. Jansson, Wendt, and Åse (2008) maintain that the feminist approaches to memory work can help to 'locate cracks and ambivalences in the already known, and open up for understandings and interpretations that take us beyond the discursively given' (2008, 230).

How can these methodological principles be applied in the study of points of memory and corresponding narratives? Feminist memory work 'emphasizes lived experience, that which is close, tangible, and concrete' (Jansson, Wendt, and Åse 2008, 230). The introduction of women and gender introduces a shift away from rational individual choices to social relations, and this helps to better understand power structures as rooted in everyday practices.

To follow the principles identified by feminist memory theorists, it becomes neces-sary to record 'mundane' stories, pay attention to 'insignificant' events of everyday life, and analyze intersections of individual and collective narratives, forgetting and silences. ('Forgetting' could include traumas experienced by other, often marginalized, groups. 'Silences' could refer to experiences that are considered as shameful or too painful to be shared openly.)

Many feminist memory theorists would likely abstain from an assertion that narratives capturing gendered experiences could be treated as representative of greater trends or beliefs held by large groups. Instead, these theorists are likely to ask the readers to respect and celebrate the individuality of each story. This position is consistent with one important goal of feminist memory work, which is to identify the uncertainties and contradictions in dominant narratives about the past and highlight the tensions between such dominant narratives and lived, individual women's experiences.

Attention to individual women's experiences helps feminist memory theorists to gain insight into power structures, oppressions, and silences that often are lost in 'gender-blind' analyses of memory. Feminist scholars acknowledge the possibility that some painful gendered experiences, such as rape or misogynist treatment, may never become part of oral testimonies because of prevailing cultural norms. Engaging in feminist analysis implies asking questions not only about the events described in the narrative but also about the omissions.

Aldona's story: partisan war, displacement, and memory work

Following the path pioneered by Hirsch and other feminist scholars of traumatic memory, this article studies the points of memory described in the biographical narrative of Aldona Vilutienė (neé Sabaitytė), a memory entrepreneur,[2] former partisan messenger, and deportee. Since 2009, I have been interested in uncovering narratives of women who were directly affected by traumatic events of World War II and the postwar eras and found their own ways to address trauma through political activities. Aldona's life story stands out due to her passionate and non-compromising devotion to memory work. An author of three books, she spent many years creating a museum in Marijampolė, which institutionalizes a version of the 'fighting and suffering' paradigm.

I conducted a semi-structured interview with Aldona Vilutienė on 13 June 2013, in her home in Marijampolė.[3] The interview was loosely structured around the two main themes of armed resistance and deportation, in addition to her activities as a memory entrepreneur. The article follows a structure in line with the interview. References to other memoirs and relevant sources, including the books written by Aldona, are made to illustrate the functions and impact of the points of memory and tensions between dominant discourses and individual accounts.

The historical period that is covered in depth in Aldona's story, the postwar era, including the Stalinist period, is usually prominently featured in narratives of women in Lithuania. As Dalia Leinartė, who conducted interviews with Lithuanian women, points out, her respondents delivered a clear and logical narrative of events that took place prior to World War II, during World War II, and during Stalinist rule. When describing the events that took place after the Stalinist period, the narratives lost their coherence (Leinartė 2016, 13). Aldona's oral testimony included long sections on the war of resistance, imprisonment, deportation, and memory work; however, admittedly, World War II and the Holocaust were missing from her discussion.

For the first theme (the armed resistance), I analyze one relevant point of memory buttons that resistance fighters wore on their uniforms. Aldona Vilutienė was a partisan messenger, and a story about finding buttons for resistance fighters was an important part of her testimony. For the second theme, I explore *vizitėlės*, or pieces of embroidery, made by Lithuanian deportees in prison camps and places of deportation in the Soviet far north. Many women prisoners, including Aldona, made these pieces of embroidery. Currently these points of memory can be found in personal collections and deportation and resistance museums in Lithuania, and they are also described in memoirs written by former deportees and former resistance fighters. They are capable of eliciting strong emotions and an immediate connection with the traumatic past among those who are familiar with everyday life in prisons and forced exile. These items are called *relikvijos* (relics) by the former partisans, deportees, their descendants, and memory entrepreneurs supporting the 'fighting and suffering' paradigm.

Political changes, traumatic memories, and the museum

Jenny Edkins argues in *Trauma and the Memory of Politics* (2003) that there is a close link between political changes, the creation of democratic entities, and traumatic memories. During the times of major political upheavals, previous order and institutions are replaced. Previous traumas are remembered and new traumas may be created. In the words of Edkins, 'forms of statehood in contemporary society, as forms of political community, are themselves produced and reproduced through social practices, including practices of trauma and memory' (2003, 11). Dominant views on trauma and memory supported by the state emerge, and they influence how people remember events such as war; however, in democratic entities, those views can be contested and challenged. Thus, a search for a coherent narrative that includes references to the past is part of the political process and is essential for ontological security of the state and society.

Aldona Vilutienė's narrative about her political struggles to create a museum telling her version of the story about the postwar resistance and deportations and gain broader recognition for this narrative sheds light on the ways that the processes related to changes in political realities, the creation of statehood, and traumatic memories analyzed by Edkins unfold on a local level. During *Atgimimas* in the late 1980s, there were many attempts by former deportees and political prisoners to establish museums telling the story of 'fighting and suffering.' These deportees and prisoners depicted the postwar years as a heroic fight against the Soviet Union and labeled the Stalinist deportations as 'genocide.' Nine museums established by the former deportees and political prisoners have survived to this day. Seven of them, including the museum started by Aldona, function as *Kraštotyros muziejai* [museums of local history] and are supported by local governments. The remaining two museums are supported by private funds. In 2012, a group of parliamentarians initiated a request for the government to make these museums into fully state-supported institutions (Vėta 2012), but this request did not yield results. *Lietuvos gyventojų genocido ir rezistencijos tyrimo centras* [The Genocide and Resistance Research Center of Lithuania], on the other hand, is a government agency.[4] This Center was a successor to the Commission on Research into Stalinist Crimes, a non-governmental organization created in 1988. Aldona Vilutienė and many other memory entrepreneurs outside of the capital have pursued their memory politics independently from the Genocide and Resistance Research Center in Vilnius.

Aldona started her memory work aimed at telling the story of 'fighting and suffering' during the same year, when a non-governmental organization called *Tremtinys* [deportee] was created in Marijampolė. Aldona became the leader of this group. She starts her story with a reference to 1993 – the year when out of numerous initiatives pursued by the museum *Tremtinys* were born. The birth of the museum was one of the most memorable events in Aldona's life:

> My work went beyond normal human capacity. When I was a partisan messenger, when I was going through hell, I was thinking about it [commemoration]. Even while deported I was thinking: when I go back, then I will need to somehow immortalize the men of my partisan unit. I became a group coordinator, and we started to collect material about partisan fights, about deportation. I created an archive at home at first. There was a woman here, Petronėlė Vėlyvienė, a partisan whose *nom de guerre* [an assumed name used during resistance] was Vilija [the name of a river in Lithuania]. She told me: 'Why are you wasting time creating archives? Only a few people will see them. Create a museum!' She was right, but how to get a place for the museum? I can't tell you everything right now. I am writing a book about it. I kept a diary. When it was very difficult, I cried …. But when people found out about it [the creation of the museum] in the beginning of *Atgimimas*, we all threw ourselves into this work, like butterflies fly into the flames.

In her book of memoirs *Laiko dulkes nužėrus* [having removed the dust of time] published in 2013, Vilutienė openly describes the ideology and political goals of the museum which was envisioned as a 'crib to foster patriotism, as [a way to express] pride in those … who have not bowed their heads and genuflected against the invader' (2013, 5). This was an attempt to construct a 'trauma drama,' a story with clear heroes and villains. Such storytelling requires strategic forgetting, which means that the events that do not fit this heroic narrative are omitted.

She recalls how people 'from all over Lithuania,' having found out about the museum, came to her, told her their stories about the past, and brought her various items from prisons and places of deportation – their 'relics.' These were photographs, embroidery made by women in prisons and deportation, wooden boxes made in the Soviet far north, rosaries made out bread, albums, medals, and buttons retrieved during the reburials of resistance fighters. Aldona was determined to find ways to incorporate these items into a dramatic story about resistance to the Soviet regime told by the museum.

This determination has probably affected the structure of the museum. Similarly to the other museums of local history in Lithuania, *Tauro Apygardos Partizanų ir Tremties Muziejus* [Tauras district museum of partisans and deportation] has two major sections, focusing on the anti-Soviet partisan fights and mass deportations by the Soviet Union that took place in 1941 and after World War II. In addition, the museum includes a smaller section on *Atgimimas* ['the rebirth'] in the late 1980s, thus attempting to establish a distance between the experiences during the Soviet period and the war of resistance. The first section includes photographs, various personal items of the partisans – including buttons from their uniforms – and weapons. The second section includes photographs from the places of deportation and numerous 'relics,' including *vizitėlės* and embroidery made by women in the places of deportation. The section focusing on *Atgimimas* includes photographs depicting trips by Lithuanians to the places of deportation to retrieve the bones of the deportees and bring them to Lithuania.

Aldona's book documents numerous conflicts with the local bureaucrats who, according to the author, resisted the creation of the museum and refused to place the museum in the so-called 'Bagdonas house' – a building in which the leadership of the NKVD (a 'law enforcement' agency known for political repression) was based during the postwar years, and in which the rooms of interrogation used Petras Raslanas, a high-ranking NKVD officer, were located.[5] The walls of the building contain many bricks with inscriptions by the prisoners, and the bones of six people who were tortured in the Bagdonas house were found next to the building. Yet the attempts of Aldona and her helpers did not bear fruit to make the Bagdonas house into the resistance and deportation museum. According to *Laiko dulkes nužėrus*, 'Bagdonas house' was privatized with the help of one of the leaders of Marijampolė's union of political prisoners and deportees and is currently used for commercial purposes.

This is not the only disillusionment experienced by Aldona in her fight for the museum. In her oral testimony, she talked about the fear experienced on 13 January 1991, when clashes between the Soviet military and civilians in Vilnius took place. Aldona was worried not about her personal safety, but about the fate of the items (the 'relics') donated to her museum by the former deportees, resistance fighters, and their relatives. She wondered about the relics and her attempt to tell the truth about the past if Lithuanian attempts to secede from the Soviet Union failed. Her neighbor, a son of the partisan leader in the unit where Aldona served as a messenger, helped her to save the 'relics.' He put all of them into bags and hid them somewhere. The bags only returned in August 1991, after the putsch in Moscow was over.

Prior to 1993, the 'relics' were housed in the museum of local history where an exhibition depicting deportation and war of resistance was housed in a small room with only three displays. Aldona talked about several instances when several 'relics' disappeared from the displays. Her book includes a detailed list of the 'relics' that were stolen in 1992: rosaries made of bread, a medal and buttons that belonged to the partisans, and a piece of embroidery that she made (a little black bag used to keep rosaries). Aldona called police; however, the director of the museum told the policemen not to bother documenting the losses: 'It is not worth to make noise about these trinkets; they are of no value.'

Hurt by these words, Aldona continued to fight for a separate building for her museum. She was able to obtain rooms close to 'Bagdonas house,' in a former court hall. As noted earlier, *Tauro Apygardos Partizanų ir Tremties Muziejus* [Tauras district museum of partisans and deportation] finally opened in 1993. Aldona acquired funds from the Union of the former Political Prisoners and Deportees, the local government of Marijampolė, and the Lithuanian diaspora in the United States. Former deportees and resistance fighters served as volunteers in the museum. The 'relics' found a safer place. Recalling the loss of 'relics,' however, triggered memories about her personal experiences during the war of resistance and deportation.

The war of resistance: 'obtaining the buttons was the most difficult task'

Memory and post-memory about the anti-Soviet resistance are alive and well in Lithuania, and emotionally charged public discussions about various aspects of these fights occur periodically. As conceptualized by Hirsch (2012), *post-memory* is a term describing the feelings and the relationship that the 'generation after' has established with the trauma experienced by their parents and relatives. Post-memory is shaped by stories, images, and behaviors; however, these experiences can be so powerful that they are capable of constructing new images and new stories, or 'memories in their own right.' Imagination plays a major role in construction of post-memory (Hirsch 2012, 5). Contentious and complex issues, such as relationships between the partisans and civilians who cooperated with the local pro-Soviet authorities, have only recently begun to be studied systematically.[6] These observations underscore the need for more autobiographical accounts by those who participated in these fights or were affected by them.

The most intense warfare associated with the anti-Soviet resistance, also known as the Lithuanian partisan war, took place in 1944–1949. The resistance fighters opposed the policies of Sovietization and political repression pursued by the Soviet Union. People joined the resistance not only due to 'patriotic idealism' but also to avoid the draft and because it became almost impossible to cope with the many insecurities and terrors of civilian life (Misiunas and Taagepera 1993, 84). Recent studies on the topic include the previous experiences of the Soviet and Nazi occupations as one of the reasons for joining armed resistance (Jankauskienė 2014, 224). Fear of punishment for cooperation with the Nazis may have been among these reasons. According to the website of the Genocide and Resistance Research Center of Lithuania, it is estimated that between 1944 and 1953, there were at least 50,000 active anti-Soviet resistance fighters in Lithuania. Overall, approximately 100,000 people were involved in anti-Soviet resistance. This number includes the fighters and their helpers (messengers, supporters, and reserve fighters). Approximately 20,000 partisans were killed during the war of resistance (Genocide and Resistance Research Center of Lithuania, n.d.).

Women were active participants of the armed resistance, although the levels of their participation and exact numbers are still under-researched. A comparative study of Lithuanian women who fought in the anti-Soviet resistance and Jewish women who fought in the anti-Nazi resistance conducted by Ruth Leiserowitz (2012) found that in both cases, women were expected to perform many 'feminine' tasks that included making food and taking care of the wounded. Another study, conducted by Žaneta Smolskutė (2006), includes factual information about 250 women who were active during the war of resistance and who, based on the law *Pasipriešinimo 1940–1990 metų okupacijoms dalyvių teisinio statuso įstatymas* [the law establishing the legal status of the members of resistance to occupations in 1940–1990] passed by the Lithuanian Parliament in 1997 received *kario savanorio statusas* [the status of a volunteer fighter] from the Lithuanian Government. The stated goal of this law was to acknowledge those who fought in the war of resistance and offer monetary compensation.

In 1944 and 1945, the resistance fighters tried to gain control of the territory of Lithuania; they engaged in battles with the Red Army and the NKVD-MVD (the Soviet Secret police). The bloodiest battles took place during this time. It is estimated that between 1944 and 1945, at least 30,000 fighters, many of whom were men who were trying to avoid military draft, were active in the woods (Jankauskienė 2014, 239). Between 1949 and 1953, the resistance movement lost its strength. Following the mass deportations of 1949, collectivization in the Lithuanian villages became more successful, and the partisan movement has lost many of its supporters. The organizational structure of battle groups, present during the previous stages of resistance movement, disintegrated. The Soviet forces were able to infiltrate many units of resistance fighters and started to control their ability to communicate with each other. Thus, in 1950, only 1228 partisans were left in Lithuania. This number decreased to 139 in 1954 and 13 in 1956 (Jankauskienė 2014, 240).

The anti-Soviet resistance fighters were active in nine districts. Tauras district, where Aldona was active as a messenger from 1945 to 1949, was one of the best-organized partisan units established in 1945. From the beginning, the partisan leaders worked on consolidating their forces in the geographical region called Suvalkija. The members of Tauras district printed their own newspaper, mandated that all fighters were dressed in uniforms used by the military forces of independent Lithuania, adopted many statutes regulating the activities of the partisans, and organized entry to western Europe by three Lithuanian resistance fighters, Kazimieras Pyplys, Jurgis Krikščiūnas, and Juozas Lukša. This unit was especially strong between 1946 and 1948, taking the initiative to lead the partisan war (Jankauskienė 2014, 234–37).

The dramatic life story of Juozas Lukša (nom de guerre Daumantas) has become iconic among some circles in post-Soviet Lithuania, depicted in several films, including Vienui vieni [Utterly Alone] directed by Jonas Vaitkus in 2003 (Vaitkus 2003), and most recently Nematomas frontas [The Invisible Front] directed by Vincas Sruoginis, Mark Johnson, and Jonas Ohman in 2014 (Sruoginis and Ohman 2014). Juozas Lukša's letters to Nijolė Bražėnaitė, whom he met in Paris and married while being trained by the French intelligence, is probably the best-known love story romanticizing the masculinization of the war of resistance.

Women were active fighters in Tauras district. According to the testimony of Antanina Akelaitytė (nom de guerre, an assumed name used in resistance, Liepa, or Lime-Tree), who served as a partisan messenger in this district, two women partisans, Anelė Senkutė (nom de guerre Pušelė, or Pine-Tree) and Janina Markevičiūtė (nom de guerre Saulutė, or Little Sun), were the main players in a plot organized by a partisan leader in attracting a large number of Soviet collaborators to a party during which they were killed. This plot became known as blynų balius [the ball of pancakes] and was romanticized in several works depicting the lives of the resistance fighters (Voverienė 2004). The military activities of women, who primarily served as messengers, are featured in only one display in the museum in Marijampolė.

Aldona joined the resistance movement early. She was only 14. She recalls that the anti-Soviet partisans were very active in Vytautiškės village where she grew up with her grandmother and eight other children. Her uncle joined the partisans as well, and she remembers vividly when she saw him and his friend for the first time: 'They wore

Lithuanian uniforms, and they were already grown-ups. Their uniforms were from the times of [President] Smetona. You know, I was dazzled. I was not even fourteen yet, but I started helping them.' Her tasks included taking the resistance fighters to villages in the neighborhood, carrying and distributing their newspapers and proclamations in public places, such as roadside crosses and big trees in visible spots, and transferring objects wrapped in paper or other material from one location to another. Often she did not know she was transporting. Aldona remembers muddling through several kilometers of swamp to complete her tasks. She also collected and recorded songs and delivered notebooks with songs to the resistance fighters.[7] The fighters wanted cigarettes, and Aldona recalls that these were expensive and very difficult to get:

> I did my best [to fulfill their wishes]. However, the most mundane things that appear to be so common were the most challenging to get. For example, bandages. Even though [a pharmacist] may not ask directly why I was getting so many pieces of bandages or iodine, they saw it. But the most difficult task was … One partisan was making a uniform, and he needed Lithuanian buttons [that is, buttons from military uniforms used in independent Lithuania]. Do you understand [the gravity of the situation]: How to obtain such buttons? I was charged with a task to get them. And how to do it? Ask [people] directly? You can be suspected [of helping the partisans]. I asked my acquaintances, talked to them, asked them, maybe they knew something. It took me a month to get these buttons, but this probably was the most difficult job. You know, you are immediately suspected [of helping the partisans].

Even other dangerous tasks, such as obtaining and delivering weapons to the resistance fighters, pale in comparison to Aldona's memory about the buttons. Therefore, for Aldona (and perhaps for other messengers who were engaged in similar tasks), the buttons – simple, small objects, often retrieved during reburials of the resistance fighters – have enormous potential to pierce time and space, and elicit the feelings of insecurity and fear associated with their memories about the war. They fit the description of 'points of memory' developed by Hirsch (2012).

These buttons, together with weapons, maps, and other personal items used by partisans, are on display in the first section in *Tauro Apygardos Partizanų ir Tremties Muziejus* [Tauras district museum of partisans and deportation]. However, the display does not include any explicit references to the experiences of women, such as Aldona, who made uniforms for partisans.

Similar to the testimonies of other former resistance fighters, betrayal by her fellow fighters stands out as a painful memory in Aldona's story. She talked about three acts of betrayal – by Šeštakauskas, a villager who lured the partisans into his house to eat freshly slaughtered pork during a very cold winter of 1947 and then invited the Soviets to destroy the partisans; by Juozas Karašauskas, a wounded partisan with the *nom de guerre* Liepa who was in Šeštakauskas' house (Juozas Karašauskas mentioned Aldona's name during the interrogation); and by Birutė, a fellow messenger, who had also betrayed Aldona in captivity. It appears that Aldona was able to forgive Liepa, who was cruelly tortured after his capture in 1947:

> He was severely wounded. It looks they were beating him as well; so, he started talking … probably in the middle of March (1948). I have it written down because I was in the archives [with the KBG files]. They probably tortured him to death. There is a reference [to him being kept] in the hospital [in the KGB files]. In March, they continued to torture him, but he refused to identify people … But at some point, you know, he started revealing the names of the people, who in turn revealed others, and finally they got to me, [but only] after a year and a half …. In Marijampolė's *Saugumas* (Soviet secret service building) they made me confront Liepa. I was asked: 'Do you know him?' I said': Of course I do not.' The interrogators started cursing me.

> He [Liepa] told [them] that he knew me. I do not blame him because they put iron into his wounds or something. After his death, someone said, worms were crawling out of his wounds, a terrible thing. But he did not say much. During the confrontation they kept asking [him]: 'Is she the same one, the same one?' I was asked: 'How can you not recognize your leader?' I replied: 'What have you turned him into? How could you have made him into such a martyr?'

She was not as forgiving to her fellow messenger Birutė, who, in the words of Aldona, 'told them more than necessary.' According to Aldona, Birutė made up a story about Aldona showing up one day with a huge pile of newspapers, and Birutė refusing to take that pile.

> They beat severely for this [distributing newspapers], you know. [I was asked] 'Where did you get them from? Where did you hide them?' This was a complete lie; I never showed up at her house with newspapers. I confronted Birutė (after I was released from prison and deportation) by telling her that she said more than necessary. She told me: 'I could not have behaved differently.' I responded: 'You really did not have to tell them that.' [Her lies] really hurt me.

Betrayal is a common theme in oral testimonies of the former resistance fighters. Studies of other irregular wars suggest that betrayal – brutal intimate violence and 'malicious denunciation' – are common occurrences during such conflicts (Kalyvas 2006; Clark 2014). Academic studies of anti-Soviet resistance in Lithuania clearly demonstrate that this conflict was not an exception (e.g. Pocius (2009), Petersen (2001), Mikelevičius (2013), and Kaunietis (2006)). However, betrayal is absent from the museums in Lithuania depicting the postwar period. Perhaps representing betrayal within the 'fighting and suffering paradigm' is almost impossible; it blurs rigid lines between heroic fighters and collaborators. In public discourse, any mention of betrayal is still likely to elicit controversy and acrimonious arguments. Interestingly, the oral testimony of Aldona about Juozas Karašauskas (*nom de guerre* Liepa) and her compassion for his suffering during the torture contrasts with a statement in her book *Laiko dulkes nužėrus*, in which she writes that the goal of the museum that she has built is to instill pride in those 'who have not bowed their heads and genuflected in front of the invader' (Vilutienė 2013, 5). The everyday reality of anti-Soviet resistance was more complex. Even Liepa, whom Aldona still respects, could not withstand torture and revealed some information about his fellow fighters.

As predicted by feminist scholars studying memory, individual accounts are likely to reveal tensions between the lived experiences and political discourses. It appears that the issue of betrayal was difficult to handle in *Ištark mano vardą* [Say my name], another book authored by Aldona Vilutienė and Justinas Sajauskas, published in 1999. Aldona dutifully recorded the names of all resistance fighters active in Tauras district. She decided to exclude *menkadvasiai* [individuals with weak souls], or those who were engaged in the resistance fight but started to betray not only the idea of resistance itself but also their co-fighters, from the list published in the book (1999, 7). However, the book still mentions *noms de guerre* (assumed names used in resistance) and, in several cases, the real names of the 'biggest traitors' who were active in Tauras district, thus signaling that betrayal remains an unresolved issue and a source of tension in narratives about the war of resistance.

Imprisonment and deportation: 'there was a longing for beauty all the time'

Most resistance fighters and their supporters, if not killed in the battle, were imprisoned and later deported to distant prison camps, such as Vorkuta and Inta. During the postwar years, the conditions in prisons were brutal, with physical and psychological torture exercised by the NKVD officers to obtain information about the remaining resistance fighters and their supporters. After the return of the Soviet military forces to Lithuania, there were 12 functioning prisons there. It is impossible to determine how many people perished in these prisons between 1944 and 1953. It is estimated that in 1945 alone, 490 people died or were killed in prisons of a total of 16,591 people being kept in the 12 prisons in Lithuania. It is estimated that between 1944 and 1952, the Soviet Secret police held 186,000 people captive in Lithuania's prisons. Most of these captives were accused of participating in the war of resistance (Anušauskas 2013, 225).

Between 1944 and 1953, 142,579 of prisoners were transferred from Lithuanian prisons to prison camps. Between 1945 and 1947, at least 37,000 deportees 'disappeared' in these camps. Most individuals deported from Lithuania after World War II worked in places where they were forced to cut wood. Both women and men were subject to this type of labor (Anušauskas 2013, 235).

In 1949, Aldona Vilutienė was imprisoned in Marijampolė and Leningrad, and then forcefully moved to the prison camp in Inta and Lemju prison camp, which were part of Vorkuta camp system until 1952, located in the north of Komi Republic. The climate in both places was very rough, with winter lasting for almost 8 months. It is estimated that the number of prisoners in Intalag (the lager system in Inta) increased from 9200 in 1942 to 14,700 in 1945 and to 22,000 in 1948. ('Lager' is a term used to describe a forced labor camp.) Political prisoners were kept in the same location as criminals (Juodvalkytė-Suščenkienė 1995, 121–23). Lemju prison camp system was smaller; approximately 4000 prisoners were kept there. It is estimated that 700 prisoners were from Lithuania (Juodvalkytė-Suščenkienė 1995, 182).

The 'relics' from these places of suffering include rosaries made of bread (despite chronic food shortages, the deportees made numerous rosaries), poems and letters written on pieces of bark, small albums with images and photographs, handmade postcards, embroidery, crosses, and other religious objects (used for mass celebrated in exile). They can be found in all nine museums portraying the experiences of the resistance war and deportation and the state-supported Museum of Genocide Victims in Vilnius, which is part of the Genocide and Resistance Research Center. *Vizitėlės* – handmade 'relics' created by Lithuanian women who were deported from Lithuania and/or imprisoned between 1941 and 1953 – bear witness to activities of women in prisons and places of deportation. Several prominent themes – the images of the 'lost' homeland, flowers, and patriotic motifs – can be seen in these artifacts.

Vizitėlės are usually very small, made on dark pieces of material, imitating postcards. The images, many of which include floral motifs, are colorful, made with thread acquired from scarfs and other pieces of clothing. Justinas Sajauskas, Aldona Vilutienė's successor as the Director of the museum in Marijampolė, has described them as 'dangerous art,' referring to the fact that similar activities required needles that were difficult to obtain in prisons (Sajauskas 2011, 3). According to Sajauskas (2011), the owners of the 'dangerous art' usually hid *vizitėlės* in their coats; some carried them in these locations for at least 10 years as a memory of someone loved.

The entries on *vizitėlės* include congratulations with name days, expressions of love, and calls to remember the author of the embroidered piece.

The art of embroidery was very popular in Lithuania prior to World War II, and most women practiced it. Women who make embroidery are mentioned in Lithuanian folk songs, and those who were able to achieve mastery in this art were respected in the villages (Milašius 2013, 83). Every region had its own style of embroidery. Traditionally, the most popular colors were brown, blue, and red; each color was associated with a certain meaning (Milašius 2013, 85). In addition, *atminimai* [remembrances], or short poems, usually quatrains, written by young men and women to their friends in albums or notebooks, were very popular during the interwar period in Lithuania. According to Vita Ivanauskaitė-Šeibutienė (2013), high school students, university students, and even soldiers created quatrains with various texts, including best wishes, requests, or vows to remember.[8] Resistance fighters wrote *atminimai* as well. These texts were usually collected in notebooks or albums. *Vizitėlės* are part of this tradition. For example, a display in the Museum of Genocide Victims in Vilnius features a *vizitėlė* created by Joana Kalvaitienė, a political prisoner, in Klaipėda prison, for her husband Juozas. It reads: 'Dear Juozas, if you return from dark prison, and I would have died meanwhile somewhere; while caressing someone else, remember that my heart was beating only for you.' Similar pleas to remember were addressed to girlfriends, sisters, or mothers.

In 2011, during the 70th anniversary of the June 1941 mass deportations, *vizitėlės* emerged from relative public invisibility. Although they could be found in the displays in the resistance and deportation museums, *vizitėlės* were virtually unknown to the public. In summer 2011, the Vincas Kudirka Public Library in Kaunas held an exhibition that was devoted entirely to *vizitėlės*. This exhibition was housed in the *Seimas* (the parliament building) the following year, along with another exhibition entitled *Tikėjimo ir vilties ženklai* [Signs of Faith and Hope], which featured postcards from deportation camps and stamps used in displacement camps after World War II. Stories about *vizitėlės* were published in conservative newspapers in Lithuania, specifically, *XXI amžius* [The 21st Century], a publication that associates itself with Christian thought, *Lietuvos Aidas* [The Echo of Lithuania], which described itself as 'a nation-state newspaper,' and *Kultūra*, a weekend supplement to *Draugas*, a Lithuanian diaspora publication based in Chicago. A brief informational essay about *vizitėlės* was published in the Kaunas-based newspaper *Kauno Diena* [Kaunas Daily].

These publications portrayed *vizitėlės* as strategies of resistance and bravery, pointing out that embroidery with needles was forbidden in prisons; expressions of patriotism, referring to the images with the colors of the Lithuanian national flag and references to homeland; and expressions of religious faith (Žulys 2011). *Kultūra* described *vizitėlės* as 'witnesses of suffering and pain.' The author of the article described the embroidery pieces as 'an introduction, or "business cards", that have reached us from far away, from those who are not alive any more, and who went through torture, prison, and deportation just for their big love for their homeland' (Abromavičius 2011, 5). In the public sphere, *vizitėlės* were framed within the paradigm of 'fighting and suffering,' as gendered symbols of resistance.

The memoirs of the former prisoners and deportees published after *Atgimimas* describe embroidery in simpler, more mundane ways, as a method to create beauty in prisons and forced labor camps and deal with sadness. For example, Sister Jonė Sofija Budrytė, who, like Aldona Vilutienė, was deported to Inta, recalls grey clothing that the deportees were required to wear. In Sister Jonė Sofija's eyes, these clothes have 'made prisoners uniform, made them grey' (Budrytė 2008, 43). To create beauty, Lithuanian women were knitting, creating embroidery every moment they had, as long as they were able to get pieces of material. The dresses that women were required to wear were poorly made; thus, the deportees secretly re-fashioned them and placed embroidered collars to make them look 'more alive.' After Stalin's death, Sister Jonė Sofija brought several embroidered artifacts to Soviet-occupied Lithuania. After the disintegration of the USSR, she donated them to museums. Three collars handmade in forced labor camps are featured in a display in the museum in Marijampolė as well.

Ona Andziulytė-Liutkevičienė, the author of one of the largest and most elaborate pieces of embroidery currently on display in the museum in Marijampolė (Figure 1), wrote in her memoir that it took her at least 2 or 3 months to make a *vizitėlė*. She wrote about the need to preserve and hide her *vizitėlės* – many of them had patriotic images, and this could have been interpreted as 'anti-Soviet'. While in the camp, Ona hid *vizitėlės* in her coat for at least 6 years. Upon her return to Lithuania in 1958, she did not show them to anyone for 36 years. Ona kept her *vizitėlės* stuffed in an old sock in a basement until 1994. Only then she decided to donate her *vizitėlės* to the museum in Marijampolė.[9] The large piece of embroidery made by Ona featured in the museum includes two recognizable national symbols – the castle of Gediminas in Vilnius – the 'return' of Vilnius to Lithuania in 1939 was a memorable event – and Vytis, a national symbol featuring a knight with a sword and a shield on horseback. In addition, the piece also features a picture of a

Figure 1. Embroidery made by Ona Andziulytė-Liutkevičienė.

young woman (presumably, the artist) behind the bars in a prison, with a brief poem about a dying youth who loved the homeland and was punished for 'being born a Lithuanian.' This embroidery definitely fits the 'fighting and suffering' paradigm on which the museum was initially built.

In Aldona's oral testimony, *vizitėlės* were briefly mentioned in the beginning of her story when she remembered different items that donated for her museum during the early nineties. *Vizitėlės* were mentioned together with rosaries made of bread, which have become a recognizable symbol associated with lagers even during the times of *Atgimimas*. Aldona connects the making of *vizitėlės* and other pieces of embroidery with her time in prison and lagers.

After her capture, the most vivid memory associated with Aldona's trip to the prison in Marijampolė was the lack of air, as she was covered with a heavy tarpaulin and guarded by seven *stribai* [local collaborators with the Soviets] and seven Russian soldiers in a truck:

> I am suffocating under this tarp. I am thinking – not much left to go (until the prison), and I am removing part of the tarp to breathe. As soon as one *stribas* sees it, he hits me with the butt of his gun. The Russians did not mind [my attempts to breathe]. Finally I made a little hole in the tarp and was able to breathe this way …. And then they brought me to Marijampolė. I think that I saw the partisans (dead) lying on the road. They [*stribai*] lifted me, wrapped up in this tarp, and brought me into the prison cell.

In the prison cell, Aldona recalled noticing an empty wide bed with protruding steel springs and no covers. She recalled reaching out and opening the window and screaming. Someone told her to be quiet to avoid being transferred to *karceris* [solitary confinement]. As time went on, Aldona started making pieces of embroidery, as 'there was more time to kill,' as compared with her memories about Inta and Lemju lagers, where she had to work long hours. Embroidery was one way to escape the suffocating prison reality. Although needles or any other sharp objects were forbidden in prisons, Aldona remembered that she was able to get needles via parcels. Needles were hidden in dried honeycombs:

> If we found a larger piece [of a honeycomb], then we started to break it, [hoping to] find a needle or a piece of metal …. There were constant searches in prisons. We hid needles in our mouths. We were told to open our mouths [during the searches], but still, they could not find the needles. They were afraid to put their fingers [into our mouths]; perhaps they were afraid that we will bite them.

Technical details on how to make *vizitėlės* emerge from Aldona's narrative about her experiences in lagers. In Inta, she was engaged in preparing the ground for excavating coal. Aldona described hard labor that she was forced to do in remarkable detail, mentioning the soldiers with dogs who made sure that she and her fellow laborers did not escape and recalling removing moss, digging ditches, and trying to keep warm in an unbearable cold. After the long day, Aldona remembered returning to the barracks to her 'two pieces of wooden boards' on which she had to sleep. With several hundred other people in the barrack, she found time and space to create *vizitėlės*:

> Threaded material from parcels [that we received from Lithuania] was used for the background which was usually dark, to make *vizitėlės* look nicer. These color threads were torn from scarfs. … Underwear was another source of color threads. We even used socks. If we had a coat or a piece of clothing with lining, then [we could use it] for embroidery as well.

In lagers, we were not punished for making embroidery *per se*, but for other things. They would say: 'It is time to sleep.' They would find a reason [to prevent us from making embroidery]. Especially if *valdiškas daiktas* (a piece of state property), such as a sheet, was used, then embroidery was confiscated. Or if a Lithuanian symbol was used, then they would take embroidery away. This is why we had to hide [embroidery]. We would hide the embroidered in our coats.

I recall getting a sheet to put on the mattress [in one of the lagers]. I did not have the needed materials for embroidery. At that time, embroidery called 'richelieu' [a type of embroidery popular during the Renaissance and practiced by Cardinal Richelieu in France] became fashionable. This technique required to pull threads, then cut out pieces of the material, and then holes shaped like roses or grating appeared. So I had this sheet, and I had a piece of metal. I cut off the end of the sheet; then cut it [this piece of sheet] into two, and here it was! I had two pieces of material. When I started pulling out the threads, a female guard showed up. She said: 'What are you doing here?' I responded: 'I am making embroidery.' She asked: 'Where did you get the material from?' Then the guard punished me immediately. She put me down for one month in *būras* (severe solitary confinement). [This was] a separate building with a place to lie down, but there was very little space, and it was dark. [I was still forced to] go to work, but no food, only every third day, and no light, no electricity. I was lucky to get out from *būras* in one week.

Despite strict punishments for breaking the rules due to embroidering, it was widely practiced, especially in prisons and deportation camps. Political prisoners in lagers such as Inta and Lemju were only allowed two letters per year. Making *vizitėlės* was another way to communicate with each other and their family members, hoping that one day they will reach the intended recipient. Texts embroidered on *vizitėlės* resemble texts found on postcards or in *atminimai* [remembrances] albums, and express love for girlfriends, family members, or spouses. For example, one *vizitėlė* made by Jadvyga Galinytė, currently kept in the museum in Marijampolė, reads: 'Dear mother, pray next to the cross, let it console you. I will return when *trispalvė* [*the Lithuanian flag*] will fly again.' (Figure 2)

This *vizitėlė* was created on a dark background, and it includes national themes, thus fitting the narrative of 'fighting and suffering.' Not all *vizitėlės* have a political message. For example, a *vizitėlė* made by Birutė Liudžiūtė and titled as 'greetings from Siberia' in the museum display includes only floral motifs. (Figure 3)

Included with the works of Aldona in the museum are little black albums for memorabilia and *vizitėlės*. These artifacts are decorated with colorful floral motifs, and are featured in the section together with the other artifacts made by women in prisons and forced labor camps.

Her oral testimony depicts the communicative function of *vizitėlės*. These artifacts were meant to tell a story to the relatives and friends about the fates of women who made them. Many hoped that somehow, through their fellow prisoners who were released before them, *vizitėlės* could reach their beloved ones in Lithuania. As explained by Aldona:

The goal [of making *vizitėlės*] was to take them home, or to have someone else take them [to Lithuania], while you are still alive, so that your friends and relatives could see this artifact. The messenger would tell your family about your life here [in exile]. *Vizitėlės* were made as gifts.

Aldona was one of the first ones to be released from Lemju prison after Stalin's death. She believes that her young age – she was not yet 18 when captured in 1949 – explains her early release. Together with two other women, she traveled to Lithuania.

Figure 2. *Vizitėlė* made by Jadvyga Galinytė.

Figure 3. *Vizitėlė* made by Birutė Liudžiūtė.

She took many *vizitėlės* with her and started visiting families to deliver them. Her encounters while serving as a messenger from Siberia, delivering *vizitėlės*, reveals severe polarization in Soviet-occupied Lithuanian society. In addition, her testimony highlights emerging relationships between the people who shared a similar fate and marginalization of returning deportees:

> Some people greeted me very nicely. I developed long lasting relationships with some families. Kareivos was such a family. I visited the parents. One of their daughter was in a lager. [Later] the two women, the daughters of Kareivos, even moved to Marijampolė to be closer to me. One was a former prisoner, but the other (daughter) stayed free. I even buried them. I kept my friendship with their parents for a long time; we took photographs together.

> In most cases, people were suspicious at first, because they were not receiving (many) letters from there (Siberia), no news. Thus, when I started talking, they started crying, but then they asked questions and listened. Others invited me to stay overnight. ...

> There was poverty, and sometimes I did not have enough money to go back [to Marijampolė from the places that I visited]. The jobs were scarce; often seasonal. There was no money. And here I was in Kaunas. I nearly was run over by a Volga (a Soviet luxury car) as I was trying to find the right location [to deliver *vizitėlės*]. So here is this rich man, coming out from his work room in his big house. [He says]: "So what? Just leave them [*vizitėlės*] here. No "thank you," nothing. It was already dark outside. I do not even remember whether he said "sudiev" [a religious farewell in Lithuanian]. When I said "sudiev," he probably responded "viso gero" [good bye, a secular way to saying "farewell"]. This "viso gero" was very unacceptable to me.

The development of the 'community of fate' among people who have experienced imprisonment and deportation is depicted in the testimonies of other former deportees. Usually, return to the homeland is described as another traumatic experience, and only other people with similar traumas can understand them. Aldona's testimony suggests that most relatives of the repressed eventually warmed up to her:

> Even when I was delivering *vizitėlės*, some people were trying to avoid me. But they were a minority. Some greeted me simply, others in a more official way, and some others very nicely. We remained friends with some for the rest of our lives.

> When entering their homes, I introduced myself: 'I am an acquaintance of your daughter,' or something along these lines. I would not say that things are bad there because we [the deportees] never complained in our letters. We told our families not to worry, and that we would return soon. I used to tell the families that I was able to get out earlier, and that their relatives would come back soon as well. Since they are not able to leave now, they are sending this handmade *atminimas* (remembrance). [The family] took it from me, started crying, and kissing the 'relic.' They were happy, and thanked me.

As demonstrated by Aldona's testimony, *vizitėlės* evoked memories from different times and places – not only her experiences in prisons and lagers (these experiences are featured in the public discourses about *vizitėlės*) but also her return to Lithuania in the early 1950s, which was another traumatic experience, often marked with rejection and marginalization. When asked about the meaning of *vizitėlės* today, she pauses briefly, and then responds:

> For someone who is reflecting [on the past], they mean a lot. But I am not sure about the majority of this generation. Sometimes I look ... even in the museum, some people come and say [when looking at *vizitėlės*]: 'Oh, what is this *skuduras* (filthy rag) made of?' [They are unaware that] the whole soul, sorrow, and longing [for homeland] were put into this 'rag.' Maybe someone who is able to keep some kind of patriotism and is interested in history, interested in those times, those experiences, the hardships of people from those times [will understand] ... or maybe only those who study people ... probably not historians .... Historians somehow ....

Aldona's answer about the functions of *vizitėlės* in current society can be interpreted as ambivalence about the survival of the 'fighting and suffering' paradigm that she tried to create, as well as insecurity about the future transmission of her memories. Despite the popularity of trips to Siberia to the places of deportation among the youth in Lithuania and widespread interest in some dramatic films about the postwar era, it is difficult to predict the future of less popular representations of traumatic memories related to the resistance war and deportation, such as *vizitėlės*. To those who made them in prisons and places of deportation, *vizitėlės* represent a form of resistance, especially because making them often-implied violations of prison rules and the use of 'state property' (such as sheets). To memory entrepreneurs, *vizitėlės* are a perfect fit with the 'fighting and suffering' paradigm because they illustrate the cruelty with which the Stalinist regime suppressed individual creativity and attempts to resist it. However, as explained by Aldona, many museum visitors often have trouble making such connections. To them, 'relics' are artifacts without a real value, individual belongings that are not part of any coherent narrative. In addition, like other museums of local history, *Tauro Apygardos Partizanų ir Tremties Muziejus* [Tauras district museum of partisans and deportation] suffers from limited funding and has to rely on volunteer work. There are no in-depth textual explanations of 'relics' presented in the museum. Therefore, given various frames of references, conflicting interpretations of the points of memory, and lack of professionalism in local history museums attempting to maintain the 'fighting and suffering paradigm,' it is likely that 'pluralism of memory' – a condition when various groups compete for their version of traumatic history in a democratic society – will remain.

Conclusion

By exploring the testimony and biography of a memory entrepreneur, one of the main goals of this article was to trace various processes of memory production. Specifically, by exploring the 'points of memory,' or visual images with evocative power, in the narrative, I was interested in how memory transcends the individual level and intersects with hegemonic narratives that tend to simplify the past. Methodologically, focusing on the 'points of memory' also offers a way to individualize the study of memory.

By comparing the published accounts of Aldona Vilutienė, a former partisan messenger and the founder of a museum to commemorate partisan warfare and displacement in a provincial Lithuanian town, with her oral testimony, I was able to identify the points of tension between 'lived' experience (as articulated in her oral testimony) and the ways in which these experiences were represented in her published work. It is fair to suggest that her published work embraces the main tenets of the 'fighting and suffering' memory regime that was popular during the initial stages of democratization.

Aldona's oral testimony revealed the complicated realities of Lithuania's partisan war with betrayals and dangers associated with the 'feminine' tasks of a partisan messenger, such as finding buttons for partisan uniforms or cigarettes. These complexities and difficult moral choices that people who were alive during the partisan war had to make are absent from simplified public narratives about the period.

A focus on the 'points of memory' allows me to highlight the gender aspects of Aldona's experiences. On the one hand, Aldona's experience as a young woman is marked by self-imposed inconspicuousness; she depicts herself as 'a mere helper' of partisans charged with tasks, some of which were described as 'mundane' but were extremely difficult and dangerous to complete. On the other hand, Aldona's gender became hyper-visible in several places. There were situations, such as when she was transported to prison in a carriage with 14 armed men, one of whom was constantly beating her with the butt of his gun, when her weakness and vulnerability as a young woman surrounded by aggressive men emerged very clearly in the narrative.

The relevance and significance of gender emerge in the descriptions of 'manly' roles that Aldona and other women who served as messengers and were later deported to lagers had to perform, such as handling weapons during the partisan war and digging ditches in lagers. At the same time, their methods of coping with the greyness of the lager or prison were 'feminine' – making *vizitėlės* and other pieces of embroidery was considered a 'woman's pastime.' In these discourses, as demonstrated in this essay, women usually emerge as mothers, wives, helpers, and silent resisters, but rarely as complex historical figures influencing history and creating memory paradigms. Focusing on Aldona's roles as a memory entrepreneur who is actively promoting her own historical truth allows challenging similar reductionist views of women in wars and nation building.

As demonstrated by the study of the points of memory that emerged in Aldona's narrative, the documentation and interpretation of individual experiences, even about well-researched events, such as war of resistance or deportations, are likely to reveal tensions within public collective discourses. Sensitivity to these tensions, such as the impossibility to treat all participants of the war of resistance as heroes on the 'right' side of history, or the difficulty to portray embroidery in prisons and lagers as acts of 'patriotism' without taking the communicative function and human relations into account, is a way to challenge hegemonic narratives. It seems to me that similar approaches offer openings for 'connective memory work' (Hirsch's term 2012, 21). Such memory work implies a search for commonalities and affiliations beyond families and across various lines of difference. In addition, connective memory work is a powerful antidote to simplifying templates and exclusionary paradigms.

Notes

1. For example, in 2012, The Lithuanian Research and Studies Center in Chicago organized 'Hope and Spirit' exhibit that featured handicrafts and artifacts made in Soviet far north. Several documentaries were produced, drawing on the materials presented in the exhibit.
2. In 1993, Vilutienė founded the *Tauro Apygardos Partizanų ir Tremties Muziejus* [Tauras District Museum of Partisans and Deportation] in Marijampolė, a provincial town in Lithuania. She served as the Director of this museum until 2000.
3. A journalist from *Tremtinys* [Deportee] newspaper introduced me to Aldona Vilutienė and participated in the conversation.
4. The use of the term 'genocide' in the title of this institution has been subject to intense domestic and international scrutiny since its inception. The criticism being that the term is used inappropriately to describe the Stalinist repressions that are researched by this Institute, in addition to the Holocaust and the Soviet period. Perhaps in response to this criticism, the Museum of the Genocide Victims, an institution associated with the Genocide and Resistance Research Center, created a section on the Holocaust. There is a section, consisting primarily of photographs, on the Roma genocide in Lithuania as well. However, the largest part of the exhibit focuses on the Soviet period.

5. Raslanas was accused of organizing Rainiai massacre in 1941 when he served as the Head of NKVD in Telšiai. He was sentenced *in absentia* in 2001 for what was described as 'the crimes of genocide' in Lithuania.
6. Mingailė Jurkutė, a contributor to a new book *Partizano sąsiuviniai* [Partisan's notebooks], made this point in 2013. She identified Mindaugas Pocius' recent book on collaboration during the war of resistance (2009) as an attempt, albeit with limited success, to address the problem (Jurkutė 2013). Mikelevičius (2013) mentions a program at the Genocide and Resistance Research Center which focuses on addressing the relationships between the partisans and the civilians.
7. Today in Lithuania in some circles partisan songs are considered to be an important legacy from the postwar period and are performed during song festivals.
8. According to Ivanauskaitė-Šeibutienė (2013), *Lietuvių tautosakos rankraštynas* [The collection of manuscripts on Lithuanian folklore] holds thousands of such texts.
9. Ona Andziulytė-Liutkevičienė's essay 'Žvilgsnis į laisvę' [A glimpse of freedom] was published in Aldona Vilutienė's book *Laiko dulkes nužėrus* (2013, 128).

Acknowledgments

I would like to thank Georgia Gwinnett College for generous support during my academic leave in Fall 2015 when I worked on this essay. I would also like to thank Justinas Sajauskas for allowing me to use several images of *vizitėlės*.

Disclosure statement

No potential conflict of interest was reported by the author.

Funding

This work was supported by Georgia Gwinnett College.

References

Abromavičius, S. 2011. *Vizitėlės—Kančių ir skausmo liudytojos*. Kultūra: Draugo šeštadieninis priedas. July 23.
Ackerly, B., and J. True. 2010. *Doing Feminist Research in Political and Social Science*. New York: Palgrave Macmillan.
Andziulytė-Liutkevičienė, O. 2013. "Žvilgsnis į laisvę." In *Laiko dulkes nužėrus... Tauro apygardos partizanų ir tremties muziejaus kūrimo ir veiklos istorija, 1993-2007 m.*, edited by A. Vilutienė, 128. Marijampolė: Piko valanda.
Anušauskas, A. 2013. *Teroras 1940-1958 m.* Vilnius: Verseus Aureus.
Budrytė, J. S. 2008. *Mano kryžiaus kelio atkarpa*. Vilnius: Lietuvos nacionalinis muziejus.
Clark, G. M. 2014. *Everyday Violence in the Irish Civil War*. Cambridge: Cambridge University Press.
Davoliūtė, V. 2013. *The Making and Breaking of Soviet Lithuania: Memory and Modernity in the Wake of War*. London: Routledge.
Devereux, L. 2010. "From Congo: Newspaper Photographs, Public Images and Personal Memories." *Visual Studies* 25 (2): 124–134. doi:10.1080/1472586X.2010.502669.

Edkins, J. 2003. *Trauma and the Memory of Politics*. Cambridge: Cambridge University Press.

Genocide and Resistance Research Center of Lithuania. n.d. *Antisovietinis pasipriešinimas*.

Goldenberg, M., and A. H. Shapiro. 2013. "Introduction." In *Different Horrors, Same Hell: Gender and The Holocaust*, edited by M. Goldenberg, and A. H. Shapiro, 3–9. Seattle: University of Washington Press.

Hirsch, M. 2012. *The Generation of Postmemory: Writing and Visual Culture After the Holocaust*. New York: Columbia University Press.

Ivanauskaitė-Šeibutienė, V. 2013. "Folklorinė kūryba Balio Vaičėno gyvenime ir rašytiniame palikime." In *Balys Vaičėnas. Partizano sąsiuviniai*, edited by K. Driskius, R. Mozūraitė, and P. V. Subačius, lxi–lxxxviii. Vilnius: Tautos paveldo tyrimai.

Jankauskienė, E. 2014. "1944-1953 m. Lietuvos partizaninis karas su Sovietų Sąjunga." In *Lietuvos karai: Lietuvos XiX-XX a. nacionalinių karų sisteminė-kiekybinė analyze*, edited by G. Vitkus, 211–266. Vilnius: Eugrimas.

Jansson, M., M. Wendt, and C. Åse. 2008. "Memory Work Reconsidered." *NORA—Nordic Journal of Feminist and Gender Research* 16 (4): 228–240. doi:10.1080/08038740802441048.

Jelin, E. 2003. *State Repression and the Labors of Memory*. Translated by J. Rein and M. Godoy-Anativia. Minneapolis: University of Minnesota Press.

Juodvalkytė-Suščenkienė, A. 1995. *Tremties ir kalinimo vietos*. Vilnius: Mokslo ir enciklopedijų leidykla.

Jurkutė, M. 2013. "Balio Vaičėno rašytinis palikimas." In *Balys Vaičėnas. Partizano sąsiuviniai*, compiled by K. Driskius, R. Mozūraitė, and P. V. Subačius, xliii–lx. Vilnius: Tautos paveldo tyrimai.

Kalyvas, S. N. 2006. *The Logic of Violence in Civil War*. Cambridge: Cambridge University Press.

Kaunietis, R. (comp.). 2006. *Aukštaitijos partizanų prisiminimai*. 5th ed. Vilnius: Valstybės žinios.

Kirss, T., E. Kõresaar, and M. Lauristin, eds.. 2004. *She Who Remembers Survives: Interpreting Estonian Women's Post-Soviet Life Stories*. Tartu: Tartu University Press.

Kubik, J., and M. Bernard. 2014. "A Theory of the Politics of Memory." In *Twenty Years after Communism*, edited by M. Bernard, and J. Kubik, 7–34. Oxford: Oxford University Press.

Langenbacher, E. 2008. "Twenty-First Century Memory Regimes in Germany and Poland: An Analysis of Elite Discourses and Public Opinion." *German Politics and Society* 26 (4): 50–81. doi:10.3167/gps.2008.260404.

Lazda, M. 2006. "Family, Gender, and Ideology in World War II Latvia." In *Gender and War in Twentieth-Century Europe*, edited by N. M. Wingfield, and M. Bucur, 133–156. Bloomington: Indiana University Press.

Leinartė, D. 2016. "Silience in Biographical Accounts and Life Stories: The Ethical Aspects of Interpretation." In *The Soviet Past in the Post-Socialist Presence: Methodology and Ethics in Russian, Baltic and Central European Oral History and Memory Studies*, edited by M. Ilic, and D. Leinartė, 12–18. New York: Routledge.

Leiserowitz, R. 2012. "In the Lithuanian Woods. Jewish and Lithuanian Female Partisans." In *Women and Men at War: A Gender Perspective on World War II and Its Aftermath in Central and Eastern Europe*, edited by M. Röger, and R. Leiserowitz, 199–218. Osnabrück: Fibre Verlag.

Lothe, J., S. R. Suleiman, and J. Phelan, eds.. 2012. *After Testimony: The Ethics and Aesthetics of Holocaust Narrative for the Future*. Columbus: Ohio State University Press.

Mälksoo, M. 2014. "Criminalizing Communism: Transnational Mnemopolitics in Europe." *International Political Sociology* 8 (1): 82–99. doi:10.1111/ips.2014.8.issue-1.

Mikelevičius, L. 2013. "Partizanų baudžiamoji praktika Varėnos krašte, 1944-52." *Genocidas ir rezistencija* 1: 71–97.

Milašius, O. 2013. *Lituanistinė ir politinė publicistika*. Vilnius: Lietuvių literatūros ir tautosakos institutas.

Misiunas, R., and R. Taagepera. 1993. *The Baltic States: Years of Dependence, 1940-1990*. Berkeley: University of California Press.

Onken, E.-C. 2010. "Memory and Democratic Pluralism in the Baltic States—Rethinking the Relationship." *Journal of Baltic Studies* 41 (3): 277–294. doi:10.1080/01629778.2010.498186.

Petersen, R. D. 2001. *Resistance and Rebellion: Lessons from Eastern Europe*. Cambridge: Cambridge University Press.

Pocius, M. 2009. *Kita mėnulio pusė: Lietuvos partizanų kova su kolaboravimu 1944-1953*. Vilnius: Lietuvos istorijos instituto leidykla.

Rubavičius, V. 2007. "Neišgyvendinamo sovietmečio patirtis: Socialinė atmintis ir tapatumo politika." In *Lietuvių tautos tapatybė: Tarp realybės ir utopijos*, edited by R. Repšienė, 12–40. Vilnius: Kultūros, Filosofijos ir Meno Institutas.

Sajauskas, J. 2011. "Vizitėlės—Pasipriešinimo liudininkės." In *Vizitėlės—Pasipriešinimo liudininkės*, edited by D. Poškienė, 3–4. Kaunas: Naujasis Lankas.

Smolskutė, Ž. 2006. "Moterų dalyvavimo ginkluotame pasipriešinime 1944-1953 m. ypatumai." *Genocidas ir Rezistencija* 2 (20): 53–62.

Sruoginis, V., and J. Ohman, dir. (2014). *Nematomas frontas* [The Invisible Front]. DVD. Vilnius: Aspectus Memoria.

Vaitkus, J. (2003). *Vienui vieni*. DVD. Vilnius: Daumanto studija.

Valatka, R. 2015. *Ką pagerbė Lietuva—Partizanų vadą Generolą Vėtrą ar žydų žudiką*.

Vanagaitė, R. 2016. *Mūsiškiai*. Vilnius: Alma Littera.

Vėta, N. 2012. *Seimo valdyba Vyriausybei siūlo sudaryti darbo grupę dėl tremties ir rezistencijos muziejų status*.

Vilutienė, A. 2013. *Laiko dulkes nužėrus... Tauro apygardos partizanų ir tremties muziejaus kūrimo ir veiklos istorija, 1993-2007 m*. Marijampolė: Piko valanda.

Vilutienė, A., and J. Sajauskas. 1999. *Ištark mano vardą. Tauro apygardos partizanų vardynas*. Vilnius: Džiugas.

Voverienė, O. 2004. *Blynų baliaus karalienė*.

Žulys, B. 2011. *Vizitėlės—Menas ir pasipriešinimas*.

Memory of socialism and the Russian Orthodox believers in Estonia

Irina Paert

Usuteaduskond/Faculty of Theology, University of Tartu, Tartu, Estonia

ABSTRACT
This article focuses on the mnemonic practices of Russian Orthodox believers in Estonia. Raising a general theoretical problem of confessional memory, the article proceeds to discuss of the representation of the past in autobiographical interviews with the older generation of Russians in Estonia, born between 1910 and 1930. The mnemonic practices of the ethnic minorities are shown to differ from the public narratives (both Russian and Estonian), thereby showing heterogeneity in the memories of the Soviet past. Thus, the article concludes that the ethnic Russians in Estonia are not a coherent mnemonic community.

This article analyzes the representations of the twentieth century in the oral history interviews with older generation members of the Russian Orthodox Church who live in Estonia. The dual aim in this study is to highlight the characteristics of the memory of the members of an ethnic minority as well as to underline the significance of the religious element in their life stories. This case study will shed the light on the broader issue of how religious belief affects the ways of remembering how members of marginalized ethnic groups deal with memory. Generally, the study asks whether or not the past is remembered differently by the representatives of the ethnic minority compared to those of the titular nation group. In particular, how was the Soviet past remembered by ethnic Russians, who are regarded by ethnic Estonians in literature and popular discourse as a whole ethnic group to be instrumental in the Sovietization of the Baltic? What can be drawn from the memories of the Orthodox believers about the memory of Estonian Russians as a group? Can specific religious or theological concepts be found in the believers' narratives of the past?

Religion as mnemotechnics

The mnemonic practices of the Russian Orthodox Church have not received sufficient theoretical or empirical study. This article proposes to focus on a specific aspect of this theme while seeking guidance from the theoretical works of memory studies: the relationship between individual memories of believers and the Orthodox Church's doctrine and practices. In order to approach the issue of the memory of an ethnic minority with a focus on religious beliefs, one needs to look at the broader theoretical framework while keeping in mind that it is impossible to provide a full account of the problem of religion and memory within the scope of this article.

The leading theoreticians of memory studies, primarily Maurice Halbwachs and Jan Assmann, were also religious studies specialists who had no difficulty in evoking religion to support their theories. Halbwachs considers whether religious memory operates in the same way as collective memory 'that is nourished, renewed, fortified and enriched, without losing any of its existence' (Halbwachs 1992, 98). Drawing on Halbwachs, the French sociologist Danièlle Hervieu-Léger argues, 'In the case of religious memory, the normativity of collective memory is reinforced by the fact of the group's defining itself, objectively and subjectively, as a lineage of belief' (Hervieu-Léger 2000, 125). She brings an example of the Christian anamnesis (which refers to commemoration of Christ's Passion, Resurrection, and Ascension in the church ritual of Eucharist), which she uses in a broader sense as a form of ritual recalling of memories. Jan Assmann identifies 'invisible religion,' a term coined by Thomas Luckmann (Luckmann 1967), with cultural memory, persuasively showing how the history of world religions can uncover the paradigmatic forms of cultural mnemotechnics (Assmann 2006). Perhaps, as one of the signs of secularization or the 'mutation of religion' (Davie 2000), religious memory that once dominated the world is no longer taken for granted but is interpreted as just one of the forms of cultural memory.

Cultural memory and religion are closely related. Cultural memory, according to Jan Assmann (2011), is distinct from *ars memoriae* (the art of memory, or variety of mnemonic techniques, used in Antiquity for training of memory and in rhetoric) and from communicative memory. Cultural memory is organized, collective, grounded in the past, dependent on the writings and on the 'specialist carriers,' embodied in rituals, ceremonies, festivals, and imbued with an element of the sacred. Cultural memory is basically synonymous with 'invisible religion' (Assmann 2011). More confusion arises from the close semantic meanings of memory and tradition. As a concept with multilayered meanings (Noyes 2009), 'tradition' is closely linked with the issue of cultural memory. Peter Berger considers that religious tradition 'mediates the experience of another reality, both to those who have never had it and to those who have but who are ever in danger of forgetting it. Every tradition is a collective memory' (Berger 1980, 49). Therefore, religious traditions can be approached as mnemotechnics through which a community may make claims to their right to represent the true heirs of the sacred origin. For example, for the Russian Old Believers, the seeming immutability of medieval traditions and rituals served as important instruments to make their claim to their right to represent the Byzantine Orthodoxy.

The cultural memory of a religious group may include tradition and rites, but it also includes history, historiography, memoirs, literary texts, and the liturgy. Religion, on the other hand, provides specific religious mechanisms such as theological postulates, sacraments, or a sense of community, to cope with traumatic memories. For example, for a Christian, an empathic association with the suffering of Christ and a commandment to love one's enemy may serve as a psychological coping mechanism for personal trauma. The sacrament of confession in the Orthodox and Roman Catholic Churches may also alleviate a sense of guilt or grief.

It is possible to distinguish between institutional and autobiographical modes of remembering: the former refers to the institutional practices of commemoration and official narrative of the past; the latter works at the personal level of individual believers. These modes may interact and overlap, but never coincide completely. The autobiographical memory often operates with the narrative schemes that can be found in religious teaching, while the individual experience of suffering and violent death can be incorporated into the 'institutional' memory as martyrdom.

This theoretical framework allows a more nuanced interpretation of the autobiographical material in this article and offers a novel vista for understanding the Russians in Estonia, not only just as former Soviet citizens and members of the marginalized ethnic minority but also as believers. Religion is only one aspect of personal identity, but it is not an insignificant one. The Christian narrative provides a framework to interpret and understand the events and experiences that occurs during one's lifetime, thus bringing together individual memory with the broader framework of collective religious memory.

Marginal memories and the Russian diaspora

One can distinguish, broadly speaking, two trends in approaching the Russian minority in the former Soviet republics. First is the study of the 'New Russian Diaspora' (Shlapentokh, Sendich, and Payin 1994; Kolstoe 1995; Laitin 1998; Kosmarskaia 2006). The study of the 'New Russian Diaspora' focuses on the trauma of the fall of the Soviet Union as the basis of the social and cultural identity of the Russian minority. The specific position of the Russians, those 'children of Empire' (Kosmarskaia 2006), in the former Soviet Republics is defined not as much by their shared language and culture as it is by their shared sense of loss of their former privileged position. The fall of the Soviet Union resulted in a 'cultural trauma' for these Russians (Aarelaid and Hatshaturjan 2006), in the sudden disenfranchisement and social and cultural marginalization in the aftermath. The second trend emphasizes shared Russian culture as a basis of this common identity and focuses on the cultural production, institutions (such as schools, the church, theater, and other cultural organizations), and associations among the Russian minority through 1918–1941 (Belobrovtseva 2008, 2010; *Pribaltiiskie russkie* 2010; Danilevskii 2010). This type of study of the Russian memory in the Baltic, emphasizing shared culture, forges a sense of continuity between the Baltic Russians before the Soviet occupation and those of the post-Soviet era; proposing rhetorically to protect what appears to be the vanishing 'Russian' heritage in the Baltic, especially material and literary culture, including architecture, icons, books, and newspapers. The studies that represent the second trend predominantly focus on the period before 1941 (the White armies, cultural institutions, the Old Believer settlers, literati, musicians, actors, etc.), and mostly exclude the Soviet era.

Neither of these trends explicitly discusses religion. David Laitin's confidence that the Russian ethnic minority is largely secular has not yet been challenged (Laitin 1998). However, the statistical data reveals that Orthodox Christianity is an important marker of identity for Russian speakers in the Baltic. This signifies an ongoing process by which Orthodoxy, with its own language and culture, can be perceived as an element strengthening Russian identity among the 'new Russian diaspora.' The 2011 popula-tion census showed that 47% of the ethnic Russians in Estonia identified as Orthodox, an 8.5% increase since 2000 (*Statistikaamet*).[1]

This article attempts to highlight the religious dimension of the Russian minority's identity and demonstrate its relevance for the problems of cultural memory, the Soviet era, and ethnic identity. The analysis below can be described as a collective portrait of the Russian Orthodox who belonged to the same generation (those born in the 1920s and 1930s). For the purpose of this article, I focused on the autobiographical accounts produced by lifelong members of the Orthodox Church who lived through the Soviet era.

In general, the efforts of scholars to highlight the cultural memory of Russians in the Baltic are supported by autobiographical reflections to a lesser degree than when compared to the Estonian-speaking population. The massive national endeavor since 1989 by the Estonian Cultural History archives has built up a collection of 2500 autobiographies written by people responding to life-writing competitions. The Russian language life narratives featured in this collection make up only a meager 4% (94 stories) (Jaago 2011, 144). The efforts of a group of committed individuals resulted in the collection of a large proportion of these Russian narratives (*Estonia – moi dom* 2009).[2] The coordinators of life-writing campaigns and scholars rarely admit that the absence of narratives from the Russian-speaking population may be a result of the discord between the lives of Russian Estonians and the dominant memory culture, including the alternative memory culture of the Russian cultural elite con-structed by the efforts of the academics in Slavic departments.

Since the soliciting of written stories from the Russian-speaking subjects has not been successful, life history interviews remain an important method to gain insight into the subjectivity of the Russian-speaking citizens. The main sources for this article were long-life story interviews with seven men and women born in the 1920–1930s, conducted between 2006–2013; published memoirs complemented these primary sources (*Estonia – moi dom* 2009; Kornilii 2009; Miljutina 1997; *Tallinskii pastyr* 2001; Ivanen 2001). The interviewees, as well as the authors of the memoirs, were lifelong members of the Orthodox Church, so-called cradle Christians. Among them were representatives of the Russian diaspora in Estonia, born during the period of Estonian Republic (1918–1941) either to families of the refugees from Soviet Russia or residents in the territory of Pskov, Petšery, and Prichud'e (Peipus) Lake area, on the Estonia–Russia border. Among the interviewees were also some Russian migrants who came to Estonia either during the war or after 1945. Despite the Soviet atheist policy, some of these men and women had been baptized as children and actively practiced their faith.

This study highlights the main narrative themes in the interviews and autobiogra-phical accounts of the Russian Orthodox. These themes are analyzed against the backdrop of the narrators' experiences as believers, Soviet citizens, and as members of the marginalized ethnic minority.

Idealization of the prewar past

The life stories of older generation Russians in Estonia were characterized by a certain unity in their narrative themes, even though these themes were not always explicit. In parallel with the Estonian life stories, there was a certain idealization of the prewar period. The place of origin of the memoirists also determined the style of the auto-biographical narration. The memoirs of the Russians born in Pskov, Petšery, or Peipus – the rural territories populated mainly by the Russian speakers that belonged to Estonia during the interwar period – often seem rooted and grounded in the local landscape. Religious life in these territories was deeply connected with the life of the village community, with a sense of local identity, and was an important source of collective and individual ethics.

Three examples from written autobiographies demonstrate pervasiveness of religious worldview among the rural Russians who lived in the Estonian territories before the war. Margarita (b. 1935), born on a farmstead in Pskov Oblast, remembered her grandfather, who was regarded as a kulak (a rural capitalist) by the Soviet authorities. He told her that the kulaks were hardworking people; he instructed her to do good works and never envy others, as it was a great sin (EKLA, f. 350, V-22). Economy, morality, and Christianity were intertwined: wealth was a result of hard work, while poverty was not sin. For a simple woman, Taisiia, born in a village near Petšery in 1930, the church was the center of rural culture. She remembers the feasts of their patron saint celebrated collectively by the entire village. Children would be dressed in their best clothes, but on their way home, they would walk barefoot so that they would not spoil their best shoes. Ariadna, born in 1937 in the village Mitkovitsy in the Petšery region, described Orthodoxy as a unifying culture for the two ethnic groups that inhabited Petšery: the Russians and the Seto. 'Seto like the Russians were Orthodox. We called them half-believers, in a sense that their faith was the same as ours but the language was different. We had the same church feasts' (EKLA, f. 350, V-60).

The urban milieu has been generally characterized by a higher degree of secular-ization than rural society, yet the urban families of the Russian émigrés in the prewar Republic of Estonia managed to make religion the center of their family life. The Russian émigrés and their children were actively involved in the liturgical and social life of the Russian Orthodox community. There were special Orthodox classes, study groups, conferences organized by the Russian Student Christian movement, and pilgrimages. The Orthodox children and young people formed lifelong friendships and found their marriage partners through church connections (Kornilii 2009; Anna b. 1922–2011; Natal'ia b. 1930).

Confessional schools were closed after 1918, but religious education continued to be an important part of the school curriculum until 1940 and during the Nazi occupation from 1941 to 1944. In the Russian schools, the Orthodox clergy normally taught the Orthodox Catechism. Valentina (b. 1929), who attended a private Russian school in Tallinn before the war, remembered that the school day started with the prayers of 'Our Father' and 'Heavenly King.' She was given the task of bringing out an icon of Mary before the common prayer at her school.

Memories of the prewar era are characterized by a certain sense of nostalgia because most of the interviewees were teenagers before the war. These individuals fondly remembered family, friendship, school, and the sense of community among the émigrés, but they did not have similar positive memories of the Estonian Republic or the Orthodox Church in Estonia. Memories of the hardship and difficulties for the émigrés, who had to adapt to the laws of the Estonian republic, and the sense of being unrecognized for their contribution to the state, can be found in personal accounts (Boris, Vladimir). Metropolitan Kornilii states that despite the freedom of religion during the period of independence, the 'spiritual needs were quite limited':

people took communion and made confession infrequently and evening services were not celebrated in many churches. In schools, the task of bringing out the icon before girls, as boys, often performed the start of classes wanted to avoid doing this. Some school children had already stopped going to church and some teachers collected popular science literature published in the Soviet Union and shared it with their students (Kornilii 2009 and oral communication). Thus, we can distinguish between an idealized cultural portrait of the Russian diaspora and the state of the Estonian Orthodox Church, which is implicitly characterized as spiritually stagnant. The spiritual revival did not begin until after 1940 (Kornilii 2009, 45).

The autobiographical narratives of the Russian ethnic minority in Estonia provide an idealized picture of their social life before the Second World War, in which the Orthodox identity served as *Gemeinschaft* (community), a connection that was lost during the Soviet era. Religious rituals, collective feasts, and the veneration of patron saints serve as a basis of collective identity that was grounded in tradition. The use of religious ritual in the urban environment, in the schools for the Russian minority, suggests that, despite secularization trends, the Russian ethnic minority tried to establish a mnemonic continuity with the past. We can distinguish two aspects in which religion is significant in the memories of pre-Soviet period. One is the visible expression of religiosity in contrast to what can to be perceived as atheistic era of the Soviet period. The other is the tacit form of religious narration present in autobiographical accounts of this era, in which the period before the war and before Stalinism was the Biblical *prelapsarian* time, that is the time of Paradise before the fall of Man, the time of innocence and happiness, the time that coincides with childhood and early youth of the memoirists.

Sovietization and repression

For the age group of interest, who were in their teens before 1940, World War II and the subsequent annexation of Estonia by the Soviet Union were important events, but not completely life changing. One can hardly discern the 'narrative of rupture,' typical of Estonian life stories (Kõresaar 2004), within these testimonies. Many of my respondents were still children or students. The memories of the war on the borderlands, like Petšery and the Pskov region, were entangled. Contrary to official Russian narrative of the war, the local population often did not make a distinction between German and Soviet forces: Margarita remembers that local peasants hid in the forest first from the Russian partisans as well as later from the Germans. Natalia remembers the prisoners of war being executed and that her parents lived in anticipation of arrest. It is not clear, however, whether the Germans or the Soviets were perceived as the bigger threat. It seems that, as children who experienced the trauma of the war, they could not clearly distinguish between the 'good' and 'bad' invaders. In one interview, a respondent could approvingly speak about 'our' (Soviet) armies, referring to the advance on Narva, and then accusatively mention the Soviet bombing of Tallinn (Svetlana b. 1930).

However, in most cases, the change of political power inevitably led to personal tragedies. Boris, as stated above, was arrested as a young man in 1945 for his service in the German army. His friend Vladimir's life was marked by the fact that wore the German uniform during the war (Natalia). Many male relatives, schoolteachers, and acquaintances were imprisoned and some were executed. Viacheslav Jakobs only learned that his father had been executed in 1941 when he was arrested 15 years later in 1956.[3] The Russians living in Estonia, who had been drafted into the German army during the war, served different sentences in the camps and some were deported as kulaks. Many of the Russian émigrés, who returned to the Soviet Union after the war, enticed by the promises of the Soviet authorities, ended up in prison and labor settlements (*Tallinskii pastyr* 2001).[4] Even though many respondents were still children or young people, they remember their fear of air raids and of the military and some recall their parents' fears of the deportations and mass executions of prisoners of war. The war and subsequent change of political power altered the destinies of the members of the Russian Orthodox community; many were sent into exile, prison, or labor camps, thereby splitting families and destroying lives.

This interpretation of the Stalinist repression and postwar retribution differs from the dominant view that the repression was intended to be the genocide of the Estonian nation. The counterargument to the genocide argument deemphasizes that the repression was targeted at the Estonians as a nation, by showing the supra-ethnic character of communism and its harmful consequences for the Russians themselves. According to Boris (b. 1924) and Vladimir (b. 1930-2013), 'as soon as the Soviet Power had injected itself in 1940 it started with the arrests of the most decent and most distinguished Russian émigrés…. The Soviet power was not just Russian but Estonian too because the communists were, by and large, [ethnic] Estonians, the local ones' (Interview, 4 January 2010). Metropolitan Kornilii states that the representatives of power and the floods of migrants from the USSR, who came to Estonia in 1940 and again in 1945, were not Russians, but the 'Soviets' (*sovetskie*) (personal communication, see also Kornilii 2009).

Among the 'local Russians,' it is difficult to judge how widely accepted the distinction between the local 'Russians' and 'Soviet Russians' was. The newcomers could not speak Estonian and were regarded as less cultured and refined than the representatives of the prewar Russian diaspora (Kornilii 2009, 74, 152; Valentina). Distinctions made between the 'Soviet Union,' which is an unconditionally negative term, and 'emigration' was a typical meta-narrative of the mnemonic culture of the Russian diaspora (Fedorov 2010, 12). Valentina said that the atmosphere at her school changed. Even though the new teachers from the Soviet Union were experts in their subjects, they did not believe in God (interview, 4 May 2012). However, there are more positive evaluations of Sovietization as well. The newcomers from Russia brought with them new expertise and skills. Anna spoke with respect about a surgeon from Moscow, whom she assisted, and who encouraged her to become an urologist. In her case, Sovietization also meant the possibility of specializing in Moscow and other top clinics in the Soviet Union. Another reason for a positive reception of the annexation of the Baltic was that, after 1945, the Estonian Russians were reunited with their relatives in Russia, many of who were thought to be dead (Svetlana, Natalia). In addition, the younger generation of Russian émigrés in Estonia, who worshiped classical Russian culture, was given the opportunity to study in the Soviet Union and visit the museums in Moscow and Leningrad. 'I was walking on these streets [in Leningrad] and day-dreaming that Pushkin or Onegin would appear around the corner' (Svetlana b. 1930).

The memoirists emphasize the role of strong interpersonal networks and communality during the Soviet period. There were two aspects to this idealization of community. On one hand, being a member of a religious group made one part of a wider network of 'brothers and sisters in Christ.' Anna and Valentina, who traveled widely across the Soviet Union attending professional conferences, made contacts with other members of the Orthodox Church. Seminary graduates used these informal networks across the USSR to search for future wives among good, pious Orthodox girls.[5] Natalia (b. 1930) from Pechery, a daughter of the church choirmaster, had three suitors, from Moscow, Ukraine, and Tallinn, who made marriage proposals after their first meetings with her. The parish had often represented a combination of liturgical and social life where matters were often solved 'over a cup of coffee' at a parish priest's house (Kornilii 2009). During the Soviet period, when the number of believers was relatively small and the administrative structure weak, the relationship between the bishops, the clergy, and the parishioners was familiar and informal (Svetlana b. 1930, Interview March, 10, 2010). Attempting to avoid contact with informers in public places (including the church), believers visited their priests at home for confession, spiritual advice, or for a simple friendly chat (*Tallinskii pastyr* 2001; Kornilii 2009; Natal'ia b. 1930). This emphasis on the relationships between the believers reflects the general prevalence of informal relations in everyday life for Soviet citizens (Ledeneva 1998). Church connections provided an additional form of support for the believers: someone in church always knew someone else who could help with one problem or another.

The narratives of war and occupation in the interviews lack the perspective of the official Soviet view, which presented the Second World War as a messianic event that liberated Europe from the evil of Nazism. This official view had very clear religious overtones and also emphasized the great sacrifice that the Russian people had made during the war. Given the omnipresence of this narrative in Soviet culture, one can understand the confusion of the Russian ethnic minority whose own experiences of the war may not have been so heroic as presented by Soviet propaganda.

Religious commitment, resistance, and compliance

While churchgoing was part of upbringing and culture for 'cradle Christians,' some of my interviewees experienced a religious conversion during the war. Valentina's husband, who was conscripted by the Nazi army, was walking in his German uniform in Berlin, feeling totally alone, when he stumbled across the Orthodox Church of St. Nicholas. When he entered the church, he suddenly felt that he was no longer alone. While in the gulag, Boris had found great consolation in reading the Gospel which his mother had managed to smuggle into his parcel, and which the prison authorities had failed to confiscate.

Churchgoing was not only a way of preserving one's cultural identity, it was also a resistance to the norms and values of the new socialist society to some extent. In this respect, Russian Orthodox believers were similar to the Estonian Christians of the same generation (Altnurme 2006, 101–150; Paert 2012). This resistance was presented in autobiographical narratives not as heroic defiance of the regime but as small acts of noncompliance. Believers had to be inventive so that they could avoid Soviet parades and public events scheduled on the significant days of the Orthodox calendar.

> During the May Day parade, I told my friend that we should be in the first row so that everybody could see us. I was marching and thinking: 'It is Great Saturday [Saturday before Easter] today. I cannot forgive myself if I miss the Mass'. So together with my friend we changed our place, moving to the back of the procession, until finally we were out of it. We ran as fast as we could. (Natalia b. 1930)

Rather than emphasizing their heroic role in the fight against totalitarianism, Russian Orthodox believers underlined the arbitrariness and injustice of the Soviet system. Metropolitan Kornilii, who was arrested in 1956 for keeping religious literature published by émigrés, challenged his accusers about their lack of evidence, for deliberately tampering with evidence, and for introducing bias. (Kornilii 2009, 103)

The tightening of the Soviet policy on religion after 1958 led to the strengthening of ideological pressures against the church. Despite the constitutional right to worship and believe, families of the clergy and active parishioners were affected by the informal rules discriminating against believers. The wife of a Tallinn priest, Vasilii Lysenko, lost her job as a kindergarten teacher (Kornilii 2009); Natal'ia (b. 1930) could not continue studying music in the prestigious Gnesin sisters' music college in Moscow because of her marriage to a priest. The singers in church choirs, who could receive some reimbursement for their work, often avoided being formally registered so that their day jobs were not affected. During Christmas, it was not unusual for some ideologically minded activists to visit the homes of their Christian colleagues from work to check whether there was a Christmas tree, interpreted as a sign of religious belief (Valentina b. 1929). New regulation of the Orthodox Church in 1961 minimized the role of priests in the management of parish affairs and gave significant power to church councils (sovety) consisting of lay parishioners. The clergy joked about this regulation, calling it 'All Power to the Soviets' (which was a well-known slogan of the revolution of 1917). This was the cause of many conflicts between priests and parishioners.

Nevertheless, depending on the profession and the time period in question, keeping one's career and personal faith was not incompatible, especially in the Baltic republics, where the control of the party concerning religion was perhaps more relaxed than elsewhere in the Soviet Union. This coexistence is illustrated in the responses from several interviewees. Anna (1922-2011), one of the top surgeons in Estonia, served for 11 years as a supervisor (starosta) in one of the Tallinn Orthodox parishes. She believes that her colleagues and the authorities knew that she was a churchgoer. Valentina and Anastasia, who also were doctors, never made an effort to hide their faith. However, Svetlana (b. 1930) who worked as a teacher – a more ideologically sensitive profession – could not attend church openly but had to hide in the balcony of Alexander-Nevsky Cathedral with the church choir.

The Orthodox Church preserved the memory of the pre-Soviet years that was expressed in the veneration of the saints, including the saints associated with the royal family, such as John of Kronstadt and Seraphim of Sarov. The literature published by émigrés could be regarded as anti-Soviet; many members of the Russian diaspora had relatives and friends abroad who provided them with spiritual literature in Russian published abroad. Estonia was a meeting point for the Orthodox Soviet underground and the Russian émigré Orthodox culture, providing spiritual answers to the searches of the dissenting intelligentsia of the 1970s.

While there was no emphasis on heroic resistance, there was even less of an attempt to discuss in interviews the problem of collaboration and compliance with the regime. One case seemed to be an exception, which was a case of apostasy by the Orthodox priest, Aleksandr Osipov. He underwent a remarkable career trajectory, beginning as an Orthodox priest in Estonia to a professor of the Leningrad Spiritual Academy, and finally to a leading figure in the Soviet atheist campaign. It was not a secret that Osipov became a collaborator, reporting to the Committee for State

Security (KGB) about church affairs in the late 1940s, long before he formally split with the church in 1959 (Firsov 2004). In the memoirs of those who knew Osipov, his case is singled out as a personal apostasy, even though it became clear how much influence he had on the careers of some of the Estonian clergy.[6] Nevertheless, the believers suspected that there were other informers within the church during the Soviet era. Metropolitan Kornilii believed that his home in Vologda, where he briefly served as a priest, was bugged by the KGB (Kornilii 2009). Vladimir remembered that his father-in-law, the priest Valerii Povedskii, had been called to the commissioner's quarters in Tallinn and confronted with the accusation based on a citation from his sermon. 'What kind of "dark forces" did you have in mind when you preached in church last Sunday?,' asked the commissioner, trying to figure out the hidden political meaning of the sermon that dealt with the spiritual state of a Christian during Great Lent (Vladimir b. 1930-2013). Someone who was in church must have recorded the sermon.[7] Despite this, Father Valerii had little fear of the authorities, perhaps knowing that his reputation of an 'anti-Soviet priest' could not be damaged more than it was already. Ordinary believers also demonstrated small acts of resistance by attending the church despite the danger, and by observing Christmas and other feasts.

Religion was treated as form of resistance in the studies of the Soviet era. However, in this section, we attempted to show *religious memory* as resistance. The simple acts of reading a Gospel, praying, and keeping the church feasts and commemoration of deceased relatives could be understood as acts of defiance. These acts of defiance have strengthened their sense of belonging to a Christian community.

Secularization

The worldview of young people was rooted in religion and the church during childhood, but religion increasingly became a matter of personal choice for young people and adults during the Soviet era. The secular worldview may not have been dominant, but it could conflict with the traditional way of life. A. Prostatov, a sailor born in Tallinn, was evacuated during 1941 (when the Soviet troops retreated from Estonia) to a village in Pskov Oblast. He was brought up in a traditional Orthodox family, decided to join the All-Union Communist League of Youth (Komsomol) in 1952. Prostatov's mother took her son to see a holy man, a monk named Simeon, at the Pskov-Pecherskii monastery.

> I was struck by the unusual simplicity and modesty of the elder, by his humble abode that had a small window and a little lamp in front of the icon. He told me kindly and as a fatherly advice: "you don't have to become a Komsomol member". But I went against the advice of the elder and my mother. (EKLA f. 350, 66)

The public spaces in Soviet life – the school, the army, the workplace, and places of entertainment – became the sites of nonreligious forms of memory, including the official memory of the revolution and the Second World War. The church also had to adapt to the official ideology. During the Second World War, the Russian Orthodox Church assumed a new patriotic role, which to some extent was a continuation of Patriarch Sergii's declaration of loyalty in 1927. The policy of Metropolitan Nikolai (Jarushevich) was especially significant in endorsing the official Soviet version of the Second World War. His patriotic speeches have been regularly published in the central church periodical, the *Journal of the Moscow Patriarchate* (Jarushevich).

Valentina (b. 1929), who completed her school studies under the new school's leadership after 1945, used Metropolitan Nikolai's sermons for her school essays without disclosing the source. A letter from Bishop Isidor to the Russian émigrés in 1948, copies of which were collected by the Commissioner for Church Affairs, bears the same mark of the emerging official narrative of the war, characterized by the sacrifice of the people and the Russian mission to humanity (ERA, R 1961, 2/12, 48–49).

Memories of the Russian newcomers to Estonia: Anastasia's story

The local population regarded the Russians who came to Estonia after the war as representatives of an alien and threatening culture and value system. In the late 1940s, many of these newcomers were representatives of the party, military personnel, technical intelligentsia, teachers, and doctors. Even though it was not always evident, some of the Soviet newcomers were also brought up in religious families and surreptitiously professed belief in God. Below is the case of Anastasia Pavlovna (b. 1924). She came to Tallinn on the medical staff of the People's Commissariat for Internal Affairs (NKVD). It is difficult to treat her case as typical or untypical, but it adds interesting details to the collective portrait of the Russians migrant to the Baltic state and gives a glance to the scarce memories of 'perpetrators.'

Born to the large impoverished family of a factory worker in Izhevsk, Anastasia was one of eight children. The family was pious Orthodox, but this did not prevent the children from becoming Pioneers at school. After graduating from medical school, Anastasia was recruited to the NKVD as a doctor, serving first in Stalingrad, then at prisoner of war (POW) camps. She recalls one of her achievements as saving the lives of captured Germans who were dying from malnutrition and disease. Under the Potsdam Agreement, she accompanied trains transporting the POWs back to Germany.

After the war, Anastasia was directed to Estonia, where she accompanied the trains of the people deported from Jõgeva to Omsk in Siberia. She remembered the great secrecy of the assignment: her superiors did not tell her what the aim and task of her journey was – they only warned of its potential hardship. Anastasia vividly described the pitiful conditions of the deported people who were densely packed on the train; many of the alleged 'kulaks' were clearly from poor backgrounds. There were old people as well as small children. As a doctor, she felt responsible for providing basic medical care for those on the train, and she expressed compassion and selflessness beyond the call of duty. During the journey, she helped deliver two babies, providing all the necessary conditions for birth despite the restrictions of the special train. By chance, she was also pregnant with her first child at this time. Even though she had no authority to do so, she tried to help the deportees by giving advice and making appeals to the local administration, as she felt that injustice had been done toward some of the arrested people. On her return to Tallinn, she was commended for her work, especially for ensuring the health and safe delivery of the deported to Siberia. She kept her participation in the deportations a secret. She could not say anything about this to her Estonian friends and neighbors. The sense of injustice and tragedy remained with her and she stopped working for the NKVD as soon as she could. When I asked her about the death of Stalin in 1953, Anastasia remembered having mixed feelings of sorrow and indignation at Stalin's crimes. 'People sincerely mourned his death. They knew, however, how much beastliness took place, but we did not want to go deep into that. It was not up to us, to discuss this. We all felt that there were abuses of power. How many people had perished, for no reason!'

Both of Anastasia's children were baptized and she began to attend church regularly in the 1960s. Religious literature and prayer books were scarce, but she shared books with some other religious women. Some colleagues disapproved of her churchgoing, but she persisted. The church provided her with much firmer concepts of right and wrong. When asked about whether her husband was religious, she replied that he had a much stronger sense of morality by disapproving of abortion, which he regarded sinful. However, for women in the Soviet Union, abortion, which was illegal until 1956, was often the only way to survive, as they could not afford to bring up more than one or two children. As a doctor, she helped her female friends terminate pregnancies. This navigation between the innate sense of moral wrong and the practical need to survive was typical for many Soviet people. Anastasia's memory of Stalinism is characterized by the same dualism: on one hand, even before the 20th Congress of the Communist Party of the Soviet Union in February 1956, she recognized the crimes of the regime because her best friend had lost her father during the Great Purge. On the other hand, she is not able to share collective responsibility for the purges; in fact, the thought of collective responsibility has never occurred to her. This tension between a personal feeling of guilt that could be connected with religious identity and the lack of responsibility for the crimes committed by the regime is not atypical but reflects the memory politics of the Russian Federation.

Orthodox religion and the reflection on the past

Individual memory within the Orthodox Church cannot be understood without an awareness of the Orthodox concept of repentance (*pokaianie*). Normally, Christians take responsibility for their own sins. Repentance, which is expressed through confession to a priest, is essential in the Orthodox system of salvation; a profound, sincere repentance is compared to a second baptism that can totally wipe out all sins and impurities (St Isaak the Syrian). The influential ecclesiastical writer, Bishop Ignatii Brianchaninov (1807–1867), believed that all mortal sins (including apostasy, blasphemy, murder, adultery) could be repented, with the exception of suicide.

Even though repentance is usually regarded as pertinent for personal salvation, there are historical precedents when repentance is used collectively. The entire 'nation' can be called to repent publicly for collective sins. In 1607, the Orthodox church performed a 'Rite of All-Nation Repentance' for the massive apostasy during the 'Time of Troubles,' when the Polish and Swedish armies invaded Muscovy. In the 1920s and 1930s, some bishops demanded collective repentance from the group of the clergy who collaborated with the Bolshevik regime and modernized the church rituals (the so-called rennovationists). Bishop Ioann (Shakhovskoi) of San Francisco has also demanded 'all-nation repentance' from the Russian people for the sins of communism. In present-day Russia, some marginal groups within the church perform 'the Rite of All-Nation Repentance' that promotes collective repentance in the sin of Tsarmurder (the execution by the Bolsheviks of the Tsar Nicholas II and his family in 1918), a practice much criticized within the church (Kormina and Shtyrkov 2011). Artists have also creatively used the concept of repentance; for example, the Georgian filmmaker Tengiz Abuladze in his 1984 award-winning film *Repentance* (*Pokaianie*) that deals with the theme of Stalinist terror. In this film, the disinterment of the body of the dictator

Varlam symbolizes the Christian and political themes of repentance, justice, and retribution.

However, the prevailing image of the Orthodox Church today is that of a Church Martyr that suffered collectively under the yoke of communism. Ordinary people, therefore, have no responsibility for the crimes of Stalinism and the communist regime in general. The poet Bella Ahmadulina performed an eccentric act of repentance in front of the Estonian bohemian public in the 1980s. In a café in Tallinn, after her poetry reading, she made a deep bow in front of Estonian artists and poets asking personal forgiveness for the Soviet occupation (Skul'skaia 2003). It would be difficult to imagine ordinary people performing such acts of public exposure. The majority of the people I interviewed had low-level, nondecision-making positions. They had not been confronted with the question of responsibility. The interviewees, with some exceptions, were quite open about discussing their personal lives, perhaps, using the interview as a form of a 'secondary' confession that dealt with an issue they no longer felt to be a burden on their conscience.

Conclusion

The studies on the Russian diaspora in the Baltic republics are characterized by the excessive emphasis on Russian cultural elites before the war, whose collective identity is largely defined as secular. These studies fail to include the life stories of believers and encompass the Soviet as well as the interwar periods. Having focused on a small group of Russian Orthodox men and women born before the war, I have found several internal contradictions, discontinuities, and paradoxes that question the value of attempts to provide a coherent and unified memory identity on the basis of one religion or one ethnicity.

The autobiographical memoirs of the Russian minority in Estonia challenge and complement the existing mnemonic communities and institutional memory in several aspects. In contrast to the dominant narrative of the Second World War, typically viewed as a messianic and heroic event, the autobiographical memories of the interviewed subjects convey the messiness of the war and the arbitrary sense of injustice of postwar retribution, fear, and grief. The Soviet era lacks a clear-cut unified characterization. Stalinist repression and the Second World War stand apart from the Soviet period as a whole, as outstanding, nontypical events when martyrs and heroes were produced. Even though some respondents reflect on the violent and unjust character of the purges and deportations, they, as members of the Russian ethnic minority, do not assume any personal responsibility for the crimes of the regime. The gaps and inconsistencies concerning the memory of Stalinism in the individual life stories could be a result of the incomplete process of commemoration of the victims on the part of the Russian cultural memory politics (Etkind 2013).

Sovietization had positive and negative aspects. Socialism was a time of opportunity for professional careers and, paradoxically, either despite the ideological campaigns or because of them, the Orthodox believers had a sense of strong interpersonal links, a spirit of mutual support and authenticity. In contrast to the memories of the same generation of Estonians, the Russian memories tend to use the narratives themes of 'rupture' and 'suffering' less (Kõresaar 2004).

Religion constitutes an important part of cultural memory. The memories of the Russian ethnic minority rely implicitly or explicitly on the Orthodox understanding of repentance and forgiveness. The tacit character of these underpinnings presents problems for the researcher but it cannot be dismissed as nonexistent. These findings suggest that a more substantive contribution from theology and ethics than has been done hitherto is required for the development of interdisciplinary memory studies.

Notes

1. These calculations do not take into account the number of ethnic Estonian Orthodox (18,517 in 2000 and 20,585 in 2011).
2. The respective attempts to collect Russian-language life stories via public appeals were made by the Estonian Cultural History Archives in 1989 and in 2006–2007.
3. Metropolitan Kornilii of the Estonian Orthodox Church of Moscow patriarchate.
4. Olga Chavchavadze, born in 1934 in Paris, had returned to the USSR in 1947 following the call of Bishop Nikolai (Jarushevich), who convinced many émigrés that there was no persecution of religion in the USSR. As soon as they moved to Russia, Olga's stepfather was arrested and disappeared. She and her mother, like many other returnees, were deported to Central Asia. Only in 1956 was Olga able to leave the settlement. She eventually moved to Estonia in 1963 where she worked as a church cantor until the early 2000s. Today, she is a nun in France.
5. According to the Orthodox canon law, if a priest does not marry before ordination, he should remain celibate.
6. It was suggested that Osipov repented before his death, but those who knew him doubt that this was true.
7. Bishops had to present a copy of their sermons to the commissioners whilst ordinary priests did not have to.

Acknowledgments

The work on the article was made possible due to the grant of Eesti Teadusagentuur: [Grant Number PUT 428].

Disclosure statement

No potential conflict of interest was reported by the author.

Funding

This work was supported by the Eesti Teadusagentuur: [Grant Number PUT 428].

References

Aarelaid, A., and A. Hatshaturjan. 2006. "Diskurs kul'turnoi travmy v russkoiazychnoi srede v Estonii." *Sotsis* 10: 57–65.

Altnurme, L. 2006. *Kristlusest oma usuni: Uurimus muutustest Eestlaste religioossuses 20. Sajandi II poolel.* Tartu: Tartu University Press.

Assmann, J. 2006. *Religion and Cultural Memory. Ten Essays.* Translated by Rodney Livingstone. Stanford: Stanford University Press.

Assmann, J. 2011. *Cultural Memory and Early Civilization: Writing, Remembrance, and Political Imagination*. Cambridge: Cambridge University Press.

Belobrovtseva, I. ed. 2008. *Russkie vne Rossii. Istoriia puti*. Tallinn: Russkii Dom.

Belobrovtseva I., ed. 2010. *Russkie v Pribaltike*. Moscow: Nauka.

Berger, P. L. 1980. *The Heretical Imperative: Contemporary Possibilities of Religious Affirmation*. London: Collins.

Danilevskii, A., ed. 2010. *Memuary v kul'ture russkogo zarubezh'ia*. Moscow: Flinta-Nauka.

Davie, G. 2000. *Religion in Modern Europe: A Memory Mutates*. Oxford: Oxford University Press.

EKLA f. 350. *Life stories collection of the Estonian Cultural Archives in the Estonian Literary Museum*.

ERA. *National Archives of Estonia*.

Etkind, A. 2013. *Warped Mountain: The Stories of the Undead in the Land of the Unburied*. Stanford: Stanford University Press.

Fedorov, F. P. 2010. "Memuary kak problema." In *Memuary v kul'ture russkogo zarubezh'ia*, edited by A. Danilevskii, 5–23. Moscow: Flinta-Nauka.

Firsov, S. L. 2004. *Apostasiia: "Ateist Aleksandr Osipov" i epokha gonenii na Russkuiu Pravoslavnuiu tserkov*. Moscow: Derzhava-Statis.

Gaponenko, A. ed. [Povedskii, Vladimir, priest]. 2001. *Tallinskii pastyr. Protoierei Valerii Povedskii. Pis'ma. Propovedi. Vospominaniia*. Tallinn: Bratstvo Sv. Isidora Iur'evskogo.

Halbwachs, M. 1992. *On Collective Memory*. Chicago: Chicago University Press.

Hervieu-Léger, D. 2000. *Religion as a Chain of Memory*. New Brunswick, NJ: Rutgers University Press.

Ivanen, A. 2001. "Protoierei Rostislav Lozinskii. Vsemu mera i blagorazumie." *Mir pravoslaviia* 9. Accessed January 15, 2014. http://www.baltwillinfo.com/mp8-01/mp-14p.htm

Jaago, T. 2011. "Nõukogudeaegne migratsioon ja selle ilmnemine oma elulugudes." *Acta Historica Tallinnensia* 17: 140–149. doi:10.3176/hist.2011.2.09.

Kolstoe, P. 1995. *The Russians in the Former Soviet Republics*. London: Hurst & co.

Kormina, J., and S. Shtyrkov. 2011. "Pravoslavnye versii sovetskogo proshlogo: Politiki pamiati v ritualakh kommemoratsii." In *Antropologia sotsial'nykh peremen*, edited by E. Guchinova, and G. Komarova, 389–413. Moscow: Rossiiskaya Politicheskaia Entsiklopedia.

Kornilii [Jakobs], M. 2009. *O moem puti*. Tallinn: Sata.

Kosmarskaia, N. 2006. *"Deti imperii" v postsovetskoi Tsentral'noi Asii: Adaptivnye praktiki i mental'nye sdvigi (russkie v Kirgizii 1992-2002)*. Moskva: Natalis.

Kõresaar, E. 2004. "The Notion of Rupture in Estonian Narrative Memory: On the Construction of Meaning in the Autobiographical Texts on the Stalinist Experience." *Ab Imperio* 4: 313–339. doi:10.1353/imp.2004.0088.

Laitin, D. D. 1998. *Identity in Formation: The Russian-Speaking Populations in the Near Abroad*. Ithaca: Cornell University Press.

Ledeneva, A. 1998. *Russia's Economy of Favours: Blat, Networking and Informal Exchange*. Cambridge: Cambridge University Press.

Luckmann, T. 1967. *The Invisible Religion: The Problem of Religion in Modern Society*. London: Macmillan.

Miljutina, T. 1997. *Liudi moei zhizni*. Tartu: Greif.

Noyes, D. 2009. "Tradition: Three Traditions." *Journal of Folklore Research* 46 (3): 233–268. doi:10.2979/JFR.2009.46.3.233.

Paert, I. 2012. "Jumalaotsigud 'jumalata' maal: Usku pöördumine, traditsioon ja põlvkonnad vene õigeusuliste seas." In *Nullindate kultuur II: Põlvkondlikud pihtimused*, edited by A. Aarelaid-Tart, and A. Kannike, 150–181. Tartu: Tartu University Press.

Paklar, V. ed. *Estonia- moi dom. Zhizneopisaniia estonozemeltsev*. 2009. Tartu: Tänapäev.

Pribaltiiskie russkie: istoriia v pamiatnikakh kul'tury (1710-2010). 2010. Riga: Institute for European Studies.

Rahvaloendus [National Census]. 2011. Accessed January 15, 2014. http://www.stat.ee/rel2011

Shlapentokh, V., M. Sendich, and E. Payin, eds. 1994. *The New Russian Diaspora: Russian Minority in the Former Soviet Republics*. New York: M.E. Sharpe.

Skul'skaia, E. 2003. "Uzhin za reshetkoi s Belloi Akhmadulinoi." *Molodezh Estonii*.

Interviews

Anastasia (b. 1924) born in Izhevsk, came to Estonia in 1945. Worked as a doctor in the POW camps, in the security forces; after retiring from the forces worked in the prison service. August 6, 2011.

Anna (1922-2011), was born to a family of Russian émigrés, graduated from the Faculty of Medicine at the University of Tartu, worked in the central clinic in Tallinn, took monastic vows some years before her death. Interview December 17, 2008.

Boris (b. 1924), born in Tallinn, arrested in 1945, served a sentence in an Inta labor camp. Graduated by correspondence from a polytechnic institute, worked as a chief engineer in a mine. In 1986 returned to Estonia. Interviews March, 10, 2009; April 6, 2010. During the interview on April 6, 2010 Vladimir (b.1930-2013) was also present.

Natal'ia (b. 1930), a daughter of a choirmaster in the monastery in Petsery. Graduated from a music college in Leningrad, worked in Dnepropetrovsk before marriage to a priest. Worked as a choir mistress in Estonian churches. Interview September 1, 2006.

Svetlana (b. 1930), was born in Tallinn, graduated Leningrad Pedagogical Institute, worked as a schoolteacher of physics. Interview March, 10, 2010.

Valentina (b. 1929), born in Tallinn, worked as a doctor. Interview May 4, 2012.

Vladimir (b. 1930-2013), born in St Petersburg, lived in Estonia with his émigré-parents, worked as a driver, was married to a priest's daughter; during his spare time repaired broken gravestones in the old cemetery. Interview March 10, 2009.

The construction of continuous *self* in the life stories of former Soviet officials in Lithuania

Irena Šutinienė

Institute of Sociology, Lithuanian Social Research Centre, Vilnius, Lithuania

ABSTRACT
This article explores the discursive strategies of representation of potentially stigma-tized Soviet era experience and its integration into a coherent construct of positive *self* as shaped in contemporary discursive contexts of Lithuanian memory culture. The critical moral reflection of potentially stigmatized Soviet era experience in the life stories of Lithuanian former Soviet officials is explored as a different strategy to the 'pragmatic' normalizations strategy of representation of this experience and integration of it into positive image of present self.

Reconstruction of the continuity of the present *self* through 'biographical work' is one of the key functions of autobiographical stories created after historical upheavals: individuals recreate their life stories, often changing them over time, and find out about themselves in those stories and about the world after historical disruptions (Fischer-Rosentahl 1995, 260). In former communist countries, reconstruction of the continuity of the positive *self* was extremely problematic in the context of the hegemonic discourses at the beginning of the 1990s, emphasizing the discontinuity with the communist era. Many examples of biographical research in former commu-nist countries revealed problems in the continuous representation of communist era experience in life stories. These problems also concerned the experience of late socialism: as is shown by biographical research in Estonia and Lithuania, this era was represented poorly, or even skipped, in many life stories constructed in the 1990s (Kõresaar 2004, 36; Marcinkevičienė 2007, 28).

However, in recent years there have been changes toward more diverse represen-tations of the communist era in the public discourse of the former communist countries. Research conducted recently in post-Soviet Baltic countries indicates changes that are especially salient in autobiographical discourses. Positive representa-tions of the Soviet era are characteristic of the Lithuanian and Latvian memoirs of former Soviet officials (Ivanauskas 2011; Rubavičius 2007a, 2007b; Kaprans 2011). Similar changes are also seen in the Estonian autobiographical discourse, where the domination of interpretations within the framework of the public 'discontinuity' discourse is shifting toward interpretations along the lines of a paradigm of everyday life (Jõesalu 2010, 293). However, recent research on Lithuanian memory culture also reveals the ambivalence, contradictions, and absence of a clear consensus in the memory discourse of the Soviet era (Christophe 2013; Safronovas 2011). The purpose of this article is to contribute to the research on the processes of changing Soviet era memory discourse by exploring how individual Soviet era memories – representations in autobiographical discourse – change in the varying and controversial contexts of the Lithuanian memory culture. The aim of this analysis is to highlight some discursive strategies employed by people in their life stories in order to integrate potentially stigmatized experiences into a continuous and coherent construct of the positive *self*. Controversial contemporary contexts of Lithuanian memory culture do not provide clear cultural models for making meaning of the Soviet era experience. This study addresses the following questions: what strategies do people employ for the representation of potentially stigmatized experiences in changing stigmatizing contexts? How do these strategies help to integrate potentially stigmatized experiences into the continuous construction of the present *self*? The article is based on the analysis of three typical cases. These stories exemplify the life stories of former Soviet officials of older generations. These three stories were chosen after analyzing 24 stories of former Soviet officials in total.

The features of Lithuanian public memory culture

Life narratives express interaction between cultural discourse, material circumstances, and the experience of the individual (Bruner 2006, 102). As is formulated by sociologist Vladimir Andrle, 'We have to create a sense of shared cultural membership with our audience by constructing the self-account as fitting for the context of its telling and by drawing on shared cultural resources' (2000, 216). Many research studies reveal the complexity of the interconnections between public cultural frames and individual life narratives. In memory studies, the complexity and discontinuity of interaction between four different levels of memory – the organic-autobiographical, the inter-active-familial, the institutionalized national, and the mass mediated-transnational levels of memory – are observed (Erll 2011, 315). Empirical research on the interaction between the individual level of memory and dominant discourse of memory culture also demonstrates the diversity of the relationship between these levels, sometimes revealing the strong domination of the patterns of hegemonic discourse in the individual memory while sometimes revealing the discrepancy between both levels (Christophe 2013, 115–116; Welzer 2008). Given the complexity of the relationship between individual and cultural memory, some researchers have come to the conclusion that the question of the interaction between different forms of memory can only be answered empirically, not theoretically (Christophe 2013, 116).

After reestablishing independence, the Soviet era was radically reevaluated in the Lithuanian memory discourse, as well as in the other postcommunist countries. The new interpretation of the Soviet period was based on the concept of a 'return to normalcy,' according to which the Soviet period was viewed as an anomaly; a break in the 'normal' development of society (Niedermüller 2004, 11–27). To a great extent, the 'return to normalcy' concept expressed the discourse understanding the Soviet occupation as cultural trauma; this view was expressed informally during Soviet era, and began to be postulated openly after the fall of the USSR (Aarelaid-Tart 2006, 57–58). In the Lithuanian discourse of cultural trauma, the themes of alien, forced occupation, Stalinist repressions and the suffering of the victims, memories of the postwar period guerrilla resistance, and other forms of resistance to the regime, became topical. Furthermore, in trying to, at least symbolically, 'return' to a 'normal' society, great importance was given to the memories and myths of prewar Lithuania, approaching this period as a model for a 'normal' democratic society (Nikžentaitis 2013, pp. 523–528) and legitimizing Lithuania's belonging to the 'West' and 'Europe' (Klumbytė 2003).

The condemnation of Soviet socialism as an alien, forced occupation still remains indisputable in Lithuanian society (Christophe 2013, 117), and belongs to the hegemonic public discourse of the Soviet era memory.[1] However, despite the consensus about the general views on Soviet occupation, researchers have observed internal divisions in Lithuania's memory culture. These divisions started developing around the late 1990s, 'with deep lines of memory culture breaks lying under the surface of society's consensus' (Christophe 2013, 117). To a great extent these differences of memory discourse are related to political identities and spheres of power between two political forces – 'conservatives' and 'ex-communists' (Čepaitienė 2004, 2007; Christophe 2013, 2010; Safronovas 2011). Almost from the very beginning, attitudes toward the Soviet era became an important indicator differentiating the political identities of 'left' and 'right,' and these differences and contrapositions were expressed not only in political, but also in moral categories (Čepaitienė 2007). Though the ex-communists approved of the main statements of the anti-Soviet discourse, they implemented these sentiments in the memory culture more passively than the conservatives. The discourse of the ex-communists was mainly defensive; they attempted to show that the communists under the Soviet regime did not '"collaborate with occupants"', but that they 'worked for Lithuania' (Safronovas 2011, 356–357, Čepaitienė 2004). Meanwhile, representatives of the conservative political forces believed only disassociation and resistance to the regime were morally acceptable attitudes and behavior to exhibit during the Soviet era (Christophe 2013). In memory policy, the conservatives actively tried to implement an anti-Soviet narrative and to hegemonize this narrative (Safronovas 2011; Čepaitienė 2004).

Barbara Christophe notes that the two discourses mentioned above have relatively equal weight and there is no clear domination of one or the other. She finds this balance of power to be a specific characteristic of Lithuanian memory culture (2013, 117–123). This balance of power in supporting different interpretations of the Soviet era is partly determined by the peculiarities of the realization of the means of transitional justice.[2] In 1991, the Communist Party was condemned and forbidden, but the majority of its members had already created a new party by the end of the previous year. The new party was created on the basis of Lithuanian Communist Party after the separation of it from the Communist Party of the Soviet Union (CPSU) in December 1989. Lustration involved only those members who had remained loyal to Moscow and did not support separation (Safronovas 2011, 358). Among them, several leaders of the Communist Party were sentenced to imprisonment but the main responsibility for the injuries committed by Soviet regime was left to the repressive structures.

The law of lustration for members of the repressive structures was used as recently as 1999. However, it was difficult to prove involvement in the secret services, because some of the Committee for State Security (KGB) documents were missing. Further, after the ex-communists returned to power again in 2000, lustration went slowly; around 2007 it came to the standstill and has since become the object of political discussions (Safronovas 2011, 360). In 2012, the remaining KGB documents began to be published, but they were not detailed enough to use as evidence to prove the responsibility of specific individuals. Instead, the responsibility was shifted to one demonized repressive structure. This shifting of responsibility led to the creation of the narrative of the 'criminal KGB,' which satisfied both conservatives and ex-communists and allowed them to construct a community of victims encompassing almost the whole nation.

Together with the failures of transitional justice, the peculiarities of the laws of citizenship also exerted an influence on de-sovietization in post-Soviet Lithuania. Unlike Latvia and Estonia, citizenship and all political rights were granted to all residents of Lithuania from the beginning, including those who came from Russia and other parts of Soviet Union during Soviet era. This helped many supporters of the previous regime remain in powerful positions. For example, in 1992, ex-communists won elections to parliament. Opinion polls also show support for the ex-communists' restrained assessments of the Soviet era in Lithuania more than in other Baltic countries: in 1993 Lithuanian inhabitants assessed both the economic and political aspects of the Soviet period more positively than Latvians or Estonians (Rose and Maley 1994, 27, 35).

The positive and neutral viewpoints of the Soviet era emerged in the public discourse in the second half of the 1990s as the alternative to the dominant anti-Soviet discourse. These newly emerged viewpoints were based to a large extent on the symbolic division of the communist era life into the everyday life and politics, which is typical for memories of the postcommunist countries. Thereby, other ways of representation of the Soviet era were made possible than those of period's stigmatization and vindication. (Kõresaar, Lauk, and Kuutma 2009, p. 29) In academic discourse, after the wave of denunciation of Soviet crimes appeared, there were more full-scale studies of the history of Soviet period, where the topics of culture, economy, everyday life, 'collaboration,' and other issues began to be discussed in a more balanced way; these discussions were also reflected in the media (Čepaitienė 2004, 90).

Alternative attitudes also appeared in the discourse of memoirs, where a growing diversity of representation strategies, mostly in respect to the period of 'late Socialism,' emerged. At the end of 1990s, many memoirs of the former Soviet intelligentsia – representatives of Soviet art, science, and culture were published. In these memoirs, some aspects of Soviet culture and everyday life were represented positively or neutrally, and conformity with the regime was normalized. In so doing the 'pragmatic' pattern, emphasizing utilitarian motives (self-expression, professional advancement, etc.), prevailed and 'oppositional' aspects of pragmatic conformism were stressed as well, and equated with 'silent resistance.' 'Pragmatic' conformism was considered to be the most suitable attitude toward the regime (Gasiliūnas, Sprindytė, and Tamošaitis 2006).

At the beginning of the twenty-first century, a 'wave' of memoirs of the representatives of previous Soviet *nomenclatura* also emerged. In these memoirs, alternatives to anti-Soviet discourse strategies of representation of the Soviet era were expressed more clearly and the ex-communists' version of Soviet era history was formulated most coherently (Rubavičius 2007a). The prototypical version of this normalization logic is aptly illustrated by the title of the book by the former leader of the Communist Party, later the President of Lithuania, Algirdas Brazauskas – *Even then We Worked for the Benefit of Lithuania* (2007). According to the logic of normalization, Soviet officials are depicted in memoires as active agents in bringing about important social, economic, and cultural changes for Lithuanian society (Ivanauskas 2011, 48). The achievements of the modernization and urbanization of the Soviet era are highlighted in an attempt to dignify the activities of the Communist Party and stress the merits of the representatives of the *nomenclatura*. Regarding the issue of collaboration, only responsibility for direct repressions is acknowledged clearly. Further, responsibility is attributed not to specific individuals, but to two institutions: the KGB (Soviet intelligence agency, sometimes demonized as 'Moscow') and the institution of the Second Secretary of the Central Committee of the Communist Party of Lithuania (appointed directly by the Central Committee of the Communist Party of the Soviet Union; acted as Kremlin's instrument of control) (Rubavičius 2007a). Accusations about the collaboration of the local party leadership are dismissed as absurd with the argument that the community of 'collaborators' could be expanded to all communists, or even the whole nation.

The anti-Soviet public discourse, mostly supported by conservative political forces,[3] blames for crimes and damage performed by Soviet regime both representatives of the repressive structures and the leadership of Communist Party and other active Communists. Though the moral assessments formulated in this discourse should reduce the group of 'non-collaborators' to a small group of resistors and victims of oppression, the limits of the group of 'collaborators' are not clearly defined in this discourse and the responsibility of specific people is not mentioned (Ivanauskas 2011, 46; Christophe 2013, 122).

The anti-Soviet discourse, as mentioned, still retains features of a hegemonic discourse. This narrative dominates the official memory politics of state institutions (Nikžentaitis 2013, 526). The remaining hegemonic power of this narrative is also demonstrated by the fact that until now, people who positively view the Soviet era are stigmatized and excluded symbolically from 'the community of good citizens' (Klumbytė 2010, 296). However, the stigmatizing and excluding power of the anti-Soviet discourse seems to be diminishing. This trend is demonstrated not only by the presence and power of the discourse presenting alternative patterns for the interpretation of Soviet era experiences, but also in the ambiguity, inconsistency, and vagueness characteristic of some basic categories and judgments of the anti-Soviet discourse itself. Researchers of the current Soviet era memory culture argue that 'the phenomena of "collaboration," "resistance," and "conformity" and their forms are not determined clearly' (Čepaitienė 2007, 46), and the boundaries of the groups of the 'right people' and 'collaborators' are shifting constantly (Christophe 2013, 122). Christophe finds ambivalent viewpoints and ambiguous interpretations in the 'hybrid' discourse of history textbooks, which reflects both the official hegemonic versions of memory culture and society's conflicts and debates, and the autobiographical narratives of history teachers (2012, 2013). It could be concluded that the ambivalence and ambiguity is a specific characteristic of the Lithuanian memory culture today, giving more space for the representation of diverse Soviet era experiences in collective and individual memories, including those 'taking advantage of' the former regime (Christophe 2013, 116–122,128). In the autobiographies, ambivalence is also used as an intentional strategy for the representation of diverse and contradictory Soviet era experiences (Christophe 2013, 133–134).

Normalization and nostalgia as means of reconstructing a continuous post-Soviet self

By definition, identity implies coherence and continuity. Many scholars consider managing continuity and coherence as the main objective when producing and interpreting life stories (Linde 1993; Elliott 2006, 39–49). As Andrle states:

> Normal functioning requires that we appear to have a past, a life story to tell; that we appear to be able to give short excerpts or more extended versions from our life story as appropriate; and that these versions are sufficiently coherent to make their subject continuous despite changes, and morally adequate despite difficult choices. (2000, 216)

Normalization is one of the most common methods of making meaning of experiences of the previous era after radical historical changes, especially when attempts to construct continuous identity take place in the context of perceived potential stigmatization. For the analysis of post-totalitarian normalization, the distinction between 'pragmatic' and 'necessary' normalizations of post-totalitarian discourse introduced by the social psychologist Dan Bar-On is important. (1999, 254–278). The 'necessary' or 'soft' normalizations are characteristic to all discourses – all social roles in interaction 'need the suppression, avoidance, even deception and we could not function, pragmatically, without these levels of normalization' (1999, 264). Although all human discourses are normalized to a certain degree, according to Bar-On, the normalization existing in the post-totalitarian discourse means 'vulgar pragmatism,' in which normalization has been overused and manipulated, which is different to 'critical and ethical pragmatism,' in which normalization has been limited to its necessary level (1999, 264). He considers 'pragmatic normalization' to be a characteristic feature of post-totalitarian discourses.

Bar-On also maintains that the 'pragmatic' and 'soft' normalizations are connected to the different attitudes to totalitarian past, including strategies of normalization when coping with a potentially stigmatized experience. His research demonstrates the existence of attitudes other than the 'pragmatic' adjustment to normality toward people's own experiences in the totalitarian past – that is, the attitude of critical consideration of previous behavior in the light of today's democratic norms and values.

The attitude toward the totalitarian past, including critical moral reflection, is also connected to a different level of psychosocial adaptation in democratic society and to the processes of reconstruction of social responsibility in post-totalitarian societies (Bar-On 1999, 254–264). The most common strategy of psychosocial adaptation in democratic post-totalitarian societies is defined as 'the adjustment' of behavior to the requirements of democratic society and the ability to act effectively under multi-contextual demands (Bar-On 1999, 257). This ability to act effectively in new democratic reality does not require the critical reflection on one's own past in the totalitarian system, while reconstruction of social responsibility includes the critical moral reflection on own past behavior, emotions, and attitudes which "helps the individual learn from past experience." (Bar-On 1999, 257) Furthermore, in respect of the reconstruction of social responsibility after totalitarianism, it is not enough only to be able to admit the facts from the past: 'To reflect means … to regain one's attributional flexibility of social responsibility, one's internal moral dialog, not merely to admit it, even in the public. The act of confession is a means for reaching this goal, but not the goal itself' (Bar-On 1999, 259). Additionally, critical reflection of one's own experience in a totalitarian system is also connected to the processes of identity construction: 'reflection is not just a cognitive or psychological construction but also a moral and social construction in which not just facts are established but selves are constructed as well' (Bar-On 1999, 258). Bar-On defines the 'adjustment criteria' and 'reflective criteria' as criteria for the identification in the discourse of the two aforementioned types of attitudes toward previous experience (1999, 281). The 'adjustment criteria' correspond to the aforementioned 'pragmatic' normalizations, and the 'reflective criteria' correspond to the 'necessary' normalizations (1999, 254–278).

Nostalgia is another common strategy for establishing a positive continuous self after deep transformations of society. Fred Davis states that nostalgia is a yearning for continuity of a self (1979, 34). As Maya Nadkarni has noticed in the analysis of postcommunist nostalgia in Hungary, 'nostalgia for the everyday life of Kadar's Hungary offered one of the few safe discourses available for talking about the previous era. Because it evaded being harnessed for explicitly political ends, it provided a powerful tool for structuring collective and individual identities' (2010, 205).

Postcommunist nostalgia is a complicated and multifaceted phenomenon that is not easy to define or identify empirically in life stories. Here, nostalgia is understood as a cultural praxis that is always reflexive – its subjects are always aware of the irretrievability of the past and selectivity of a nostalgic memory (Nadkarni and Shevchenko 2004; Nadkarni 2010)). Nostalgia expresses present feelings and concerns and, in terms of identity construction, nostalgia can be an essential constitutive part of the individual's present self and their present projections of social history (Klumbytė 2009, 97).

Neringa Klumbytė reveals an important aspect of the role of nostalgia in reconstruction of a positive self-identity in life stories in an analysis of the connection between post-Soviet marginalization and nostalgia for the Soviet past. She argues:

> Nostalgia is a restorative discourse, through which an individual reclaims one's own dignity and respect by transposing himself or herself onto an idealized chronotope of the Soviet past … Nostalgia is also a way to claim recognition and inclusion in a post-Soviet mainstream society, which very often denies equal citizenship to those who long for Soviet time. (2009, 93)

This reconstruction of dignity and continuous identity through nostalgia in life stories legitimizes the part of Soviet experience and memory that is negatively assessed or ignored in contemporary public. It is the apolitical character of nostalgia that enables people to speak 'safely' about their Soviet era experience – 'not to talk about the past while talking about it' (Nadkarni 2010, 205).

Data and methods

This article is based on the analysis of written life stories of Lithuanian people that were sent in response to the life history competition 'My destiny and the destiny of my kin in the maelstroms of history' that took place between 2010 and 2011. The Department of Sociology of Vilnius University and *Versmė* Publishing House organized the competition and the author of this article was involved. Competitors were to describe their own life stories and the lives of people close to them in the context of historical events. The set of autobiographies (117 life stories)[4] reflected varied social and demographic diversity. The authors of the life stories came from a variety of different social, educational, and geographic backgrounds. More than half of the authors (74) were representatives of an older age generation born between 1924 and 1944. Thirty-three authors represented people born between 1945 and 1957 and the rest of the authors were from younger generations.[5] This analysis covers the life stories of the oldest generation.

Twenty-four life stories were chosen to represent the biographical experience of those during the Soviet era that could be considered to be potentially stigmatized in current discursive contexts. The criteria for the identification of potential stigmatization are based on the interpretation of the term 'political conformism' in the Lithuanian scholarly discourse. Political conformism means participation in implementing the regime's political power and encompasses activities such as voluntary participation in public political undertakings, active direct support of the regime through creative works and products, membership in the Communist Party, heading the central nonpolitical institutions, working for the political and party authorities, power structures, or work as a KGB agent (Klumbys 2004, 24, 2009, 53–55). Taking high-level positions at institutions that implement policies of the regime, which inevitably involves the other activities previously listed, is defined as the highest level of political conformism (Klumbys 2009, 56). The highest level of political conformism, as well as collaboration with power structures, within the anti-Soviet discourse generally is stigmatized as 'collaboration.' Therefore, the selection criterion for life stories was the respective institutional position of authors within the field of political power. The stories selected were those of people who were officials in high-level positions at country-level institutions, employees in local party and administrative structures or power structures, or leaders of local institutions [6] during the Soviet era. Two stories of representatives of the second generation of the former members of repressive structures of Stalinist era were also selected in order to represent contexts of unambiguous stigmatization in all public discourses.

All of the authors were members of the Communist Party. A diversity of professions as well as of geographical locations was reflected in the sample. Most of the authors were retired when they wrote their autobiographies.

The analysis of these life stories focused on the continuity of the narrators' presentation of *self* in the story that is on the presence or absence of incoherence and contradictions in this presentation and connections of this coherence or incoherence to the character of presentation of the narrator's potentially stigmatized Soviet era experience. The analysis of the life stories was based on insights from the field of interpretative analysis of biographic narrative interviews. The techniques of narrative analyses (especially the distinction between narration and argumentation modes in life narratives) as described by Fritz Schütze and Gabriele Rosenthal (Schütze 1983;

Rosenthal 1993) are employed. Such segments of the life narratives as *self-characterizations* (Andrle 2000, 219), *codas* (Labow 2006, 79), and the final segments of the whole story (resolution including the final *coda*) were investigated more in-depth. It was assumed that, in the written life stories, the final resolution and coda of the whole narrative usually contained in the author's summary of their present *self*, which also includes connections to the past.

The strategies of normalization in the life stories were classified according to the representation of different contexts of stigmatization in public discourse (unambiguous stigmatization or presence of alternative discourses. The contexts representing different attitudes toward the totalitarian past (as defined by Bar–On) – the presence or absence of the attitude of a 'critical moral reflection' of past experience – were also considered. Thus, the stories containing the critical moral reflection of the experience of conformity with the Soviet regime and the stories representing strategies based on 'pragmatic adjustment' were identified at the start of the analysis and both groups were analyzed separately. Within these groups, the prevailing patterns of normalization of potentially stigmatized experience were identified empirically. The cases analyzed in this study represent typical patterns in the narrative strategies of normalization (Creswell 1998, 119). Besides typical features, all the cases analyzed here also contain some unique traits.

Among the 24 stories analyzed, there were 6 stories where the experience of engagement with the Soviet regime was critically reflected upon from the point of view of contemporary democratic moral values and ideologies and where the issues of 'collaboration,' 'opportunism,' and 'responsibility' were discussed. Normalizations in the other 18 stories analyzed only corresponded to the 'adjustment' criteria: these stories represented 'pragmatic' normalizations, as defined by Bar-On. In 16 of these stories, the normalization strategies of the experience of conformity with the Soviet regime mostly followed the patterns of the alternative discourse of ex-communists. The two remaining stories reflected a different stigmatizing context: the experience of their authors is stigmatized unambiguously in all public discourses. Though all discursive strategies of coping with dilemmas produced by unambiguously stigmatizing people's experience in the anti-Soviet hegemonic discourse are used in all groups of stories, some of them are more salient in the stories representing particular contexts. As examples of the larger sample, this study analyzes three stories representing patterns of construction of continuous identity based on different normalization strategies characteristic to the contexts investigated. With respect to the discursive contexts, two cases reflect the situation when there are alternative models of normalization in public discourse and one case reflects the contexts of unambiguous stigmatization. The names of the authors are pseudonyms.

'Pragmatic normalization': Julius's story

The story of Julius (born in 1937) was, to a great extent, adjusted to the schemata of hegemonic anti-Soviet discourse. The potentially stigmatized life experience was normalized according to the schemes of the opposite 'ex-communist' discourse, and the Soviet era experience was presented by separating the political and everyday spheres. The author's life experience was presented as depoliticized in the everyday mode of narration, while the themes relevant to the dominant national narrative were more frequently presented in the mode of argumentation, revealing the narrator's present position or illustrated by the stories and characters of other people. The terminology in the narrative was inconsistent: sometimes the exalted rhetoric of the ideology of Lithuanian nationalism ('our holy land,' 'Revival,' and so on) was mixed with phrases of Soviet ideology when speaking about everyday life.

The leitmotif of Julius's narrative experience of the Soviet era is the advancement of a man, born to a very poor family, to a higher social position. Julius became a forester, later advanced to a middle-ranking position in the Ministry of Forestry, and also worked in the Council of Trade Unions. After the restoration of independence, he continued in the Ministry of Forestry until his retirement. The theme that seems to be relevant for Julius is the transition out of poverty; poverty dominates his childhood memories and also frequently appears in later periods. The story of advancement from poverty to a higher social and economic status seemed to be the main construct organizing the presentation of the narrator's Soviet era experience. However, this construct is latent to a great extent, while the greatest part of the story presents the themes of the dominant anti-Soviet narrative.

The sequence of life events in the story was frequently interrupted by themes of the dominant anti-Soviet narrative. More attention was paid to themes corresponding to the national narrative than to personal experience. For example, references to school contains only 'patriotic' episodes, such as a time when he accidently saw a bunker of partisans, a memory of singing patriotic songs, or a discussion of the stories of teachers who, as he found out later, were involved in the resistance. The theme of 'collaboration' with the communist regime was thematized only as a theme of belonging to the Communist Party, and was normalized according to the 'national-communist' pattern of 'work for the benefit of the nation.' This normalization was explicitly formulated in a 'national-communist' justification of membership of the Communist Party: 'if not us, then the newcomers, Russians, would have taken higher Soviet posts.' This pattern of normalization was also expressed in the positive character of a 'national-communist,' 'patriotic' leader of the branch in which the narrator worked,[7] who appears in the story just after the episode of the author's joining the Communist Party and in many other episodes of the story about professional work. The story listed a number of aspects illustrating the content of this character's 'work for the benefit of Lithuania': he 'trained own professionals,' 'not always obeyed the requirements of the Communist Party,' 'admitted ex-deportees to work,' and so on. However, Julius did not mention any aspects of resistance to the Party's requirements in his own professional activities. He presented his own professional work in a depoliticized way, depicting the political sphere as peripheral. Thus, the image of Julius as a 'national-communist' was also contradictory.

The story of the post-Soviet era was also constructed within the frame of a hegemonic anti-Soviet narrative, presenting the identity of 'a patriotic Lithuanian nationalist' and, in this case, the presentation of life events corresponded to this identity. His post-Soviet life continued with his participation in the popular movement for independence and various activities associated with 'work for the nation' (mostly as work for the protection of the nature and reconstruction of ethnic heritage). However, his story of life in the post-Soviet period also seemed to have signs of normalization: only the events consistent with the anti-communist discourse were highlighted and presented in detail.

The resolution and coda at the end of the whole narrative revealed the author's attempts to come to terms with the discontinuities produced by the normalization of the story according to the schemes of the anti-Soviet discourse. Although, in parallel with the anti-Soviet discourse, the author relied upon the patterns of discourse of ex-communists, he also used additional strategies to help to make meaning of the controversial experiences of the past and present and to build a coherent self-image. The coda of the life story contained categorical criticism of present society and positive judgments about Soviet times that were explicitly formulated only in this part of the story. The ambiguity and ambivalence in this part of the story also revealed the lack of consistency in the terminology of the story: it included enthusiastic support for the independent state expressed in the exalted rhetoric of nationalist ideology as well as swinging criticism of contemporary society, expressed in the angry rhetoric and use of some terminology from the Soviet era. The content of the criticism toward contemporary society was consistent with typical themes of postcommunist nostalgia; the themes of poverty and wealth inequality, which was relevant to the author's experience, were particularly stressed. Most of the criticism toward the current times was expressed through nostalgia about the hopes and goals of 1988–1991. In his criticism, the author displayed the popular pattern of argumentation for overcoming the contradictions of the postcommunist experience, which has been identified by Christophe as being present in the Lithuanian public discourse and history textbooks. Anti-capitalist and anti-western resentment is commonly expressed in instances like this. The split between rich and poor is emphasized and assessed as unjust and unfair to the ordinary people, who bravely took part in the mass movement of 1989–1991 and do not deserve the unjust 'nomenclature capitalism.' Instead, the cynical and greedy rulers, as opposed to the ordinary people, are blamed for the injustice (Christophe 2010, 13–14). This strategy also 'redirects the nostalgia which frequently leads to a glorification of the Soviet past to the miracle year of 1989 which is turned into an epitome of national and social unity' (Christophe 2010, 14). The story of Julius expressed this 'redirection' of nostalgia, which was also reflected in the statement summing up the criticism of the present – 'this is what we fought for.' However, potential nostalgia for Soviet times was only explicitly expressed once in the story, with reference to better access to education in Soviet times:

> If I brought the times when our family was short of bread to the current times, I would definitely have no access to studies. I could not afford being a forestry officer whom my mother wanted me to become so much. I could not afford textbooks, notebooks and other learning supplements that pupils can hardly carry in their bags now. (Julius [1937] 2011, 20)

Though nostalgia and the anti-western argumentation helped to solve contradictions raised by controversial contemporary experiences, the narrator also probably understood that this nostalgia does not correspond to the present *self*-image of 'patriotic Lithuanian nationalist'. As if in an attempt to mitigate his positive judgment of Soviet times, to a certain extent, he treats his advancement during the Soviet era as accidental: 'My wife and me, we were the lucky ones. We both were younger children in our families and we both completed education.' The coda of the story also contains other attempts of the author to overcome the inconsistencies and contradictions of the self-image of 'patriotic Lithuanian nationalist' as presented in the normalized story. Here, he attempted to transfer the image of contemporary 'patriotic self' into the Soviet era. This was demonstrated in the final summary of the story: here he formulated a claim concerning his anticipation of regaining independence that seems false as it was not confirmed by any facts of the life experience:

We lived through a very interesting time. War, Soviet terrorism, kolkhozes, the Revival. In Soviet times I believed that the rebirth would come. I thought I was born in independent inter-war Lithuania, and I would die independent, too. My dreams came true. (Julius 1937, 21)

There was one more group of arguments in the final part of the story that showed the author was not certain about the sufficiency of the strategies used for constructing the continuity of *self* in the story. He tried to justify the connection of contradictory past and present 'political selves' without critical reflection on past behavior and expressed support for the argumentation that only behavior in the present period matters for the present image of a person. This argumentation was expressed in his opinion about two contemporary leaders: a former leader of the Lithuanian Communist Party and a former activist of oppositional culture:

Many people assess the Sąjūdis[8] leaders Algirdas Brazauskas and Vytautas Landsbergis differently. I dare call them leaders, as they both deserve that. They both toiled honorably for Lithuania's sake, but only in a different way .... Those two men are the same to me. They have paid their duty to the Motherland by liberating it from the Soviet heel. (Julius 1937, 21)

Hence, the story of Julius demonstrated the pattern of 'pragmatic' normalization, largely oriented to public relevance, where the presentation of life experience is, to a great extent, adjusted to the schemata of the hegemonic anti-Soviet discourse. This adjustment resulted in some incoherence and discontinuities in the presentation of *self* in the story. By separating the political sphere from the 'nonpolitical' everyday life, Julius also rejected part of his experience of conformity with Soviet regime, which was normalized in accordance with the 'national-communist' pattern of the discourse of ex-communists. This pattern, however, is of little help in representing the personal experience of conformity and of integrating it into a positive and coherent *self*. This was especially shown in the final part of the story, where the author's feelings of discontinuity and the incoherence of his image of the positive present self were indicated.

Critical moral reflection and revealing the ambivalence of the soviet experience: Vytautas's story

The story of Vytautas (born in 1942) demonstrated his attempt to reflect critically on his experience of the Soviet period by applying contemporary moral and ideological criteria and the principle of ambivalence as the main framework for making meaning of his experience during the Soviet era. The main part of the story was written in the narrative mode, and explicit argumentation appeared only in the abstract at the beginning and in the final summary of the story. Schütze considers that narrations transmit former experience, whereas argumentations represent the perspective of the present (Schütze 1983; Rosenthal 1993). Though there were a lot of implicit arguments expressed through narratives in Vytautas's story, this indicates that, to a great extent, the life story was primarily based on the author's experience.

The problem of establishing connections between the two periods of life separated by anti-communist turn as a historical 'break' was explicitly formulated by Vytautas as the main aim of the story, and was reflected in the title of the story – *In the break of regimes and systems*. His main concern, established at the outset of his story, seems to be the issue of collaboration that is avoided on 'pragmatically normalized' stories.

From the angle of collaboration, Vytautas reflects on the problem of continuity between the Soviet and the post-Soviet era experience:

> Did people like me, educated differently by the parents and the Soviet system, collaborate? Did we believe in the bright future of communism? Did we conscious, ideologically contribute to the development and consolidation of socialism? And where are we now, after the restoration of independence? How do we express our patriotism, Lithuanian belongingness, the desire to strengthen the state? Is everything fading away after the euphoria and enthusiasm of standing in the Baltic Way?
>
> I think I'll try to answer some questions by telling about myself. With some others – it's much more difficult. We were under devastation of the totalitarian system, combined with a well thought-out upbringing. Time has shown that it was temporary, false, misleading, and alien.
>
> Yes. We did collaborate. Helped to create a regime based on the unfortunate ideology. No. We were committed to the pursuit of our professions. Professionally, inquiringly, dutifully. (Vytautas [1942] 2011, 1–2)

Both strategies of the representation of the Soviet era experience analyzed here – critical reflection upon a potentially stigmatized experience in terms of contemporary moral values and the revelation of the ambivalence and ambiguity of the Soviet era experience – are interconnected in the story. The principle of ambivalence in the story was selected consciously, and it allowed the author to freely narrate the ambiguous and contradictory (from the viewpoint of contemporary contexts) experience, without reticence on the problems of guilt and responsibility.

The ambivalence of the life experience of former Soviet officials in the Soviet era was revealed in the story while also revealing the insufficiency of categorical judgments of hegemonic discourse. Vytautas pointed out that life in Soviet reality was more complicated, and, therefore, categorical judgments based on 'black or white' were too narrow. The ambivalence and controversy of life during the Soviet era was narrated also with the help of positive 'others'. In this context, the image of the author's father appeared to be very important. This image of a positive 'other' served to reflect on both types of experiences and attitudes – opposition to and collaboration with the system. Vytautas described his father as a progressive, interwar farmer and the noncommunist 'kolkhoz chairman' of the postwar period. His father served in the Red Army during the war, but 'was never proud of military awards.' He communicated with the Soviet authorities in the postwar period and, simultaneously, helped partisans and relatives in exile. In Vytautas' story, the father's character, representing ambivalent experience, served as an important model of positive identification and one of the principal tools to articulate the ambivalence of Soviet time. At the same time, legitimizing the father's position of collaboration fulfilled the need to secure a positive image of the family. The father's image allowed him to show the ambiguity and ambivalence of collaboration while in the position of the chairman of the collective farm (Vytautas also held this position for some time), and belonging to the Communist Party:

> My father had agricultural knowledge and, therefore, was appointed by the authorities to chair the collective farm. There were partisans in the surrounding forests and one of our relatives was among them. Ideological chairmen would have problems, but partisans didn't touch my father. My father's career ended after two years and we came back to our native village. (Vytautas [1942] 2011s, 6)

The quoted fragment illustrates the professional nature of the chairman's work, the 'nonideological nature' of the father, and his relationship with partisans who are treated as heroes in the contemporary discourse. The insufficiency of unambiguous evaluations of Soviet era experience was also revealed through a number of other characters and stories. For example, Vytautas relays a story about a Russian military officer who participated in the deportation of the Vytautas's relatives and, according to his father, was wiping tears as 'most army men were normal and understanding people.' Vytautas also describes a postwar Party instructor who was 'a brave and sincere person,' a skilled agricultural professional, and many others. These stories display a popular interpretation pattern, particularly with regard to postwar times, in which the moral values of people, professional work, support of 'ordinary people,' and even the ability to maneuver between two fighting forces – anti-Soviet partisans and Soviet power structures in order to avoid victims – was regarded by people as more important than political or ideological positions (Christophe 2012, 15–17).

The experience of involvement in the Communist Party, *Komsomol*, and his father's service in the Red Army was presented as 'collaboration' to some extent. Vytautas did not legitimize his joining the Communist Party and did not justify membership by 'national-communist' or other similar arguments. Rather, he confirmed his ideological indoctrination which was, however, normalized as 'naïve: "I naively thought by myself: In what way is it possible not to be with the current powerful might"' (Vytautas [1942] 2011, 12). However, the disapproval by his father, which the author described right after the story about joining the Party, again revealed the ambivalence of Soviet life, demonstrating loyalty of his family to oppositional to Soviet regime prewar traditions and values, thus also revealing the complexity of choices between loyalty and disloyalty to the regime as well as entanglement of loyal and disloyal social belonging during Soviet era:

> So far, painful memories and a scar in the heart are left. When my district government appointed me to the position of the 'kolkhoz chairman,' my dad asked me whether I belonged to the Party. He knew that without it a person would not be appointed to such a position. I affirmed it. A cruel answer. 'My son, a tree was growing and one branch withered. It was cut off. You're now that branch in our family.' All the time we communicated after that, I felt coldness. It still hurts me. (Vytautas [1942] 2011, 12)

The continuity of *self* of Vytautas was to a great extent based on the narrative of his professional work during the Soviet era. Vytautas worked as a stock-raising professional (later, as a kolkhoz chairman and director of a huge stock-raising farm). His professional experience was structured within the framework of a collective story of *communist-era professionalism*, similar to the stories analyzed by Vladimir Andrle in research conducted in the Czech Republic; these stories were used as a mean to avoid potential stigmatization in the life stories of men and women who had successful careers under communism; (2000, 223–24);. It was not by accident that Vytautas' story began with an episode about choosing a profession, and the motif of continuing successful professional activities was one of the most important factors describing his present life and identity in the final coda of the story. The story of *communist-era professionalism* was told by depicting characters who were good professionals. In the story of the author's professional career, positive characters were hard working, highly skilled professionals, who may or may not have been Party members, thus showing the distinction between political and professional spheres. Value was especially given to the professionals who were most efficient and innovative at work. Again, an important role was given to the image of his father. This image served to express, *inter alia*, the conflict between a professional career and the political sphere, which also played a significant role in the story of Vytautas's professional activities:

> It was hard for my father to run the kolkhoz. I know it very well, because I've tried that 'managerial bread' myself. Operational activities were clear and pleasant for him. But then … there was Party's policy that should be pursued. That was a problem. There were many inexpert Party activists trying to dictate their rules at the sittings of the board. He said he could hardly stand throwing one of such 'experts' out of a window together with the frames. (Vytautas [1942] 2011, 7)

To a large extent, the story of the author's work in the Soviet period was presented as a struggle for high quality, professional, effective work; it contained many stories about overcoming the obstacles emerging from the Party leadership and Soviet staff members (including the non-communists), who were dishonest in their work.

Similarly to the Czech stories analyzed by Andrle (2000, 223–225), the story of Vytautas questioned the anti-Soviet dominant discourse, both by segregating professional activities from the political sphere, and by providing examples of highly skilled communist professionals, thus disclosing the exaggeration of the negative influence of the political dimension on the professional sphere in the anti-Soviet discourse. Characterizations such as 'He was a communist, but a straight person and a competent professional' (Andrle 2000, 225) were also present in the story. However, the story as a whole did not unambiguously support the argument that 'one had to be politically astute to sustain conditions for doing a job well' (2000, 225). The connections between the political and professional sphere in the story of Vytautas were presented as more complicated and ambivalent. Though the image of the representatives of political institutions as impeding professionalism dominated, there were also noncommunist staff members who were dishonest. In line with the schemata of the anti-Soviet discourse, the author associated this dishonesty with the Soviet system, which destroyed the prewar habits of honest work. Moreover, the *leitmotiv* that links the stories of *communist era professionalism* to the prewar period (consistent with the models of anti-Soviet discourse) was expressed in the image of his father, who also transmitted to Vytautas the *habitus* of honest and innovative work from the prewar period. While narrating the story about his professional activities, the author emphasized the continuation of this *habitus* as a milestone in constructing the continuity of his own *self*. Therefore, Vytautas' story of *communist era professionalism* combined arguments from different discourses – some arguments challenged the stereotypes of anti-Soviet discourse, while others seemed to be consistent with them. Thus, in the story of *communist era professionalism*, the narrator also argues for ambivalence as an interpretative principle.

The narrative of the movement for independence was also presented clearly, and the continuity of professional work experiencing new opportunities played an important role in the narrative of the post-Soviet period.

Thus, the continuity and coherence of Vytautas's identity was constructed through the continuity of the 'professional self,' by discussing and mitigating the categorical judgments of the anti-Soviet public discourse by revealing the ambivalence of life in the Soviet era, and by establishing the connection to the prewar period of independence in line with some anti-Soviet discourse themes. The open reflection of the potentially stigmatized Soviet era experience of conformism helped to integrate this experience into the more coherent *self*. The presence of the reconstruction of social responsibility that is connected to the moral reflection of the experience of the totalitarian era that looks problematic from the point of view of contemporary values and norms (Bar–On 1999, 257) can also be seen in this story. Although Vytautas did not put himself among those most responsible for 'helping create the regime', (Vytautas [1942] 2011, 2) his reflections indicated that he would probably behave differently if he lived in a totalitarian system now or in the future. This was also implied by the conclusive assessment of the main benefits of independence for him in the life story, where the moral aspect is emphasized: 'Above all, the feeling that someone is behind you and above you has disappeared. Totalitarianism was ruining personality' (Vytautas [1942] 2011, 34).

Objective ambivalence, as a principle of interpretation of the Soviet era experience, enabled the author to identify certain benefits of the Soviet era for him, namely (like in Julius' story), good educational opportunities. However, there was no nostalgia in Vytautas' story, as it does not contain disenchantment with or criticism of the present (the author compared the Soviet era access to education with that in prewar Lithuania). Yet, unlike in Julius' story, Vytautas presented controversial experiences and interpretations intentionally within the interpretation space allowed within the framework of ambivalence. Ambivalence, as a tool of interpretation, encompasses both positive and negative assessments, thus helping to lessen and reconcile the contradictions between them.

Blame, guilt, and dispute of public discourses: Elena's story

The third story of Elena (born in 1940), portrays a version of unambiguous discursive stigmatization. The story demonstrated the thematization of experiences related to the most difficult memories, those creating the greatest tension in remembering post-Soviet society – blame and guilt. The author of the story is the daughter of a man who participated in carrying out Stalinist repressions in the postwar period. In Lithuanian memory culture, Stalinist repressions and their executors are viewed in a categorically negative light and this negative evaluation belongs to the hegemonic part of the public memory culture. Therefore, unlike in the case of 'collaboration,' there is an unquestionable and unambiguous interpretation model prevailing in Lithuanian memory culture with regard to this type of experience. Former members of the organizations that carried out the Stalinist repressions, as well as their family members and relatives, usually tend to conceal or deny such experiences in the biographical interviews conducted in between 2001 and 2002[9] (Šutinienė 2003, 60–61). In the stories written in 2010 and 2011, two representatives of the second-generation have thematized this experience of their family members; however, one of them chose a strategy similar to denial – she reported about her father's participation in repressive structures, but refused to interpret or discuss said participation, saying 'it is too early to speak about this complicated period.' To defend her own positive image and that of her family, another second-generation representative, Elena, chose strategies that dispute the public discourse and the strategy of nostalgic criticism of the present.

The story of Elena revealed the significance for her identity of a sense of stigmatization and exclusion, created by the present discursive contexts. In general, the story was constructed as a 'counter narrative' (Andrews 2005, 110) and was organized around the stigma of her father's experience. Approximately half of the story consisted of direct argumentation polemicizing with the statements of the dominant anti-Soviet discourse and criticizing present society; indirect argumentation was also expressed to a large degree. The narrative of life experience presented was fragmented, with few facts and an inconsistent time line.

In terms of her current economic, social, and symbolic status, the author seemed to be a 'winner' who expressed satisfaction with her present life and the opportunities provided by the new system. In her case, the protest-triggering feeling of exclusion seemed to be related to the stigmatization of her family's Soviet experience in present contexts. Another biographical context likely to determine the sense of exclusion in present society was the experience of work in the local *Komsomol*, Party authorities, and other Soviet institutions that required a certain degree of political loyalty. In this case, the feeling of stigmatization may have also been enhanced by the memories of stigmatization personally experienced by Elena, the daughter of a *stribas* (a Lithuanian word derived from the Russian word '*istrebitel*,' a member of the postwar local structures involved in repressions).[10] Her experience of being stigmatized was related to the environment in the local area where she was working in the 1950s. In this period, people in local communities still remembered the postwar repressions, and the members of repressive structures, commonly called '*stribai*' by locals, were condemned: 'The phrase '*stribas*' daughter' was the lash discouraging from any initiative'(Elena [1940] 2011, 17).

Like other stories from people of her generation, Elena's story was to a primarily narrated within the framework of the anti-Soviet discourse. The story aimed to combine both – consent to the principal statements of the anti-communist discourse and opposition to the particular schemata and statements of this discourse. As a result, the story contained many contradictions and direct arguments often contradicting the implicit ones. This dual nature was also a characteristic of the present self-image that Elena had. In the self-characterization developed in the story she presented herself as a winner, who expressed satisfaction with her present life. At the same time, the sense of marginalization was expressed in the characterizations of other people, whom she described as wantonly wronged by the elite, humiliated, helpless 'worthy and decent' men, whose (and her own) dignity she protects by means of protest and nostalgia.

The main theme of direct dispute against the public discourse that Elena used to defend the positive image of her family was judging the activities of partisans who fought against the Soviet occupation in the postwar years (officially called *bandits* in Soviet times) and the *stribai* who were involved in carrying out the Stalinist repressions (officially called *people's defenders*). These issues are also debated in the present public discourse, questioning the unambiguous hero-izing of the partisans, but do not provide justification for executors of the Stalinist repressions (Veidas 2007; Pocius 2009). Elena, in contrast, invoked the argumentation of the official Soviet discourse where participants in the anti-Soviet resistance were portrayed in a negative light as 'bandits,' while members of the repressive structures were seen as heroes. In doing so, she also employed the rhetoric of the official Soviet discourse (*defenders of people, bandits, The Great Patriotic War*, and so on). These changing and ambivalent present contexts of Lithuanian memory culture enabled the author not to ignore her father's complicated experience and, in order to maintain the positive identity of her family, to use the official Soviet discourse schemes that are denied in the public discourse and omitted from it. In German discursive contexts, which are unambiguously negative about national socialism, representatives of the second- and third- generations of Nazi families do not contest the judgments of the public discourse but, advocating for the positive image of their families, try to marginalize and blur the participation of their family members in these activities (Welzer 2008). Elena had no intention of critically reflecting on or judging her father's experience (she did not raise the question of her father's role in the repressive structures), but unconditionally defends him. The questions of guilt and responsibility are insufficiently debated in the public space. In Lithuania, as in other postcommunist countries, the effect of 'transitional justice' 'spares society the much needed self-examination of the past and past behavior' (Kiss 2009, 138).

The other part of the argumentation was the criticism of present society, describing the decline, instability, and disillusionment of the present. Considering that Elena's story was largely constructed within the framework of the anti-Soviet discourse, nostalgia for Soviet times was implicit in her story, whereas nostalgia for the 'singing revolution' of the 1988–1991 (which, according to Christophe (2010, 14), 'redirects nostalgia which frequently leads to a glorification of the Soviet past to the miracle year of 1989'), was expressed explicitly. This nostalgia reflected the same pattern of argumentation as in Julius' story. In Elena's story, the same feelings and claims as characteristic of Soviet era nostalgia (Klumbytè 2009, 109) were transposed mostly to nostalgia for, in her words, the 'unfulfilled ideas and dreams' of the 'singing revolution.' Feelings of marginalization, as well as an appeal for respect, dignity and recognition, were expressed more in Elena's story than Julius's: she frequently defended the dignity of 'decent and honest' people who 'believed in the bright idea of liberation' but who now are 'helpless,' 'neglected,' and 'humiliated and despised in public institutions.' In parallel, the contraposition between 'ordinary men' and 'the mighty' was emphasized. Value was attached not only to the experience of the 'singing revolution,' but also to the Soviet era experience: in her story 'ordinary, decent men' now wantonly wronged by the cynical authorities were those who 'honestly worked all of their lives' in Soviet times, too. Anti-capitalist and anti-western attitudes were also strongly articulated in the following argumentation: 'All the ideas and dreams have been suppressed, blanketed, blown away, and killed by a rapidly sprouting capitalism. Material things penetrating from the space of a better, easier, different political system have become the core axis of life and the center of forces.'(Elena [1940] 2011, 23). However, this argumentation is also ambivalent in that implicit nostalgia for Soviet times was accompanied in the story by mistrust of both political systems.

In terms of the integration of Elena's Soviet era experience into the continuous construction of *self*, this argumentation is of little help. Although projecting present disappointments onto the hopes of the 'singing revolution' contributed to the reconstruction of the positive image of the present *self*, fragmentary nostalgia for Soviet times manages to integrate into this image only a small part of the Soviet experience. The small degree of integration is due to the fact that Elena's opposition to dominant anti-Soviet discourse attitude contrasts not with the interpretation of socialism, but with 'unfulfilled dreams' of the 'singing revolution.'

The author's former loyalty to the Soviet system was also thematized in a form of protest, by openly opposing the anti-communist discourse, which considers only resistance attitudes to be acceptable. She described her 'Soviet-friendly' position in a demonstrative and sarcastic manner, and thus expressed her protest against the negative valuations of such a stance and the defense of her positive identity: 'Always busy at work and social organizations, without having the slightest idea of choosing a path of moral resistance' (Elena [1940] 2011, 24).

Unable to reconcile the conflicting discourse positions (and her two 'ideological selves'), the Elena declared all political systems and ideologies as erroneous, thus relativizing the evaluations of her own and of her father's experiences: 'History will put all the finishing touches. It is just. But ideology is a real prostitute' (Elena [1940] 2011, 12). Elena tried to reconstruct her identity by denying both the past and current political and ideological systems. Therefore, continuity of the *self* through continuity of life experience was constructed only within the sphere of family life, separating this sphere of life from social and ideological identifications. Yet, even when representing this experience, the author paid greater attention to the history of earlier family generations, while the history of her own and of her family's life was presented only fragmentarily. Her family history and memories of her child-hood and youth were presented in the narrative mode, while her later experiences, including her work for the Soviet authorities, was only briefly reported. The family story was often intertwined with explicit and implicit protest-triggering argumenta-tion. In family and personal life history, an important role was given to 'fate,' which evidences the author's refusal to be considered in the role of an active subject (Schütze 1983).

The author's confusion in the face of irresolvable controversies, at the same time, reflected her position of helplessness and of being a victim of changing political systems and ideologies. Although this position was not consistently maintained throughout the story, it suggests an important principle, which structured the pre-sentation of the author's experiences, and, to a certain extent, her family's experiences, and was reiterated in the argumentation. For example: 'Nobody cares of you, and never did. No matter whether Utopian socialism ideas were flying in your backyard or it was full of promotional promises carpeted by ideological kites' (Elena [1940] 2011, 25). These feelings were also reflected in the fate *leitmotif* in the family history. Mistrust and detachment from all political systems and ideologies were explicitly formulated in the final summary of the story: 'There were no great disappointments in my life. Maybe it's because I didn't have vain illusions. I am proud of, trust in and rely upon my family only. If you don't have a firm foundation, all ideologies you believed in wear off, all honors and awards turn sour.'(Elena [1940] 2011, 26) However, this summary also expressed contradictions of the construction of the present *self*, as her own family life, though declared as most important, was thematized in a fragmen-tary way in the story.

The case of Elena illustrated a strategy of representation of past experience under the impact of unambiguous postcommunist stigmatization, when 'stigmatizing aspects of life, although in some cases constituting small fragments of peoples' past lives, became the defining biographical pole, around which all other events were "(re) constructed"' (Miller 2003, 111–112). Elena chose the strategy of defending her own and her family's positive identity by disputing the discourses stigmatizing her family's experience. However, this strategy, in the same way as the direct adjustment to the schemata of the anti-communist discourse, was of little help in representing the ambivalent Soviet experience and integrating it into a positive and coherent *self*. Although the varying and ambivalent contexts of Lithuanian public memory culture allowed the author to thematize guilt-related experiences more freely and to rely upon Soviet-time models of interpretation not recognized in this culture, they do not help much in reconciling contradictions when trying to construct coherence.

Conclusion

In contemporary Lithuanian memory culture, especially at the official level, the domination of the stigmatizing Soviet era discourse still persists. However, there are also features indicating the decrease of its stigmatizing power. This is reflected in the ambiguity, vagueness, and ambivalence, characteristic of some forms of this discourse, as well as in the positive and neutral interpretations of Soviet era experiences in autobiographical discourses. This article explored how former Soviet officials of the older generation use autobiographical discourse to integrate their potentially stigmatized experience, shaped by the controversial contexts of Lithuanian memory culture, into a continuous construct of the positive self. The article was based on the analysis of three typical cases selected from 24 life stories written as a response to the 2010–2011 life history competition 'My destiny and the destiny of my kin in the maelstroms of history.'

The analysis demonstrated that older people who have experience of cooperation with the 'system' inevitably have to resist the stigmatization of their experience created by the negative assessments of the Soviet era in the anti-Soviet discourse. The stories of former Soviet officials reflected both the lasting stigmatizing impact of the anti-Soviet discourse, creating discontinuity with their past experience, and the influence of changes of public memory discourse that enable to establish a more continuous relationship with this period. The life stories in question were constructed more or less in the frame of the anti-Soviet discourse and this is also characteristic of the recently written Estonian autobiographies of the older generation (Jõesalu 2005, 2010). In addition, in all stories, strategies of direct and indirect resistance to the anti-Soviet discourse were used, and diverse discursive strategies of normalization were employed. The patterns of 'pragmatic' normalization prevailed in the life stories, in a similar way to the discourse of the memoirs of former 'nomenclatura' and intelligentsia in Lithuania (Rubavičius 2007a, 2007b) and of former Soviet officials and intelligentsia in Latvia (Kaprans 2011). However, the life stories also showed that there are some new strategies of representation of the potentially stigmatized Soviet era experience that, so far, have been absent from the autobiographical discourse of Lithuanian former Soviet officials. In terms of constructing the continuity of the present *self*, the strategy of critical moral reflection upon the potentially stigmatized Soviet experience helps to thematize this experience more freely and comprehensively, as well as to integrate it into a more coherent present self-image, than the strategies of 'pragmatic' normalization. Still, the strategy of 'critical moral reflection' is far less common than that of 'pragmatic normalization.' Psychological research suggests that the level of adaptation in a democratic society, which includes critical reflection on and learning from past experience, is not easily achievable for a post-totalitarian individual: in this transition, 'one has to relearn or reinvent the flexibility to doubt and ask questions' and 'resume the social responsibility,' as well as 'to unlearn the rigidity and the shrinking of social responsibility' (Bar-On 1999, 255). One of the most important factors influencing the development of more critical attitudes toward controversial issues of the past seems to be the 'memory work' in public discourses (Alexander 2004; Cohen 2001).

Last but not least, the life stories provide insights into the autobiographical strategies which disclose the ambivalence of life in the Soviet times, thereby contributing to a more liberal thematization of the diverse Soviet experience, and to conciliation of controversies that are difficult to avoid. In both cases of 'pragmatic normalization' controversies between the presented images of the Soviet and post-Soviet 'selves' appear to be more persistent. Revealing ambivalence as an intentional model of interpreting Soviet era experience (together with the critical moral reflection of stigmatized experience) aims to conciliate these controversies. Such findings add an empirical argument to the existing research suggesting that conscious ambivalence in the Lithuanian autobiographical narratives can serve as an effective tool, creating the space for voicing inherently controversial Soviet-time experiences in which 'there is no need to be reticent about guilt' and 'alternatives for guilt-attracting behavior can be identified' (Christophe 2013, 133).

Notes

1. According to Foucault, some discourses are hegemonic and so rooted that they are invisible, taken for granted, and not scrutinized (Foucault 1998, 12–15).
2. Transitional justice is 'the full range of processes and mechanisms associated with a society's attempt to come to terms with a legacy of large-scale past abuses, in order to ensure accountability, serve justice and achieve reconciliation.' (UNSG 2010):
3. Hegemonic anti-Soviet discourse is created and supported not only by the right wing political elite; the post-Soviet public includes many former dissidents and political prisoners, many intellectuals and the younger generation, as well as the new elite, among others (Klumbytė 2009, 95).
4. This collection of autobiographies can be found at the Department of Sociology, Vilnius University.
5. The limits of the cohort generations used in the analysis have been defined by the sociologist Sigita Kraniauskienė on the basis of empirical biographical research of generations' identity and the classical theory of 'political generations' by Karl Mannheim (Kraniauskienė 2004). Similar generational limits have also been identified by the Estonian sociologist Aili Aarelaid-Tart, comparing the Estonian political and historical timeframe (which is comparable to Lithuania) and the calendar lifetime of a generation. The only difference is that in case of Estonia the *Republican* and *Stalinist Generations* include only people born before the Soviet time (1920–1939) (Aarelaid-Tart 2006, 29; Johnston and Aarelaid-Tart 2006).
6. The sample did not include the life stories of people whose activities during the Soviet period could be attributed to 'activist conformism' activities, which the scholars described as a lower level of political conformism; it covers all the items listed above in the definition of conformist activities, except working at the institutional power positions (Klumbys 2009, 55–56). The activist conformism in the form of the Communist Party membership is mentioned most often in the life stories. During the late Soviet period the overall level of public conformism was increasing and the distinction between the activist conformists and the rest of the society remained but still was gradually weakening. With respect to the party membership the 'most important distinction, *us – them* was drawn between communists who were close to the power centres and those who were at a distance from them' (Klumbys 2009, 56), 'belonging to the Communist Party even if condemned, was not considered as betrayal, but as careerism' (Klumbys 2004, 24) and in the post-Soviet discourses was generally not stigmatized. Therefore, the life stories of the 'ordinary communists' or the ones who otherwise participated in the 'activist conformism' undertakings, but did not have higher institutional positions have not been incorporated into the sample.

7. Characterizations of other persons in the life story usually tally with the narrator's self-characterizations – either as direct opposites or as positive identifications (Andrle 2000, 219).
8. Sąjūdis is the political organization which led the struggle for Lithuanian independence in the late 1980s and early 1990s.
9. In the study conducted in 2001–2002, the memory of Stalinist period among representatives of older generation in local communties of Lithuanian periphery was investigated. The aim of the study was to identify the interpretative patterns of reminiscing of this period and attitudes toward the moral issues of 'memory work' among three groups of representatives of the older generation with different biographical experiences: The formerly repressed people, the people related to the execution of repressions (members of repressive structures or family members of the same generation), and 'ordinary' people not connected directly to both groups. Some former members of the repressive structures totally refused to tell their life stories, some used to omit this period or denied their belonging to the structures. Those who recognized their participation refused to speak about it in detail.
10. In Lithuania the *'istrebitel'* battalions were organized in 1944 and in 1945 and renamed as *'liaudies gynėjai'* – 'defenders of people'; they primarily participated in NKVD operations against partisans and in carrying out deportations.

Acknowledgments

I am very grateful to Ene Kõresaar for her thoughtful critiques and suggestions. I would also like to thank Martins Kaprans, Raili Nugin, and the three anonymous reviewers for their valuable remarks and comments. Translated by Diana Andrejevienė.

Disclosure statement

No potential conflict of interest was reported by the author.

References

Aarelaid-Tart, A. 2006. *Cultural Trauma and Life Stories*. Helsinki: Kikimora Publishers.
Alexander, J. C. 2004. "On the Social Construction of Moral Universals: The "Holocaust" from War Crime to Trauma Drama" In *Cultural Trauma and Collective Identity*, edited by J. C. Alexander, Eyerman, R., Smelser, N. J., and P. Sztompka, 196–263. Berkley: University of California Press.
Andrews, M. 2005. "Living Counter–Narratives." In *Qualitative Research Practice*, edited by Clive Seale, Giampierto Gobo, Jaber F. Gubrium, David Silverman, 110–113. London: Sage.
Andrle, V. 2000. "Neither a Dinosaur nor a Weathercock: The Construction of a Reputably Continuous Self in Czech Post – Communist Life Stories." *Qualitative Sociology* 23 (2): 215–230. doi:10.1023/A:1005434900668.
Bar-On, D. 1999. *The Indescribable and the Undiscussable. Reconstructing Human Discourse after Trauma*. Budapest: Central European University Press.
Brazauskas, A. 2007. *Ir tuomet dirbome Lietuvai*. Vilnius: Knygiai.
Bruner, J. 2006. "Life as Narrative." In *Narrative Methods*, edited by P. Atkinson, and S. Delamont, Vol. 1, 99–116. London: Sage.
Čepaitienė, R. 2004. "Lietuvių istorinės sąmonės tyrimų perspektyvos: Ideologinis problemos lygmuo." *Politologija* 35: 84–100.
Čepaitienė, R. 2007. "Sovietmečio atmintis - tarp atmetimo ir nostalgijos." *Lituanistica* 4 (72): 36–50.

Christophe, B. 2010. "Remembering Communism – Making Sense of Post-Communism. An Analysis of Discursive Strategies in Lithuanian Textbooks." *Eckert. Beiträge* 10.

Christophe, B. 2012. "Verhandlungen über den Sozialismus. Geschichtslehrer als Schnittstelle zwischen individuellem und kollektivem Gedächtnis." *Eckert. Beiträge* 1.

Christophe, B. 2013. "Dviprasmiškumas kaip įrankis? Lietuvos istorijos mokytojai kaip kultūrinių socializmo interpretacijų reikšmių vertėjai." In *Atminties daugiasluoksniškumas. Miestas, valstybė, regionas/ Multilayered Memories. City, State, Region*, edited by A. Nikžentaitis, 11–136. Vilnius: Lithuanian Institute of History.

Cohen, S. 2001. "Memory Wars and Peace Commissions." *Index on Censorship* 30 (1): 38–48. doi:10.1080/03064220108536869.

Creswell, J. W. 1998. *Qualitative Inquiry and Research Design*. London: Sage.

Davis, F. 1979. *Yearning for Yesterday: A Sociology of Nostalgia*. New York: Free Press.

Elliott, J. 2006. *Using Narrative in Social Research*. London: Sage.

Elena. [1940] 2011. "Autobiography. Competition 2010-2011." Department of Sociology, Vilnius University, unpublished manuscript.

Erll, A. 2011. "Locating Family in Memory Studies." *Journal of Comparative Family Studies* 42 (3): 303–318.

Fischer-Rosentahl, W. 1995. "The Problem with Identity: Biography as Solution to Some (Post)-Modernist Dilemmas." *Comenius* 15: 250–265.

Foucault, M. 1998. *Diskurso tvarka*. Vilnius: Baltos lankos.

Gasiliūnas, V., J. Sprindytė, and Tamošaitis, R. 2006. "Atmintis be atminties. Apie atsiminimų knygas kalbasi literatūrologai." *Metai* 11: 96–108.

Ivanauskas, V. 2011. *Lietuviškoji nomenklatūra biurokratinėje sistemoje: Tarp stagnacijos ir dinamikos*. Vilnius: Lithuanian Institute of History.

Jõesalu, K. 2005. "'The Right to Happiness' – Echoes of Soviet Ideology in Biographical Narratives." *Berliner Osteuropa-Info* 23: 91–99.

Jõesalu, K. 2010. "The Meaning of ‚Late socialism': Analyzing Estonians' post-communist memory culture." *Asia-Europe Journal* 8: 293–303. doi:10.1007/s10308-010-0269-4.

Johnston, H., and A. Aarelaid-Tart. 2006. "Generations, Micro-Cohorts and Long-Term Mobilization: The Estonian National Movement 1940-1991." In *Cultural Trauma and Life Stories*, edited by A. Aarelaid-Tart, 122–152. Helsinki: Kikimora Publishers.

Julius [1937] 2011. "Autobiography. Competition 2010–2011." Department of Sociology, Vilnius University, unpublished manuscript.

Kaprans, M. 2011. "Normalizing the Cold War Habitus: How Latvian Autobiographers Cope with their Soviet-time Experience." Social Memory of Latvia and Identity. Working Papers 6. Riga, Valsts Petijumu Programma Nationale Identitate.

Kiss, C. 2009. "Transitional Justice. The (Re)Contruction of Post-Communist Memory." In *The Burden of Remembering. Recollections and Representations of the 20th Century*, edited by E. Kõresaar, E. Lauk, and K. Kuutma, 119–138. Helsinki: Finnish Literature Society.

Klumbys, V. 2004. "Dar kartą apie kolaboravimą ir konformizmą." *Kultūros barai* 2: 21–25.

Klumbys, V. 2009. "Lietuvos kultūrinio elito elgsenos modeliai sovietmečiu." PhD thesis., Vilnius University, Vilnius.

Klumbytė, N. 2003. "Ethnographic Note on Nation: Narratives and Symbols of the Early Post-socialist Nationalism in Lithuania." *Dialectical Anthropology* 27: 279–295. doi:10.1023/B: DIAL.0000006191.13635.ba.

Klumbytė, N. 2009. "Post-Socialist Sensations: Nostalgia, the Self, and Alterity in Lithuania." *Lietuvos etnologija: socialinės antropologijos ir etnologijos studijos* 9 (18): 93–116.

Klumbytė, N. 2010. "Memory, identity, and citizenship in Lithuania." *Journal of Baltic Studies* 41 (3): 295–313. doi:10.1080/01629778.2010.498188.

Kõresaar, E. 2004. "Memory and History in Estonian Post-Soviet Life Stories. Private and Public, Individual and Collective from the Perspective of Biographical Syncretism." PhD-thesis., Tartu University Press, Tartu.

Kõresaar, E., E. Lauk, and K. Kuutma. 2009. "The Twentieth Century as a Realm of Memory." In *The Burden of Remembering. Recollections and Representations of the 20th Century*, edited by E. Kõresaar, E. Lauk, and K. Kuutma, 9–36. Helsinki: Finnish Literature Society.

Kraniauskienė, S. 2004. "Identiteto tyrimo metmenys: Kartų identiteto paieška XX a. lietuvių autobiografijose." *Sociologija. Mintis ir veiksmas* 2: 40–51.

Labow, W. 2006. "Some Further Steps in Narrative Analysis." In *Narrative Methods*, edited by P. Atkinson, and S. Delamont, Vol. 1, 75–97. London: Sage.

Linde, C. 1993. *Life Stories. The Creation of Coherence.* New York: Oxford University Press.

Marcinkevičienė, D. 2007. *Prijaukintos kasdienybės 1945-1970 metai. Biografiniai Lietuvos moterų interviu.* Vilnius: Vilniaus Universiteto leidykla.

Miller, B. 2003. ""Portrayals of Past and Present Selves in the Life Stories of Former Stasi Informers."." In *Biographical Research in Eastern Europe: Altered Lives and Broken Biographies*, edited by R. Humphrey, R. Miller, and E. Zdravomyslova, 101–114. Hampshire: Ashgate.

Nadkarni, M. 2010. "'But It's Ours': Nostalgia and the Politics of Authenticity in Post-Socialist Hungary."." In *Post-Communist Nostalgia*, edited by M. Todorova, and Z. Gille, 190–214. New York: Bergham Books.

Nadkarni, M., and O. Shevchenko. 2004. "The Politics of Nostalgia." *Ab Imperio* 2: 487–524. doi:10.1353/imp.2004.0067.

Niedermüller, P. 2004. "Der Mythos der Gemeinschaft. Geschichte, Gedächtnis und Politik im heutigen Osteuropa." In *Umbruch im östlichen Osteuropa. Die nationale Wende und das kollektive Gedächtnis*, edited by A. Corbea-Hoisie, R. Jaworski, and M. Sommer, 11–27. Innsbruck: Studienverlag.

Nikžentaitis, A. 2013. "Atminties ir istorijos politika Lietuvoje." In *Atminties daugiasluoksniškumas. Miestas, valstybė, regionas*, edited by A. Nikžentaitis, 517–538. Vilnius: Lietuvos istorijos instituto leidykla.

Pocius, M. 2009. *Kita Mėnulio pusė: Lietuvos partizanų kova su kolaboravimu 1944–1953 metais.* Vilnius: Lietuvos istorijos instituto leidykla.

Rose, R., and W. Maley. 1994. *Nationalities in the Baltic States. Studies in Public Policy 222.* Glazgow: University of Strathclyde.

Rosenthal, G. 1993. "Reconstruction of Life Stories. Principles of Selection in Generating Stories for Narrative Biographical Interviews." In *The Narrative Study of Lives*, edited by R. Josselson, and A. Lieblich, 59–76. London: Sage.

Rubavičius, V. 2007a. "Neišgyvendinamas sovietmetis: Atmintis, prisiminimai ir politinė galia." *Colloquia* 18: 1–15.

Rubavičius, V. 2007b. "Nomenklatūrinės atminties diskursas ir tapatumo politika." *Kultūros barai* 9: 6–12.

Safronovas, V. 2011. "Lietuvos atminimo politikos tendencijos po 1990 metų." In *Nuo Basanavičiaus, Vytauto Didžiojo iki Molotovo ir Ribbentropo: Atminties ir atminimo kultūrų transformacijos XX-XXI amžiuje*, edited by A. Nikžentaitis, 337–378. Vilnius: Lithuanian Institute of History.

Schütze, F. 1983. "Biographieforschung und Narratives Interview." *Neue Praxis* 13 (3): 283–293.

Šutinienė, I. 2003. "Sovietinio laikotarpio atminties bruožai autobiografiniuose pasakojimuose." In *Socialinė atmintis: Minėjimai ir užmarštys*, edited by I. Šutinienė, 13–54. Vilnius: Eugrimas.

UNSG. 2010. "United Nations Approach to Transitional Justice." UNSG 2010, March 2. Accessed 16 June 2016. http://www.unrol.org/files/TJ_Guidance_Note_March_2010FINAL.pdf

Veidas. 2007. "Kodėl Lietuva drovisi didžiuotis partizanų žygdarbiu?" Discussion. Veidas 7, February 15.

Vytautas. [1942] 2011. "Autobiography. Competition 2010-2011". Department of Sociology, Vilnius University, unpublished manuscript

Welzer, H. 2008. "Collateral Damage of History Education: National Socialism and the Holocaust in German Family Memory." *Social Research* 75: 287–314.

Between improvisation and inevitability: former Latvian officials' memoirs of the Soviet era

Mārtiņš Kaprāns

Institute of Philosophy and Sociology, University of Latvia, Riga, Latvia

ABSTRACT
This article deals with the autobiographies of former Soviet officials that have been published in Latvia since the 1990s. In particular, it focuses on three interrelated layers of biographical narrative: construction of social identity, strategies for avoiding the stigmatization of collaboration, and comparisons between the Soviet and post-Soviet experience. The article contends that former officials in their memoirs use a pragmatic representation of the Soviet past as the major locus of their positive identity. Through this genuine representation of the past, autobiographers emphasize virtues that might be accepted by a post-Soviet neoliberal society.

The transitional period of the 1990s was a time of difficulty, a time when postcommunist societies were faced with a great force of memory which, as Augustine (1991, X, 17.26) describes, was an awe-inspiring mystery and a power of profound and infinite multiplicity. In Latvia, though, the social memory of the 1990s was embedded in the negative representation of the Soviet past, situated at the heart of a new political memory, and reinforced by the national politics of historical justice.[1] Along with reconciliatory intentions, this politics, specifically the lustration proposals (e.g. introducing vetting measures toward the former Soviet officials, opening KGB archives), prompted heated debates (see Pettai and Pettai 2014; Zake 2010). The negative representation of the Soviet past, as scholars have noted, emphasized two major themes: suffering from and resistance to the nondemocratic Soviet regime (cf. Onken 2007; Aarelaid-Tart 2003; Budryte 2002). That, however, provided limited options for coping with existential anxiety vis-à-vis the Soviet era. People were usually implicitly encouraged to see themselves either as victims or ardent opponents of a totalitarian regime. To be sure, the hegemony of negative representation in Latvia and elsewhere created a complicated problem of how to assess the entire Soviet era.

The 1990s was a particularly uneasy time for those who had explicitly collaborated with the Soviet regime and had implemented Soviet policy, such as public officials, active party members, and *nomenklatura*. In Latvia, people from former ideological and law enforcement institutions avoided engaging in public memory work. Nevertheless, former Soviet officials, henceforth referred to as 'former officials,' have published a number of memoirs since the 2000s, and their voice has become more pronounced in the mass media. Notwithstanding the dominance of a negative representation in political memory, Latvian biographical discourse has supported objectification of a pragmatic representation of the Soviet era since the 1990s. The pragmatic representation highlights the ability to accommodate the Soviet regime and to achieve privately or socially important goals during the Soviet era (Kaprans 2012b). This article argues that the pragmatic representation that has emerged outside Latvia's memory regime, in the memoirs of former officials, opens new discursive avenues for the Latvian social memory to understand the late Soviet period.

The Latvian social memory of the Soviet era echoes the characteristics of a broader memory region across the Baltic states. The Baltics have been identified as having distinctive cultures of remembrance, with a strong anticommunist consensus concerning recent history (Troebst 2010; cf. Ekman and Linde 2005). However, the latest dynamics of Latvian, Estonian, and Lithuanian social memory challenges such an anticommunist assumption. The transformation of the image of the Soviet period is especially observable within biographical discourse and popular culture where, unlike in the 1990s, people are more willing to reflect on topics that require a balanced view of the Soviet era. Numerous memoirs written by the former members of the Soviet Lithuanian *nomenklatura* have challenged the traditionally negative view of the *nomenklatura* by claiming that they worked for the benefit of the nation (Ivanauskas 2012). Likewise, Estonian scholars have suggested that in the 2000s, memories of daily Soviet life replaced repression and resistance as the major themes of Estonian life stories, and that they expanded the biographical perspective, supplementing the political ethos of rupture with a sense of continuity at the level of everyday life (Jõesalu and Kõresaar 2013; Aarelaid-Tart 2010, 45; Jõesalu 2005, 92; Anepaio 2002). Even Baltic commemorative discourse about Stalinist repressions, which mobilized people during the period of national revival in the late 1980s, switched from historical memory to a more individualized approach (Budryte 2005, 188). In short, the social memory of Baltic societies over the previous decade has experienced a certain emancipation from the hegemony of anti-Soviet representation, encouraging former officials to construct what Mark calls 'a democratic autobiography' (2010, 136).

By analyzing the autobiographies of former Soviet Latvian officials and representatives of various ideological institutions, this research contributes to the understanding of the shifting social memory in the Baltics and perhaps, to what one may call the east European memory (see Wawrzyniak and Pakier 2013). To tackle paradigmatic changes, I focus on three interrelated layers of biographical narrative: construction of social identity, strategies for avoiding the stigmatization of collaboration, and comparisons between the Soviet and post-Soviet experience. Clearly, these layers cannot grasp the whole individual experience, nor can they fully depict the complexity of postcommunist memory work. Nevertheless, these are important structural tenets that reveal the specificity of postcommunist biographical discourse.

Social representations of the past

By telling life stories, people show their 'will to remember' the recent past. Nora (1989, 19) suggests that by ignoring this will, 'we would quickly drift into admitting virtually everything as worthy of remembrance.' This will, of course, is not transparent; it is driven by different and sometimes overlapping motifs, which shape the creation of cognitive images of the past and define what we might tentatively label as an idiosyncratic construction of personal history. Since the 1990s, Latvian scholars have been exploring post-Soviet life stories largely as individual histories (cf. Bela 2012; Saleniece 2005; Bela-Krūmiņa 2003; Skultans 1998). However, when life stories become part of the public sphere, as memoirs in bookstores, for example, the inner cognitive images of individuals are propelled into the formation of *social* representations of bygone times. Apart from empirical differences, methodologically, the remediation of the past through public memoirs refocuses the analytical strategy from individual cognitive processes to the relational aspects of meaning making.

By *social* representations, I mean a system of shared values, ideas, and practices that people manifest when communicating about the past. Social representations revolve around conceptual *themata* (source ideas, image concepts) that express essential and generic properties of particular historical periods and encapsulate intentions of particular mnemonic communities. Conceptual *themata* reveal themselves through various pragmatic manifestations or methodological themes (on the concept of social representations, see Marková 2005; Wagner and Hayes 2005; Moscovici 2000). Jovchelovitch (2012, 442) insists that 'Historical narratives fix meaning in the central core of social representations, are resistant to change and endure over time but they are neither frozen nor stable: it is their very flexibility and imaginative characteristics that give them resilience.'

In the 2000s, social representation theory (SRT), which underscores this study, has looked forward to connecting with the 'nonparadigmatic, transdisciplinary, centerless enterprise' (Olick and Robbins 1998, 105) of collective memory. Acknowledging that the SRT as well as collective memory perspective is critical of their forerunners, they still can be read as an extension of the Durkheimian tradition that views society through social facts. SRT, postulated by the social psychologist Serge Moscovici (2008) in the early 1960s, has created an interdisciplinary field where the past is seen as a social object and collective memory is a shared representation of this social object (see Wagoner 2015; Marková 2012; Jovchelovitch 2012; Liu 2005; Liu and Hilton 2005). Such representation is constructed, legitimized, and transformed through various discourses about the past, including biographical discourse. Therefore, social representations, first and foremost, are dynamic rather than static, as one may presume from the common understanding of the term *representation*. In this perspective, autobiographers are not just isolated and lonely storytellers but also memory agents who mold the past by adding a subjective dimension as well as furthering the memory discourse. As SRT particularly addresses the agency-structure issue, it becomes a useful explanatory approach, not exclusively for social psychologists, but for a wide range of social scientists interested in the relations between postcommunist autobiographies and larger mnemonic processes, such as political memory or myth making.

Arguably, social representations of the past resemble constructs offered by professional historians. Both laymen representations and professional constructs attempt to explain retrospectively what has happened in the past. Historians create a rather reified universe, however, by using rule-bound archival work and careful interpretations of findings, whereas common people converse about historical periods daily and informally, thereby creating a consensual universe where 'society is seen as a group of individuals who are equal and free, each entitled to speak in the name of the group and under its aegis' (Moscovici 2000, 34). A freely accessible and dynamic public sphere open to dialogue that tolerates differences is a crucial prerequisite for generating a consensual universe and, hence, competing social representations. Under such conditions, social representations of history, by definition, cannot be a silent enterprise; there is constantly, as Howarth (2006) stresses, a struggle over the meaning of reality among hegemonic and oppositional representations in society. In democratic societies, this struggle often fosters cognitive *polyphasia* within individuals as well as within the mnemonic community.

The concept of cognitive *polyphasia* implies that 'different and incompatible cognitive styles and forms of knowledge can coexist within one social group and can be employed by one and the same individual' (Voelklein and Howarth 2005, 434). Since representations of the past always involve diverse voices, cognitive *polyphasia* illustrates 'the expression of multiple identities, the forging of cognitive solidarities, and importantly, communication between cognitive systems as the motor that adjusts, corrects and transforms knowledge' (Jovchelovitch 2012, 444). I argue that cognitive *polyphasia* is a fundamental concept in Latvian biographical discourse, as it prompts changes in representational practices with regard to the Soviet period.

Latvian post-Soviet autobiographies

Latvian autobiographical literature, as an essential part of post-Soviet biographical discourse, has experienced fluctuating growth. Yet, the number of autobiographies that reflect upon life during the Soviet period has consistently increased. The authors of these autobiographies mainly represent two age cohorts: those born in the 1920s and those born in the 1930s. These cohorts may be associated either with two successive generations or with two units of the same generation; the former group consciously experienced World War II and Stalinist repressions, while the latter group formed a generational core in the 1960s and more actively experienced the liberalization of the Soviet regime (see Kaprans 2012a).

Men representing different groups of the former Soviet intelligentsia (writers, composers, actors) have written the majority of post-Soviet autobiographies. Besides the intelligentsia, there are two other groups of publicly active autobiographers: former officials and deportees (those who were exiled to Siberia).[2] Deportees have published their life stories over the last 25 years both as individual autobiographers and as contributors to public collections of memories. Former public officials have become active relatively recently, but they still take certain precautions. The owners of publishing houses, who dominate the field of Latvian autobiographies, confirm that former Soviet officials avoid publishing their memoirs largely because of a disinclination to be publicly exposed as a former official and to protect themselves from being stigmatized; this disinclination is another reminder of the hegemonic effect of negative representation.[3] However, these three major groups of autobiographers should not be perceived as mutually exclusive; some representatives of the Soviet intelligentsia were deported and Soviet institutions later employed some former deportees. So, a single autobiographer may embody different identities; hence, analytically, it is better to define these groups as distinct mnemonic communities rather than closed social categories. The remaining autobiographers who do not fall into any of these groups may be viewed as individuals defined more by their occupation (priests, teachers, sportsmen, etc.) than as part of a self-aware mnemonic community.

Latvian autobiographical narratives vary stylistically, ranging from purely intimate self-reflections to broader recollections of public life and events. Quite often a mixture of genres appears: fragments of diaries, letters, statistics, short biographies of other people, and fictional texts supplement a retrospective narration. Some autobiographers also imitate the professional style of texts written by historians: they refer to private and public documents, quotations from other autobiographies, bibliographies, appendices, and so on. Moreover, many autobiographies reflect upon particular political time frames, such as life in Siberian exile, the 1960s, or the revival of Latvian self-determination in the late 1980s. Yet, a common thread running through these narratives is the somewhat weak reference to interwar Latvia.

A synthetically constructed category of former officials consists of diverse social groups. On one hand, it includes individuals who worked in Soviet institutions but were not directly responsible for *ideological work* and most likely did not join the Communist Party, such as policemen, foresters, and heads of shops. Another large group is the *nomenklatura*, who took key administrative positions approved by the Communist Party. The classification described by Voslenskii (2005, 148–51) suggests that Latvian autobiographers represent the staff *nomenklatura*, as well as the elected *nomenklatura*. The staff *nomenklatura* had various positions in the party apparatus that were approved by more senior people in the party hierarchy, but included in the latter group were the members of the *nomenklatura* elected to supreme councils and district councils. Unlike other postcommunist countries, the secretaries of the Communist Party of Latvia (CPL) did not publish their memoirs even though members of the top-level staff *nomenklatura* did (Johansons 2006; Liepiņš 2008, 2003; Dzenītis 2002; Āboltiņš 1992). Memoirs of former officials often attract the attention of the Latvian mass media, which use them as sources of information about the Soviet period. Some of these memoirs are received positively, since they speak about unfamiliar experiences and historical details. Conversely, memoirs are criticized for factual imprecision and for the autobiographer's inability or disinclination to discuss particular historical events and people. In this study, I analyzed 10 memoirs written by people who have worked in Soviet institutions, nine of which were published in the 2000s. These memoirs were selected in order to embrace the different levels of the Soviet administrative ideological system. Such diversity provides multifaceted qualitative data that are useful in extrapolating the different dimensions of analytical categories and in establishing relations between these categories.

Positive or negative identity?

In autobiographical narratives, the use of *we* instead of *I* changes the experience from an individual experience to a shared one. The opposite process turns a shared experience into an individual one; thus, social identity to some extent is always expressed through self-identity, and *vice versa*. However, both levels (*we* and *I*) are normally shaped by the social representation of the past. Namely, when former Soviet officials reflect either on in-group relations or on their relations with those outside the group, it is not just the retrospective anchoring of multilayered identities; it is also the way that social representations of the Soviet era are manifested and modified in the long term.

A useful vantage point from which to understand how former officials interpret their reconstructed Soviet identities is to see how autobiographers retrospectively depict the horizontal and vertical relations that affected their mutual positioning in the Soviet regime. As Jõesalu and Kõresaar (2012) demonstrate in their analysis of the life story of an Estonian industry manager, the main objective of their narrator was to manage the vertical and horizontal networking of Soviet everyday life. Presumably, horizontal relations might highlight social cohesion whereas vertical relations entail hierarchical roles and 'power motifs' (see McAdams 1988, 69–104).

At the horizontal level, former officials serve as a reference group for solidarity, outstanding professionalism, and altruism. Horizontal relations that are portrayed in Latvian memoirs often help to frame the autobiographer's positive identity. For example, Jūlijs Beļavnieks (2011, 77), the chairman of the famous *kolkhoz* 'Madliena,' recalls how his colleagues at the District Executive Committee supported his resistance to an absurd ideological demand to increase the potato harvest at 'Madliena.' Jānis Dzenītis, Soviet-era Minister of Justice and Attorney General (2002, 133), does not hesitate to express satisfaction with his supportive colleagues and professional achievements in Soviet Latvia: 'I was keen on my job, felt prepared enough for it, and believed that others also appreciated what I did. They appreciated me at all levels, even at that indefinable national level.' Along with individual satisfaction that clearly illuminates professional qualities, working for the benefit of society is also a common theme that displays the everyday duties and social responsibility of various former officials (cf. Kargins 2005, 67; Ulmanis 1995, 144; Āboltiņš 1992, 12–13).

The interplay between former officials' self-identity and social identity observable in these biographical self-presentations shows how people struggle to find *interpretive keys* that can open doors to positive identity which is associated with the Soviet-era professionalism and social responsibility and lock doors to potentially negative identity that may emerge from reflections on ideological work and conformism. Nevertheless, sometimes, Latvian autobiographers feel comfortable enough reflecting on the exclusivity of their potentially stigmatizing social status. Edmunds Johansons, the last chairman of the Latvian Committee for State Security (KGB) (2006, 39), emphasizes that KGB employees belonged to the elite of Soviet society and, incidentally, KGB informers were chiefly motivated by a well-developed sense of patriotism and loyalty to their country rather than by fear of sanctions. Furthermore, the omnipresent and omnipotent image of the KGB might be exaggerated, as Johansons suggests in his memoirs, which were criticized by the Latvian mass media:

> When I started to work at the KGB, I was surprised by the prevailing public opinion about Cheka's eyes and ears as if they were everywhere. The society believed in the enormous size of the KGB's staff. That, of course, was complimentary: it's pleased to work in an institution that was assumed to be so mighty by society. In fact, the number of employees wasn't more than a thousand. (2006, 54–55)

Conversely, the description of vertical relations among former officials triggers in-group comparisons. Usually, that results in a critical appraisal of superior institutions and senior officials who, unlike subordinates (autobiographers), are depicted as ideologically inclined hardliners and simply inert persons. As Beļavnieks recalls:

> In the first years [of taking on the chairmanship of the kolkhoz 'Madliena'], I regularly sent letters and petitions to superior institutions complaining about various unsolved problems.... Although I received well-timed replays along with the regulations of that time, the positive outcome normally was quite insignificant or the solutions of identified problems were delayed. (2011, 127)

Throughout his memoirs, Beļavnieks continually describes his daily struggle with the Soviet institutions responsible for agricultural policy. In fact, the ostensibly innocent Beļavnieks' remark highlights Soviet hierarchical relations with a prag-matic *kolkhoz* situated at the bottom and useless governmental institutions at the top. Another account of Soviet everyday life comes from Uldis Lasmanis, who worked in the Soviet trade system. Lasmanis (2006, 274) describes his job as the director of a Soviet shop as involving great responsibility. It demanded a knowl-edgeable, skillful, and physically strong person; therefore, he assumed that mem-bers of the party *nomenklatura* did not covet the position. Here again, professionalism is contrasted with an ideologically inclined Significant Other (the party *nomenklatura*). Such juxtaposition obviously separates the autobiographer from ideologized interactions and obligations within the Soviet administrative system. On the other hand, it brings to the fore the autobiographer's ability to do things professionally, regardless of ideological hurdles. Furthermore, the dis-course of professionalism often addresses micro-resistance practices (bypassing the Soviet laws, saving cultural heritage, etc.), which convey daily attempts to over-come the ideological absurdities of the Soviet state. Like other groups of autobio-graphers, the majority of former officials do not normally interpret these daily subversive activities as some kind of heroic ordeal, although sometimes they were nationalistically motivated. Nevertheless, this micro-resistance redefines colla-boration as a unidirectional activity and as an official's complicity with the regime. Instead, the dialogical nature of compliance and autobiographer's agency is emphasized, thus downplaying the conformism discourse provided by the negative representation of the Soviet era.

The memories of vertical relations may also lead autobiographers to the victim identity, a subtype of positive identity in many postcommunist societies whose dominant attitude toward the communist period is arguably embedded in victim-hood nationalism (see Lim 2010). Although not widespread, victim identity appears when former officials recall how their superiors in the party and the autobiogra-pher's workplace humiliated them for ideological and selfish reasons. For example, several former employees of Soviet law enforcement institutions allude to the early 1980s as a turning point in their careers. During the short reign (1982–1984) of the General Secretary of the Communist Party of the Soviet Union Yuri Andropov, former KGB generals, and those who held the most important positions in the KGB in Moscow started a derogatory ideological cleansing in the Soviet republics. 'We were suspected of being nationalists, as well as being linked to criminals and bribery,' recalls Aloizs Blonskis (2000, 155–56), who worked for many years in the criminal police, 'All sorts of intrigues, passions, accusations, and insults emerged and consequently, working became harder and harder. Ultimately, it was not possible to bear the brunt of all that.'

Vertical relations are at the core of former officials' negative identity as well. They trigger reflections on obedience and collaboration during the Soviet era. However, rarely is penance or the self-criticism of former officials seen as an underlying attitude toward collaboration with the regime. By and large, explicit reflections on a stigma-tized experience are episodic and appear when autobiographers reveal their suscept-ibility to ideological brainwashing or cowardice and fear of supporting individuals who were unjustly accused of anti-Soviet behavior (cf. Beļavnieks 2011, 53, 280; Liepiņš 2003, 85, 86; Āboltiņš 1992, 14, 71). Edvards Berklavs, Vice-Chairman of the Council of Ministers in Soviet Latvia (1956–1959) and the iconic leader of the so-called national communists in the 1950s, has written,

It's very hard to acknowledge that you have spent part of the best years of your life in illusions. Even now, I can't fully understand why I didn't see much earlier how terrible the party (CPSU) was, which had committed such incredible mass killings; (...) Even in hindsight I can't understand why I was so foolish. In 1940, I was already 26 years old. (1998, 12, 57)

Despite the unwillingness or inability to assess their own collaboration, those from the lower ranks of the Soviet administration are used to associating themselves with the critical discourse characteristic of the intelligentsia's memoirs. These former officials reinforce the image of greedy and incompetent party functionaries who intended to demoralize the professional state administration and to distort many good ideas by blindly following the dictate of the Communist Party. When Nagel (2004) interviewed managers of communist enterprises from the German Democratic Republic (GDR) 10 years after the fall of the Berlin Wall, managers emphasized their individual accomplishments and downplayed their responsibility for the former regime and its mishaps by blaming the communist elite. Latvian autobiographies, like the GDR managers' life stories, illustrate this universal strategy of former officials in postcommunist societies in coming to terms with their past. That is, by making superiors the scapegoats, or making minor subgroups, like party functionaries, within the reference group, or by extrapolating the scapegoat as an alien out-group, such as the communist elite or Moscow functionaries, former officials establish a positive identity. According to Tajfel and Turner (1979), such strategies of social identity demonstrate the social creativity of former officials. Moreover, blaming the elite can even be observed in the memoirs of the elite itself. For example, Dzenītis (2002, 117, 182, 189, 270) regularly criticizes the Soviet elite as being responsible for the collapse of the USSR. Apparently, a never-ending vertical relation of the Soviet political system provide everyone with an opportunity to relocate responsibility symbolically to imagined party, elite, or *nomenklatura* and present one's self as an executor rather than a decision-maker. Moreover, if we follow Jaspers' (2000) argument and differentiate the issue of guilt, then we will notice that former officials in their memoirs focus on political guilt rather than on moral guilt. As moral guilt 'exists for all those who give room to conscience and repentance' (Jaspers 2000, 57) vis-à-vis their explicit conformism in the Soviet era, it is obviously more risky to address moral guilt. Moreover, such reflections might actually undermine the scapegoat strategy applied exclusively toward superiors. Political guilt, in turn, is narrower and more manageable, as it holds liable only those who explicitly took strategic and decisive decisions that had a destructive impact on the broader public.

Vertical relations do not always lead to comparison and confrontation. Along with critical depictions, one can find memories about fruitful cooperation with particular superior officials who are characterized as professionals possessing a strategic vision of how things should be done. Anrijs Kavalieris, the former Vice-Minister of the Internal Affairs of Latvian Soviet Socialist Republic (LSSR) (2002, 15), exemplifies this *soft hierarchy* based on his experience in the Prosecutor's Office:

The Prosecutor's Office was run by Mednis, the prosecutor who wasn't just an excellent organizer but also very demanding of his subordinates and himself. His attitude towards novices wasn't as if they were just a cheap labour force or hindrance, as sometimes happens nowadays. He intentionally attempted 'to create an investigator' out of me.

These ideologically loyal but, in the autobiographers' opinion, agreeable characters symbolize moral soundness, and their appearance in biographical narratives, as Andrle

(2000, 225) has suggested, might be viewed as a collective story that challenges the dominant stereotype of ideologically obsessed communists. Nevertheless, superior officials who have such positive images are rarely found. The image shifts from autobiography to autobiography, revealing not merely the controversy around a particular person, but also the presence of different social representations of the Soviet era. For example, in many post-Soviet autobiographies, Eduards Berklavs is commonly associated with resistance to Soviet Russification and the industrialization policy.[4] Yet, he is critically appraised by other autobiographers, estimating his anti-Russification measures as unreasoned and voluntary, which resulted in assessment of employees based on their nationality rather than on their professional skills (Beļavnieks 2011, 270).

By the same token, the concept of moral soundness is helpful for highlighting the positive aspect of working in Soviet institutions. For example, Jānis Liepiņš (2008, 146), the assistant of Jānis Kalnbērziņš,[5] admits: 'I felt confident about my capability to serve for the first person of the country, because I knew that such duties are assigned to those who are the most gifted.' Beļavnieks (2011, 143), in turn, explains his election to the Latvian Socialist Soviet Republic Supreme Council as a gratuity from top-level officials for successfully running a *kolkhoz*. Hence, it is more appropriate to speak about the *multiple hierarchies* that link the autobiographical narratives of former officials. The concept of multiple hierarchies has a higher explanatory value than that of a single hierarchy because it shows how vertical relations transform in post-Soviet biographical discourse. Furthermore, multiple hierarchies can be also applied to the autobiographies of the Soviet intelligentsia as an analytical category, where assumptions about the rigid binaries of the Soviet regime and intelligentsia are occasionally revised (see Kaprans 2010a).

Normalizing the stigma of party [*Komsomol*] membership

Goffman (1986) defined 'stigmatization' as the process by which the reaction of others spoils normal identity. In light of the anti-Soviet representation of the past, publicly expressed support for the Soviet system or appreciation of Soviet administrative practices may also spoil one's normal identity in contemporary Latvia. Former officials, however, avoid speaking about the collaboration as a stigmatizing experience.[6] In fact, instead of spoiling normal identity, former officials prefer to reinterpret stigmatizing experiences.

The condemnation of the CPL has invariably been part of post-Soviet memory politics in Latvia. Clearly, that has made membership in CPL a stigmatizing experience. However, the autobiographers whose life stories I have analyzed tend to justify their party membership. On one hand, some former officials clearly admit that they do not regret joining the party. For example, Beļavnieks (2011, 299) was a member of the CPL for 32 years, and he does not feel sorry about that because he obtained experience in the party that was useful in solving economic problems in *kolkhozes* and in learning how to work with a variety of people. On the other hand, former officials highlight the inevitability of party membership if one wanted to have or maintain a successful career; many argue that membership was not motivated by ideological beliefs. Thus, living with double standards – being member of CPL without believing in the communist ideals – as a consciously cultivated state of mind is commonly used as a major justification for Soviet-era conformity. Sometimes, acting in accordance with double standards is even compared to 'the guerrillas' underground activities' (Liepiņš 2008, 100).[7] The same justification strategy applies to joining the *Komsomol*, the youth wing of the party, where future party leaders were developed. Autobiographers contend that *Komsomol* membership should not be stigmatized, because many of today's politicians and entrepreneurs actually obtained leadership skills and had the opportunity to change the Soviet regime from within. The former *Komsomol* leader Āboltiņš has admitted that practical activities in the *Komsomol*

> Were certainly more important than an abstract ideological struggle. There was a double meaning behind these activities: we sought to do useful work instead of screaming ideological slogans. It was a school of practice, a good opportunity to advance the skills of organizing and learning how to persuade people about the usefulness of your plans. (1992, 15)

Incidentally, the reviewers of Āboltiņš's memoirs received this pragmatic attitude positively. For example, the poet and Āboltiņš's contemporary, Māris Čaklais (1992), sympathized with Āboltiņš's active but severely restricted position while working in Soviet institutions. Likewise, party or *Komsomol* autobiographers provide prosaic reasons to deconstruct any ideological attachment for joining the party, pointing to the various material and social advantages received from membership in ideological organizations or from undertaking ideological duties. Notable benefits included travel throughout the USSR or internationally, or acquiring their own flat (Lasmanis 2006, 385; Artmane 2004, 180; Āboltiņš 1992, 10).

Apart from these somewhat pragmatic arguments, more apathetic explanations of joining the Soviet ideological organizations are offered. The former president of Latvia, Ulmanis (1995, 143), managed the public utility establishment in Riga during the Soviet period, and he argues that the party and *Komsomol* – both of which he joined – were simply structural units of the Soviet machinery. Similarly, Vija Artmane, the famous actress and vice-chairperson of the Soviet Peace Committee (2004, 301), insists that she did not know about the riskiness of becoming a member; 'just one thing was clear: successful and loyal people, both old and young, were invited to join the party.' These cases illustrate how autobiographical subjects, in order to reduce moral responsibility for their compliance, turn themselves into objects influenced by the *force majeure* of powerful ideological organizations and functionaries. Sebre (2010, 33), who has also analyzed this kind of strategy in Latvian life stories, defines the strategy as the mechanism of psychological self-defense. Notwithstanding psychological self-defense, the explicit passivity (but not necessarily self-victimization) concerning Soviet collaboration should similarly be interpreted as a cultural practice legitimized by Latvian public discourse. That is to say, the autobiographers' emphasis on a missing agency is a discursive practice that is preferable if one wants to normalize one's collaboration experience. Through such a normalization discourse alternative meanings are attached to the negative representation of the Soviet era, challenging the condemnatory understanding of collaboration that dominates Latvia's political memory. Thereby normalization is a biographical strategy that helps to maintain what Giddens (1991, 35–69) has called 'ontological security.'

The separation of formal ideology from meaningful activities, so characteristic of many Latvian memoirs, is evidently presented as an essential part of the survival kit of those who explicitly supported the regime. It agrees with what Yurchak (2006, 93–98) wrote about the last Soviet generation – those born in the 1950s and 1960s. Following the formal guidelines of Soviet ideology, the final generation engaged in the performative reproduction of authoritarian discourse that was a crucial precondition to be able to do meaningful work. Yurchak, however, did not thoroughly discuss the equally important question of how a post-Soviet context has influenced the motivation to exploit this dichotomy for explaining conformity within the regime. Jõesalu (2005, 93) clarifies this point by linking it to the post-Soviet de-ideologization of the past. That is, the motivation to differentiate professional responsibility and ideology is embedded in the present necessity of managing the past performance. Such a necessity, as Andrle (2001, 829) suggests, might spring from the desire to create a morally adequate self. If the strategy of double standards normalizes the collaboration experience and is seen as socially acceptable behavior, then there is another social phenomenon that lies behind the normalization. In light of Aarelaid-Tart's contention (2010, 52), one may argue that this strategy signalizes the presence of cultural trauma in post-Soviet biographical discourse. A reference to intentional double standards or double consciousness may be used effectively as justifiable rhetoric, but not straightforwardly annul the fact of deliberate conformism that autobiographers avoid addressing. By remediating this cultural trauma, the autobiographers and their readers are confronted with a moral dilemma: whether to accept the imperative of hegemonic negative representation that stigmatizes those who collaborated or tolerate the autobiographer's humane desire not to be permanently labeled as a collaborator or traitor.

Arguably, there is a generational discrepancy in how participation in the *Komsomol* or other forms of collaboration are seen. Older autobiographers who experienced life in interwar Latvia and whose formative period occurred during a time of tremendous social change in the 1940s are more likely to self-criticize or moderately acknowledge their naivety or idealism as an impetus for joining the party and supporting Communist ideology (Liepiņš 2003, 85; Dzenītis 2002, 42–43; Berklavs 1998, 350). However, those born in the 1940s and 1950s are more focused on stressing double standards, opportunism, and cynicism as everyday strategies (Kargins 2005, 74; Ulmanis 1995, 92; Āboltiņš 1992, 10). Older autobiographers, who represent the first generation of 'builders of communism,' are also more likely to claim that external processes forced them to support the system, whereas younger autobiographers emphasize the inner locus of control in relations with Soviet institutions. Such generational differences in terms of where the locus of control is placed reveal another dimension of how the topics of rupture and continuity interact in post-Soviet biographical discourse (see Jõesalu and Kõresaar 2013). Ignoring these differences may lead to a simplified interpretation of the normalization discourse.

Overall, though, the normalization of CPL or *Komsomol* membership and ideological activities put forward utilitarian motives, which in comparison with the motifs behind self-criticism and penance have a higher probability of being converted into post-Soviet normality. In other words, professional and personal advancement, as well as a realistic and self-confident approach to the system one had to live in, are virtues that might be accepted by a post-Soviet neoliberal society as general characteristics of positive identity. Thus, utilitarianism – especially if it was directed at increasing the well-being of society – manifests itself as an alternative to the collaboration perspective propagated by advocates of negative representation. That also explains why genuine, but more universal political convictions like support for antifascist ideas, as observed in the life stories of former East Central European communists (Mark 2010, 152–64), are rarely used by Latvian autobiographers to justify collaboration. Namely, memories about the political engagement with ideas, which cannot be contextualized in the discourse of a nationalizing state (Brubaker 1996) or professionalism contradict the virtue of utilitarianism and most likely would be interpreted as signs of allegiance to the Soviet order.

Comparing two eras

Comparisons between Soviet and post-Soviet experiences are a common feature of Latvian autobiographical narratives, as I have noted elsewhere (Kaprāns 2010b). This also applies to the memoirs of former officials. Their comparisons illuminate the organizing themes of the social representation of the past as well as the present status quo. Regarding post-Soviet autobiographies, we may delineate two different dimensions of inter-experiential comparisons: post-Soviet progress and criticism of post-Soviet reality.

Post-Soviet progress is a rather obscure theme in the autobiographies of former officials, as well as that of other mnemonic communities. By progress, I mean situations in which people openly admit that life is better today than it was under the Soviet regime. This ethos sporadically appears in the memoirs of those who worked in Soviet law enforcement institutions. For example, they allude to the superiority of the post-Soviet legal system and to the fact that contemporary law enforcement institutions are compelled to make their regulations more transparent, and to be more democratic and free from obtrusive ideological demands (cf. Kavalieris 2002, 17, 90; Blonskis 2000, 36, 127). Likewise, some other autobiographers believe that today's youngsters have greater opportunities; they are not as restricted and brainwashed as the autobiographers' generation was during the Soviet period (Berklavs 1998, 57; Ulmanis 1995, 88).

On the other hand, criticism of post-Soviet conditions is more conspicuous. One recurrent theme of this criticism is the argument with present day interpretations of the Soviet period, and the emphasis on the lack of understanding among historians, politicians, and journalists about how complicated life was then. This line largely challenges the false image of Soviet officials created after Latvia regained independence. For instance, Āboltiņš (1992, 10), who was the first former official to publish memoirs in the early 1990s, objected to the idea of the nomenklatura as a privileged class, claiming instead that 'We are mistaken now for insisting that back then the middle stratum of the nomenklatura could immediately obtain all the material benefits that they desired. There were physical as well as social problems and procedures that interfered with that' (see also Beļavnieks 2011, 282; Kargins 2005, 67).

The appraisal of current democracy is another theme that emerges. Although the representatives of Soviet law enforcement institutions are among those who point to post-Soviet progress, they are quite willing to highlight various shortcomings, which one can see in the work of law enforcement institutions nowadays. They emphasize that the Soviet state paid more attention to maintaining order on the streets and preventing crimes, and the fight against corruption was more successful. In the opinion of these individuals, the Soviet judicial system also was more effective, and instead of merely sensationalizing crimes, the press attempted to influence its readers (Kavalieris 2002, 72; Blonskis 2000, 100–103; Zlakomanovs 2000, 148). Along with this criticism of rather mundane everyday practices, more fundamental doubts are cast on the rapid transformation of the post-Soviet economy, which degraded outstanding collective farms and industry (Beļavnieks 2011, 229). As a result, this skeptical attitude toward current democracy and its pillars reveals its favor toward the Soviet era. However, it also exposes the disillusionment about how democracy and the market economy have developed. In particular, sharp criticism emanates from the feelings of former officials that antidemocratic processes are still continuing in the post-Soviet period and that nothing has changed since the collapse of the USSR. Such dissatisfaction often manifests as cliché-ridden frustration: people expected life to be better, but that did not happen. Instead people got poorer and only a weak, corrupt state remained after the breakdown of the USSR. Lasmanis expresses this mood:

> Now, in the independence era, the power of money predominates, whereas then, to a certain extent, the party and, of course, the Cheka's rights to call everyone ruled... We can judge variously, but in comparison with the Soviet-era telephone rights, more and more facts prove that there are the rights of money and capital in the free world. Practically, it means that the verdict of the courts depends on one's capacity to hire a lawyer. (2006, 427, 467)

The presence of the Soviet legacy is another broad theme discussed by former officials. The Soviet legacy is partly related to the criticism of Latvian democracy, but, beyond discussing political failures, autobiographers illuminate the current post-Soviet everyday practices that emanate from the Soviet legacy. Notably, former officials, unlike the Latvian intelligentsia, do not speak about the corrupted political elite as an inheritance from the Soviet era, nor do they addresses the issue of communists who have remained to power in post-Soviet Latvia. Instead, they emphasize peculiar Soviet practices, such as laziness, alcoholism, submissiveness, or exaggerated collectivism, that, in some way, continue to corrupt society. Āboltiņš (1992, 75) concludes that, 'We are still condemning the ability and desire of an individual to be more excellent than other individuals. It comes from our socialist past. It is the philosophy of crowd' (see also Liepiņš 2008, 87; Blonskis 2000, 151; Ulmanis 1995, 178). However, none of these former officials project the lingering of the Soviet legacy to themselves, which might express self-criticism and jeopardize their positive image; in other words, the inability to get rid of the Soviet legacy is associated with collective responsibility. Perhaps an emphasis on collective responsibility might also be interpreted as an implicit and unintended indicator of the Soviet legacy.

If the Soviet legacy bears the negative meaning of past experience, then the degradation of post-Soviet social relations demonstrates just the opposite – a sort of moral superiority of Soviet society. This criticism mostly applies to professional relations, which in post-Soviet conditions have deviated from the earlier standard. As former officials argue, the work ethic nowadays is rooted in a sense of impunity, it sometimes discredits individuality and a sense of responsibility or it eradicates modesty and mutual respect. This lamentation of the lost merits can be vividly illustrated by Ulmanis' reflections on relations between teachers and pupils:

> Now it seems to me that teachers have got used to everything and have learned to ignore impudence. Now different relations prevail in school. To a large extent, the respectful distance between teacher and pupil is lost; many regulations of inner order and discipline are lost. [We] do not have pupils' uniforms anymore; everyone dresses and adorns oneself as they like, in line with their imagination and opportunities; girls start to use cosmetics too early. I even can imagine that during the break pupils might have a smoke with the teacher. (1995, 86–87)

In contrast to the current socially disoriented reality, Soviet society is depicted as more disciplined and law-abiding; and even if antisocial behavior, like stealing or teenage fighting, did exist then, it, as suggested by some autobiographers, was normally based on some sort of morality or implicit humane rules of behavior (Blonskis 2000, 32–33; Ulmanis 1995, 81–82). A number of autobiographers are particularly upset by the lifestyle of members of post-Soviet society who have lost serious purpose in their lives, which built the individual's character and triggered, 'the crystallization of the moral core of personality' (Zlakomanovs 2000, 136).

Although there is a certain amount of criticism toward the Soviet social order, sympathies vis-à-vis the Soviet era may raise the question of what role post-Soviet nostalgia plays in the memoirs of former officials. As Boym (2001, 41–56) has stated, nostalgia should not be perceived as just a desire to return to a lost time. Besides 'restorative nostalgia,' there is also 'reflective nostalgia,' which includes both irony toward the past and a critical attitude toward the present. Whereas restorative nostalgia is based on continuity and reproduction of the past, reflective nostalgia upholds the past as a crucial and unrepeatable part of one's identity project. Nadkarni and Shevchenko (2004), however, insist that the reflective and restorative components may be present in any nostalgic practice, and the salience of a particular component, as well the mutual relationship between components, is determined by generational boundaries and distinct memory politics. Considering these two dimensions of post-Soviet nostalgia, it seems that former officials most likely exhibit restorative nostalgia: they do not clearly support the renewal of the Soviet Union, but they express a longing for stability, predictability, and social security, which, they argue, was intrinsic to the Soviet system. Nevertheless, this restorative nostalgia is largely characteristic of the first generation of the builders of communism (born in the 1920s and early 1930s) but rarely appears in the memoirs of those who represent the last Soviet generation (born in the 1950s).

Conclusion

Superficially, the memoirs of Latvian former officials appear to reveal relationships between negative (anti-Soviet) and positive (pro-Soviet) social representation: how they come together in making meaning of the Soviet period and the autobiographer's identity. Yet, as I have sought to demonstrate in this study, there is always an area that does not belong to either representation. This is the area into which multiple hierarchies and pragmatic depictions of conformism fall and where 'multidirectional memory' (Rothberg 2009) comes into being.

The vast majority of former officials, I have argued, use this alternative mnemonic area as the locus of their positive identity narrative. From there, former officials can show their complicity in the Soviet era as neither principally undermining the conceptual themes of negative representation nor those of positive representation. Namely, if you wanted to realize your professional ambitions or to work for society you had to collaborate with the regime. This kaleidoscopic area, where either cunning or submissive behavior can be morally justified by today's standards, provides Latvian former officials with opportunities to normalize stigmatized experiences. Hence, the main contention of this study is that the organizational themes of normalization discourse are not just the *in situ* emanations of negative or positive representation; they are relevant indications of a new form of social representation that has become more salient in the 2000s. I have already called it a pragmatic representation of the Soviet era, presented at the beginning of the paper, which does not simply combine the conceptual themes of negative or positive representation but offers a genuinely alternative mindset, emancipating participants in biographical discourse.

Though pragmatic representation is apparent in various groups of Latvian auto-biographers, memoirs of former officials are prototypical examples. The Latvian mass media, which facilitate the discursive elaboration of post-Soviet autobiographies, find this type of representation to be uncomfortable because it does not fit into the self-evident field of politicized negative representation or polemical positive representation. Here, in accordance with the social representation theory, we may encounter semantic barriers, such as the threat of stigmatization or undermining one's identity (Gillespie 2008) if one conveys the Soviet past through pragmatic representation too explicitly. The interaction between the officially mythologized structure of the Soviet period and biographical attempts expand their rigid relations suggest that pragmatic representation is still an *anticipatory representation*, which 'plays a crucial role when social actors reconstitute a common understanding of the world they share' (Philogène 2001, 127).

Manifold knowledge is inherent to pragmatic representation for it may concurrently invoke positive, as well as negative, connotations of the Soviet period, not completely degrading it, but maintaining a morally manageable distance from this past. Arguably, the distinctiveness of pragmatic representation is triggered by cognitive *polyphasia*, which is a decisive prerequisite for biographical improvisation. Cognitive *polyphasia* enables individuals to construct an autobiographical narrative in the manner described by Kõresaar (2001, 48) when many different lives and types of biographies (career biography, apartment biography, travel biography, hobby biography) are entangled in a single narrative, which mediates the Soviet past through multiple frames. Both cognitive *polyphasia* and a relatively polyphonic Latvian public discourse about the Soviet period (see Kaprāns 2010c, 2009) have encouraged former officials to merge their conflicting ideas. The autobiographers' need for a morally adequate identity is an evident driving force of these complex processes. It is noteworthy, though, that cognitive *polyphasia* 'emerges primarily when members of groups are coping with new conditions during their life-time' (Wagner and Hayes 2005, 235). In this sense, not only inter-experiential comparisons, but also predominantly the autobiographies of Latvian former officials per se, have been responses to new post-Soviet conditions.

At end of this paper, however, I want to challenge pragmatic representation by drawing attention to a vital question posed by Zygmunt Bauman (2003, 6): where is the boundary drawn between one's doings and the conditions under which one acted (and by definition, could not have acted otherwise) in the course of the narrative? Among other issues, Bauman's question sheds light on the intriguing dialectics between post-Soviet biographical improvisation and the Soviet conditions in the past under which former officials could not have done other than collaborate. Eventually, Bauman takes us back to the agency-structure problem. On the one hand, this concern emphasizes the emancipating qualities of pragmatic representation, which legitimizes agency, especially when compared with negative or positive representation. However, it also draws attention to moral relativism as a cultural practice, which nurtures pragmatic representation and entitles former officials to overcome the structural limitations imposed by post-Soviet political memory.

Notes

1. For the conceptual differences between social and political memory consult Assmann (2004).
2. Around 60,000 Latvians were exiled to Siberia during the two largest Stalinist deportations, which occurred in 1941 and 1949. Exile as a traumatic episode appears in practically all the autobiographical narratives as a direct or mediated experience.
3. Semi-structured interviews were carried out with five owners of publishing houses in September 2011.
4. Eduards Berklavs (1914–2004) was the leader of the so-called Latvian national communists who in the late 1950s fought against the Soviet nationality policy. Berklavs was dismissed from the post of the vice chairman of the Council of the Ministers of LSSR in 1959 and was administratively exiled to the Soviet Russia. Berklavs became one the leaders of the dissident movement in Soviet Latvia and played an active role during the period of national revival.
5. The First Secretary of the Central Committee of the Communist Party of Latvia (1940–1959).
6. The Latvian intelligentsia is more open to speaking about this issue in their memoirs (cf. Purs 2006; Vulfsons 1997).
7. Scholars interested in Estonian biographical discourse have pointed to double consciousness as a pivotal strategy for postwar generations of various professional groups (see Wulf and Petri 2010; Aarelaid-Tart 2003).

Acknowledgements

The research was supported by the European Union through the European Social Fund (Mobilitas grant No. GSHRG409MJD) and by Latvia's Government Commission for KGB Research.

Disclosure statement

No potential conflict of interest was reported by the author.

Funding

This work was supported by the European Union through the European Social Fund: [Grant Number GSHRG409MJD]; Latvia's Government Commission for KGB Research [grant Contract Number VDKKOM-D/11].

References

Aarelaid-Tart, A. 2003. "Estonian-inclined Communists as Mariginals." In *Biographical Research in Eastern Europe: Altered Lives and Broken Biographies*, edited by R. Miller, and E. Zdravomyslova, 71–99. Aldershot: Ashgate.

Aarelaid-Tart, A. 2010. "The Theory of Cultural Trauma as Applied to the Investigation of the Mindset of Estonians under Soviet Rule (Based on the Biographical Method)." In *Inheriting the 1990s: The Baltic Countries, Studia Uralica Upsaliensia*, edited by M.-K. Baiba, Vol. 37, 38–64. Uppsala: Edita Västra Aros.

Āboltiņš, J. 1992. *Biju biedrs, tagad kungs*. Rīga: Neatkarīgā Cīņa.

Andrle, V. 2000. "Neither a Dinosaur nor a Weathercock: The Construction of a Reputably Continuous Self in Czech Post-communist Life Stories." *Qualitative Sociology* 23 (2): 215–230. doi:10.1023/A:1005434900668.

Andrle, V. 2001. "The Buoyant Class: Bourgeois Family Lineage in the Life Stories of Czech Business Elite Persons." *Sociology* 35 (4): 815–833. doi:10.1177/S003803850100815X.

Anepaio, T. 2002. "Reception of the Topic of Repressions in the Estonian Society." *Pro Ethnologia* 13: 47–65.

Artmane, V. 2004. *Ziemcieši. Mirkļi no manas dzīves*. Rīga: Pētergailis.

Assmann, A. 2004. "Four Formats of Memory: From Individual to Collective Constructions of the Past." In *Cultural Memory and Historical Consciousness in the German-Speaking World Since 1500*, edited by C. Emden, and D. Midgley, 19–37. Oxford: Peter Lang.

Augustine. 1991. *Confessions*. Translated by Henry Chadwick. Oxford: Oxford University Press.

Bauman, Z. 2003. *The Individualized Society*. Cambridge: Polity Press.

Bela, B. 2012. "Everyday Life, Power, and Agency in Turbulent Latvia: The Story of Otto Irbe." In *Baltic Biographies in Historical Crossroads*, edited by A. Aardelaid-Tart, and L. Bennich-Björkman, 37–52. London: Routledge.

Bela-Krūmiņa, B. 2003. "Relationship between Personal and Social: Strategies of Everyday Life in the Process of Radical Social Changes." *Pro Ethnologia* 16: 9–19.

Beļavnieks, J. 2011. *...bet tā bija*. Rīga: Trīsdesmit seši.

Berklavs, E. 1998. *Zināt un neaizmirst*. Rīga: Preses nams.

Blonskis, A. V. 2000. *No ierindnieka līdz ģenerālim*. Rīga: Likuma Vārdā.

Boym, S. 2001. *The Future of Nostalgia*. New York: Basic Books.

Brubaker, R. 1996. *Nationalism Reframed: Nationhood and the National Question in the New Europe*. Cambridge: Cambridge University Press.

Budryte, D. 2002. "'We Call It Genocide': Soviet Deportations and Repression in the Memory of Lithuanians." *Bridges* 9 (3/4): 223–253.

Budryte, D. 2005. *Taming Nationalism? Political Community Building in the Post-Soviet Baltic States*. Aldershot: Ashgate.

Čaklais, M. 1992. "Epitāfija reformkomunismam." *Laiks*, November 11.

Dzenītis, J. 2002. *Sava laikmeta vilnī*. Rīga: J. Dzenītis.

Ekman, J., and J. Linde. 2005. "Communist Nostalgia and the Consolidation of Democracy in Central and Eastern Europe." *Journal of Communist Studies and Transition Politics* 21 (3): 354–374. doi:10.1080/13523270500183512.

Giddens, A. 1991. *Modernity and Self-Identity: Self and Society in the Late Modern Age*. Stanford: Stanford University Press.

Gillespie, A. 2008. "Social Representations, Alternative Representations and Semantic Barriers." *Journal for the Theory of Social Behaviour* 38 (4): 375–391. doi:10.1111/jtsb.2008.38.issue-4.

Goffman, E. 1986. *Stigma: Notes on the Management of Spoiled Identity*. New York: Simo & Schuster.

Howarth, C. 2006. "A Social Representation Is Not a Quiet Thing: Exploring the Critical Potential of Social Representations Theory." *British Journal of Social Psychology* 45: 65–86. doi:10.1348/014466605X43777.

Ivanauskas, V. 2012. *Lietuviškoji nomeklatūra biurokratinėje sistemoje: Tarp stagnacijos ir dinamikos (1968–1988 m.)*. Vilnius: Lietuvos istorijos institutas.

Jaspers, K. 2000. *The Question of German Guilt*. New York: Fordham University Press.

Jõesalu, K. 2005. "'The Right to Happiness'. Echoes of Soviet Ideology in Biographical Narratives." *Berliner Osteuropa Info* 23: 91–99.

Jõesalu, K., and E. Kõresaar. 2012. "Working through Mature Socialism: Private and Public in the Life Story of an Estonian Industry Manager." In *Baltic Biographies in Historical Crossroads*, edited by A. Aarelaid-Tart, and L. Bennich-Björkman, 68–85. London: Routledge.

Jõesalu, K., and E. Kõresaar. 2013. "Continuity or Discontinuity: On the Dynamics of Remembering 'Mature Socialism' in Estonian Post-Soviet Remembrance Culture." *Journal of Baltic Studies* 44 (2): 177–203. doi:10.1080/01629778.2013.775849.

Johansons, E. 2006. *Čekas ģenerāļa piezīmes: Atmoda un VDK*. Rīga: 1991. gada barikāžu dalībnieku biedrība.

Jovchelovitch, S. 2012. "Narrative, Memory and Social Representations: A Conversation Between History and Social Psychology." *Integrative Psychological and Behavioral Science* 46 (4): 440–456. doi:10.1007/s12124-012-9217-8.

Kaprans, M. 2012a. ""Constructing Generational Identity in Post-communist Autobiographies: The Case of Latvia." In *Life Writing Matters in Europe*, edited by M. Huisman, A. Ribberink, M. Soeting, and A. Hornung, 259–278. Heidelberg: Winter Verlag.

Kaprāns, M. 2009. "Padomju pieredzes (re)konstrukcija biogrāfiskajos vēstījumos: Latvijas lokālās preses analīze (1995–2005)." *Latvijas Arhīvi* 1/2: 162–194.

Kaprāns, M. 2010b. "Social Commentary as Biographical Work: Post-Communist Autobiographies in Latvia." *Auto/Biography Studies* 25 (2): 249–263. doi:10.1353/abs.2010.0028.

Kaprans, M. 2012b. "Normalizing the Cold War *habitus*: How Latvian autobiographers cope with their Soviet-time experience." In *The Baltic Sea Region and the Cold War. Tartu Historical Studies*, edited by O. Mertelsmann, and K. Piirimäe, Vol. 3, 261–277. Frankfurt am Main: Peter Lang.

Kaprans, M. 2010a. "Retrospective Anchoring of the Soviet Repressive System: The Autobiographies of the Latvian Intelligentsia." In *Between Fear and Freedom: Cultural Representations of the Cold War*, edited by K. Starck, 193–206. Newcastle: Cambridge Scholars Publishing.

Kaprāns, M. 2010c. "Padomju laika reprezentācija jaunākajā latviešu prozā (2000–2006)." In *Laiku atšalkas: žurnālistika, kino, politika*, edited by O. Proskurova, 189–202. Rīga: LU SPPI. http://www.szf.lu.lv/fileadmin/user_upload/szf_faili/Petnieciba/sppi/mediji/Laiku_atsalkas.pdf

Kargins, V. 2005. *Nauda un cilvēki*. Rīga: Atēna.

Kavalieris, A. 2002. *Pusgadsimts kriminālistikā*. Rīga: Valters un Rapa.

Kõresaar, E. 2001. "A Time Ignored? About the Role of the Soviet Period in Biographies of older Estonians." *Ethnologia Fennica. Finnish Studies in Ethnology* 29: 45–55.

Lasmanis, U. 2006. *Dēla gadsimts*. Rīga: U. Lasmanis.

Liepiņš, J. 2003. *Es sadarbojos ar KGB un CIP dubultaģentu Imantu Lešinski*. Rīga: Atklātais sabiedriskais fonds 'Latvietis'.

Liepiņš, J. 2008. *Sarkano okupantu orģijas Latvijā*. Rīga: Biedrība "Domas spēks".

Lim, J.-H. 2010. "Victimhood Nationalism in Contested Memories: National Mourning and Global Accountability." In *Memory in a Global Age*, edited by A. Assmann, and S. Conrad, 138–162. Basingstoke: Palgrave Macmillan.

Liu, J. H. 2005. "Social Representations of Events and People in World History Across 12 Cultures." *Journal of Cross-Cultural Psychology* 36 (2): 171–191. doi:10.1177/0022022104272900.

Liu, J. H., and D. J. Hilton. 2005. "How the Past Weighs on the Present: Social Representations of History and Their Role in Identity Politics." *British Journal of Social Psychology* 44 (4): 537–556. doi:10.1348/014466605X27162.

Mark, J. 2010. *The Unfinished Revolution: Making Sense of the Communist Past in Central-Eastern Europe*. New Haven: Yale University Press.

Marková, I. 2005. *Dialogicality and Social Representations: The Dynamics of Mind*. Cambridge: Cambridge University Press.

Marková, I. 2012. "Method and Explanation in History and in Social Representations." *Integrative Psychological and Behavioral Science* 46 (4): 457–474. doi:10.1007/s12124-012-9210-2.

McAdams, D. P. 1988. *Power, Intimacy, and the Life Story: Personological Inquiries into Identity*. New York: Guilford Press.

Moscovici, S. 2000. *Social Representations: Explorations in Social Psychology*. Cambridge: Polity Press.

Moscovici, S. 2008. *Psychoanalysis: Its Image and Its Public*. Cambridge: Polity Press.

Nadkarni, M., and O. Shevchenko. 2004. "The Politics of Nostalgia: A Case for Comparative Analysis of Post-Socialist Practices." *Ab Impero* 2: 487–519. doi:10.1353/imp.2004.0067.

Nagel, U. 2004. "Maintaining a Sense of Individual Autonomy under Conditions of Constraint: A Study of East German Managers." In *Biographical Methods and Professional Practice: An International Practice*, edited by P. Chamberlayne, J. Bornat, and U. Apitzsch, 131–148. Bristol, UK: Policy Press.

Nora, P. 1989. "Between Memory and History: *Les lieux de mémoire*." *Representations* 26: 7–24. doi:10.1525/rep.1989.26.1.99p0274v.

Olick, K. J., and J. Robbins. 1998. "Social Memory Studies: From 'Collective Memory' to the Historical Sociology of Mnemonic Practices." *Annual Review of Sociology* 24: 105–140.

Onken, E.-C. 2007. "The Baltic States and Moscow's 9 May Commemoration: Analysing Memory Politics in Europe." *Europe-Asia Studies* 59 (1): 23–46. doi:10.1080/09668130601072589.

Pettai, E.-C., and V. Pettai. 2014. *Transitional and Retrospective Justice in the Baltic States*. Cambridge: Cambridge University Press.

Philogène, G. 2001. "From Race to Culture: The Emergence of African American." In *Representations of the Social: Bridging Theoretical Tradition*, edited by K. Deaux, and G. Philogène, 113–128. Oxford: Blackwell.

Purs, L. 2006. *Aizejot atskaties*. Rīga: Signe/L. Purs.

Rothberg, M. 2009. *Multidirectional Memory: Remembering the Holocaust in the Age of Decolonization*. Stanford: Stanford University Press.

Saleniece, I. 2005. "Latvian 20th Century History from the Perspective of Oral History Sources. The Views of Russians from Eastern Latvia." *Pro Ethnologia* 19: 33–42.

Sebre, S. 2010. "Pride, Suspicion and Trust Represented in Narratives from Latvia During the 1990s." In *Inheriting the 1990s: The Baltic Countries, Studia Uralica Upsaliensia 37*, edited by B. Metuzale-Kangere, 26–37. Upssala: Edita Västra Aros.

Skultans, V. 1998. *The Testimony of Lives: Narrative and Memory in Post-Soviet Latvia*. London: Routledge.

Tajfel, H., and J. C. Turner. 1979. "An Integrative Theory of Intergroup Conflict." In *The Social Psychology of Intergroup Relations*, edited by W. G. Austin, and S. Worchel, 33–47. Monterey, CA: Brooks/Cole.

Troebst, S. 2010. "Halecki Revisited: Europe's Conflicting Cultures of Remembrance." In *A European Memory? Contested Histories and Politics of Remembrance*, edited by M. Pakier, and B. Stråth, 56–63. New York: Berghahn Books.

Ulmanis, G. 1995. *No tevis jau neprasa daudz*. Rīga: Liktenstāsti.

Voelklein, C., and C. Howarth. 2005. "A Review of Controversies about Social Representations Theory: A British Debate." *Culture & Psychology* 11 (4): 431–454. doi:10.1177/1354067X05058586.

Voslenskii, M. 2005. *Nomenklatura*. Moskva: Zakharov.

Vulfsons, M. 1997. *Kārtis uz galda!* Rīga: Liesma.

Wagner, W., and N. Hayes. 2005. *Everyday Discourse and Common Sense – the Theory of Social Representations*. Basingstoke: Palgrave Macmillan.

Wagoner, B. 2015. "Collective Remembering as a Process of Social Representation." In *The Cambridge Handbook of Social Representations*, edited by G. Sammut et al., 143–162. Cambridge: Cambridge University Press.

Wawrzyniak, J., and M. Pakier. 2013. "Memory Studies in Eastern Europe: Key Issues and Future Perspectives." *Polish Sociological Review* 183 (3): 257–279.

Wulf, M., and G. Petri. 2010. "Generating Meaning Across Generations. The Role of Historians in the Codification of History in Soviet and Post-Soviet Estonia." *Journal of Baltic Studies* 41 (3): 351–382. doi:10.1080/01629778.2010.498210.

Yurchak, A. 2006. *Everything Was Forever, Until It Was No More*. Princeton: Princeton University Press.

Zake, I. 2010. "Politicians versus Intellectuals in the Lustration Debates in Transitional Latvia." *Journal of Communist Studies and Transition Politics* 26 (3): 389–412. doi:10.1080/13523279.2010.496327.

Zlakomanovs, N. 2000. *Izmeklēšanas priekšnieka atmiņas*. Rīga: N.Zlakomanovs.

We were the children of a romantic era: nostalgia and the nonideological everyday through the perspective of a 'Silent Generation'

Kirsti Jõesalu

Department of Ethnology, University of Tartu, Tartu, Estonia

ABSTRACT
This article focuses on the generational self-understanding of women born in the 1940s in Estonia. Their self-understanding is analyzed through nostalgia and private–public remembering and is based on 21 life stories. The life stories primarily focus on the everyday experiences from the late socialism era. These women are more likely to give examples not in accordance with dominant national discourse, and their voice has not been heard in the public discourse. The article shows that experiences from the private sphere also have an influence on the formation of generational consciousness.

Introduction

It is common for life story narrators to make closing statements that can be read as the key to the whole life story (Kirss 2005, 34; Kõresaar 2011, 345). *Life goes on!* (*Elame veel!*)[1] – this short statement summarizes many life stories that were recorded at the dawn of the new millennium. The narrators wanted to show that despite the hardships experienced in the past, life will continue. Closing statements of this kind enable the narrators to emphasize that they are looking forward to the future while also referring to the difficulties of the recent past. The article focuses on the narrative memory of late socialism from the point of view of the generation born in the 1940s. In these life stories, the phrase 'Life goes on!' directs the reader's attention to the narrators' experiences during the hard times in the aftermath of World War II and in the transition years of the 1990s. It also serves as a point of reference to years that witnessed a better life, such as the period of 'late socialism' from the 1960s to the 1980s (see Yurchak 2005, 31; Jõesalu and Kõresaar 2013).

The article discusses the interpretations of 'late socialism' that have been added to post-Soviet memory culture through autobiographic memory practices by women of the postwar generation. By interpreting their written autobiographical accounts through the prisms of public–private relationships and everyday experiences, the article seeks to determine whether or not there are discursive practices common to telling the life stories of postwar women and whether a generational consciousness (Corsten 1999) can be detected. The article is divided into six sections: an analytical framework is provided by introducing the concepts of nostalgia and the 'Silent Generation'; the life stories are contextualized and introduced, and different aspects of remembering late socialism are observed.

The life stories featured in this article were written by women at the turn of the millennium, and represent a significant paradigm shift in Estonian post-Soviet memory culture (Jõesalu and Kõresaar 2013). The analyzed collection of life stories played a significant role in letting late socialist experiences be remembered in their own right. Until the new millennium, 'late socialism' was typically seen through the lens of the hegemonic discourse on the victory of capitalism over socialism in which the Soviet period was remembered as a disrupted era in Estonian history. In the 1990s, post-Soviet Estonian memory culture focused on experiences from the interwar period of independence and on the pivotal events of the 1940s and 1950s. These experiences were represented by most of the narrators born in the 1920s whose narratives became an important core part of official memory policy (cf. Kõresaar 2005), while the experiences of other generations remained in the background. In this framework, the period of late socialism was reduced to a comment on the discourse of the 'long rupture.'[2] The development of memory culture during the twenty-first century has, however, introduced diversity into the interpretations of the late socialist period (Jõesalu and Kõresaar 2013).[3]

Nostalgia and the experiences of the 'Silent Generation'

The transition of society from socialism to a liberal capitalist democracy in post-socialist countries had a profound impact on the ways in which the recent past is remembered. In the study of post-socialist memory cultures, nostalgia has proved to be a much-used concept – different aspects of nostalgia have been addressed in the literature, including examples from Hungary, Romania, Bulgaria, East Germany, and the former Yugoslavia (Todorova and Gille 2010; Velikonja 2008; Petrovic 2010).[4] The US-Bulgarian historian Maria Todorova, paraphrasing Marx, even noted that 'a specter is haunting the world of academia: the study of post-communist nostalgia' (2010, 1). Todorova also reminds the reader that there are other ways of interpreting the pasts of East and Central Europeans aside from *Vergangenheitsbewältigung [coming to terms with the past]* by questioning the dominant understanding of nostalgia as something negative or as a mere longing for the past (2–4). Anthropologist Dominic Boyer has pointed to the hidden hierarchies inherent in the understanding of nostalgia: he claims that from the Western European and the US perspective nostalgia is often seen as something which is common to Eastern Europeans, a sign of their backwardness in comparison with Western Europeans (Boyer 2010). Todorova emphasizes that while dealing with the question of nostalgia we should determine who is speaking about nostalgia, what the agents of nostalgia are, and what this nostalgia expresses (2010, 7–8).

In life stories written in Estonia between 2001 and 2004, nostalgia appears as a counter-memory (Berdahl and Bunzl 2010)[5] to the hegemonic discourse about the Soviet past, bringing up issues that have been silenced. The narrators reminisce about the late socialist era nostalgically; they give meaning to the complicated present through nostalgia (56). As we observe who is speaking about nostalgia or about being nostalgic, the question of generational belonging also arises.

Bernd Weisbrod has shown that the concept of 'generation' has predominantly been defined through (public) political events, which are primarily based on the experiences of men, and many of these definitions of what generation is go back to Mannheim's work on generations (Weisbrod 2007; Niethammer 2005).[6] While questioning the adequacy of a political, male-centered definition of generation, Weisbrod suggests that politics of generation-making could be examined in more detail and that 'Silent Generations' should be brought back into focus of generational research (2007, 31). Generational consciousness need not necessarily be connected with a historical event; it could also be defined through everyday experiences and the narration of those experiences. Those generations whose experiences have not yet been publicly heard could thereby be defined as 'Silent Generations.' The silenced dimensions of experiences could create connectivity within a generation in the same way as participation in demonstrations (which – as the example of the 1960s generation demonstrate – constitutes one of the experiences creating the self-consciousness of a generation) (Silies 2009, 112). Further, nonpublic communication rather than participation in public and political debates can bring about a shared sense of belonging for certain age groups (Silies 2007, 28).[7] Catriona Kelly suggests in this context a perspective that stresses the importance of a common narrated experience, which could be connected to the private, not the public sphere (2007, 165–166).

In this analysis, those born in Estonia in the 1940s are seen as members of a 'Silent Generation' who have not been able to make their voice heard at a national level (Kelly 2007, 168).[8] During their formative years, in the second half of the 1950s and the beginning of the 1960s, no major political events took place that could be interpreted as being formative in creating the sense of generational belonging. In the context of Baltic life experiences, those born in the 1940s can be labeled as a 'Soviet generation': they were born into and socialized in Soviet society, and spent the greater part of their working lives in Soviet Estonia. The only society they were familiar with until the 1990s was Soviet society.[9] As a rule, this generation received a better education than their parents and nearly one in five of those born in the 1940s received higher education (Katus, Puur, and Sakkeus 2005). They spent their childhood at home looked after by their mothers or grandmothers, which differed from the experiences of their children who mostly went to kindergarten (e.g. Raleigh 2012). For these narrators, the period of late socialism was filled with learning and working; this was a time of self-realization and family building. The 1960s and 1970s were also a time of economic prosperity in society in general, and the working and living environments of individuals improved as a result.

Between 1991 and 1994, after the Singing Revolution and regaining the independence, radical reforms took place in Estonian economy. This period has been called 'a time of extraordinary politics' (Lauristin and Vihalemm 2009, 5). Many state owned companies were closed down or restructured, which forced many of the working population to find new roles in the transforming society (e.g. Roth 2004; Helemäe and Saar 2006; Nugin 2015). During the transitional years, women born in the 1940s had to adapt to the new working relations, and sometimes had to retrain in a new profession. In the early years of capitalism, work experiences gained during the Soviet era were underestimated and new managers generally preferred to hire people without any significant work experience from the Soviet period. The status of some professions also changed, for example, among others, that of teachers, who were often criticized in the changing society as representatives of out-of-date experiences (see Kõresaar 2004).

Thus, two main periods emerge as central in the studied narratives: the improvement of everyday life in the 1960s and 1970s, and the dramatic changes in the 1990s. These experiences can be considered as shared by the analyzed group, which could contribute to the formation of generational consciousness. This 'Silent Generation' can be seen as one of the main agents in diversification and re-democratization of late socialism in Estonia. By taking an active role in life writing at the beginning of the twenty-first century, those life story writers made visible the role of nostalgia as counter-memory in the development of memory culture: in this generation's life stories experiences from late socialism are mediated through the prism of nostalgia, which in turn helps the authors to give meaning to the complicated present.

Life stories in a particular setting: bringing one age group into focus

Life stories have formed an important part of the building of a new national identity in Estonia (Hinrikus and Kõresaar. 2004) as well as in Latvia (Bela 2009) since the late 1980s. While oral history projects have been central in Latvia (Bela 2009), the main life story collection in Estonia consists of written autobiographical accounts at the Estonian Cultural History Archives of the Literary Museum (KM EKLA).[10] These stories have mostly been sent to the Archives in response to the various life-writing campaigns organized by the Estonian Cultural History Archives and the Estonian Life Stories Association since the end of the 1980s. While life story research has been quite popular in Estonia (Kirss, Kõresaar, and Lauristin 2004; Kõresaar 2005; Kirss 2009; Kõresaar and Jõesalu 2016), it still appears that life stories sent in as a response to the campaign about life in the ESSR have received less attention from researchers (the two notable exceptions are Lauristin 2004; Lember 2007), and the perspective of women born in the 1940s have received even less attention.[11]

All in all, the pivotal events from the 1940s and 1950s have received more attention, at least within the Baltic context, than the period of late socialism. The questions of gender identity and nationalism have emerged as important topics in connection with deportation and survival (Elksnis Geisler 2011; Lazda 2005; Kirss 2005; Davoliūtė 2005). In Lithuania, women's experiences between 1945 and 1970 have also been explained in the framework of post-socialist remembrance culture (Leinarte 2010). In Estonia, Aarelaid-Tart has interviewed her peers with whom she studied history at university in the mid-1960s and contextualized their experiences in a generational framework along the lines of broader biographical research (Aarelaid-Tart 2012a).

The present analysis mostly draws on the autobiographical accounts sent to the Estonian Cultural History Archives (ECHA) from 2001 to 2004 in response to the life-writing campaign: *My Life and My Family's Life in the Estonian Socialist Soviet Republic (ESSR) and in the Republic of Estonia* (organized in 2000–2001, 330 life stories were collected).[12] From among these, 34 life stories by women born between 1936 and 1952 were selected for closer study. Twenty two of the women were born in the 1940s, with an equal number born during and after the war. Stories from women born during the 'margin years' (1936–1939, seven stories; and 1950–1952, five stories) were also included in the study. As usual for Estonian life-writing campaigns, the participants come from different social backgrounds: contributing to life-writing campaigns has been seen as important by many different people, from teachers to collective farm (*kolkhoz*) workers. Most of the narrators lived in villages and small towns, but some came from the capital, Tallinn.

It emerged that women born in the independent Republic of Estonia (i.e. before 1940) use different ways of narrating and would identify themselves with the republic through the year of their birth. Via this association with their birth year, these women would connect their personal stories with the national narrative. However, these women born before 1940 employ similar narrative practices as younger women when describing the division of their lives between public and private duties and generational affiliation. In addition to the unpublished life stories, published autobiographical accounts by women of the same generation are also included in the analysis (Lauristin 2010; Tungal 2008, 2009; Tarand 2008). These published authors are prominent in the fields of culture and politics, yet this group is underrepresented in the collection of life stories from the Archives.

The focus on women's experiences derives from the concentration of women's stories among respondents to the 'My life and my family's life in the ESSR' campaign. It is notable that stories from women are the most numerous especially within the postwar generation, while less than five stories were sent to the Archives by men born in the 1940s. One reason for this could be that the appeal was directed more toward everyday experiences than the main historical events, and this encouraged women to send their narratives to the archive. Results of other campaigns have been more gender balanced.

Another factor influencing the topics of the collection 'My life and my family's life in the ESSR,' besides its methodological focus on everyday experiences, was the effect the postcommunist decade had on its main respondents. The post-Soviet transformation had a different effect on women than men. Men were more likely than women to emerge as 'winners' in the new economic system. (Sotsiaalministeerium 2016, Anderson and Vöörmann 1996). Women, however, especially those with small children and those approaching retirement were among the most vulnerable groups (Hansson 2003, 133; Helemäe and Saar 2006). The authors of the analyzed life stories belong to the latter group: at the time of writing their accounts, the women had just or almost reached retirement age.

Among other sociopolitical changes, the new retirement system affected the generation born in the 1940s and early 1950s. During the Soviet era, the retirement age for women was 55; under the new system, those born in 1944 could first retire in 2002 at the age of 58, while others, born after 1944, retired even some years later. The changes in retirement policy significantly changed expectations concerning one's life trajectory. This meant that many of women had to work up to 5 years more than they had expected to in the beginning of their work life during mature socialism. In the changed economic situation, women in their 50s, in particular, found it difficult to keep their jobs as many positions had been either restructured or liquidated. Paradoxically, retirement could improve one's material situation: the pension, which had been quite small, was still a fixed and regular income compered to one's unemployment benefits.[13] Therefore, retirement could have ended (or alleviated) precarious situation for many women. This kind of precarious situation also heavily influenced the choice of topics in these life stories as well as the ways in which the late socialism years are remembered.

In the following pages, a close reading of the life stories is presented through the lens of the public–private relationship, by asking how the narrators of the stories relate to the public understanding of the Soviet past. In order to relate those stories to the public understanding of the Soviet era, the narrators' conceptualizations of themselves as mothers and employees is examined, as well as their generational self-description.

Placing one's story into the public (national) framework

The autobiographical accounts sent to the ECHA in the twenty-first century are not characterized by political ideas and ideologies, but by everyday discourse. National ideology that would prevail in the public and the private discourses of Estonian society in the 1990s was much less observable in these stories than those of previous generations. In the research on the Estonian post-Soviet life writing by the prewar generation (mainly by those born in the 1920s), Kõresaar discusses the overlap between private and individual and collective and national discourses (2005). In the life stories highlighted in this paper, an overlap of the individual and the national typically occurs in situations when family members are directly affected by violence (primarily the deportations of 1949).

In comparison with earlier generations, women born in the 1940s were more likely to display attitudes in their life stories that are not in accordance with the dominant national discourse. A vivid example of difference in attitudes is the interpretation they give to the role of partisans, the so-called *Forest Brothers*.[14] In the Estonian national historiography, and even more in the public discourse available elsewhere (e.g. in media discussions and in published memoires), the partisans were perceived as important members of the anti-Soviet resistance movement (see Laar 1993, 2007). However, rather than just praising their heroism, the women born before 1940 questioned the dominant narrative by stressing dubious aspects of the partisans' deeds. Life story writers tend to remember the fear they felt as children in the 1940s, and recall violent deaths in villages. In the example below, the narrator describes the cruel deaths of villagers by hand of a notorious partisan. She was also very critical of how this partisan had been represented in the historiography of the 1990s, especially the Prime Minister and historian Mart Laar's description of this particular partisan as a 'freedom fighter.'

> There was a great fear of being in the forest at night: from behind any tree a partisan [Forest Brother] from the notorious Ilp gang could jump out and harass you. Several of Ilp's victims are buried in the cemetery near my mother's grave. To this day, I remember the funeral of the young *komsorg* [local secretary of Young Communist League] [–]

> In the next grave rests an elderly couple, whom Ilp killed with an axe in their sleep at their home. What kind of a man of principle and freedom fighter can this murderer be? Many Saaremaa residents are very disturbed by Mart Laar having made Ilp into a national hero. It seems that everyone acknowledges his own kind. (Ruth, b. in 1941, life story submitted in 2001, KM EKLA F. 350, 1309, 2)

While the some authors of these life stories may not see partisans in a heroic light, many find praiseworthy aspects about representatives of the Soviet system. In another example, a *partorg* [local party secretary] is described as a nice person, a feature that definitely does not belong to the dominating narrative about the Soviet era:

> The positions of directors and *partorgs* were replaced. One of the nice ones was NIKOLAI LUMI (local party secretary). His wife worked at the library. I remember his kindness when I, a bundle of rags, was allowed to participate in activities at the library. I was imbued with such a sense of genuine politeness there. They had a little daughter, 4–5 years old. These three were killed by the partisans one evening in May, as they were unsuspectingly approaching their apartment. (Ene, b. 1942, life story submitted in 2001, KM EKLA F. 350, 1236, 1–2, capital letters added by life story narrator)

The life stories cited above were written 15 years ago, but it is interesting to note that even 10 years later Aarelaid-Tart, a member of the same generation, felt as if her memories of the Stalinist era, especially of the partisans, had no place in the public discourse (see Aarelaid-Tart 2012b).[15]

In addition, another focal theme in the contemporary Estonian national story appears to be the idea of continuity with the prewar Republic of Estonia. The continuity was often created in the life stories written at the end of 1980s and beginning of 1990s through describing the experiences of previous generations and using examples from one's own life in the Estonian Republic before the Soviet occupation in 1940. However, the Estonian folklorist Tiiu Jaago has noted that the topic of family continuity is no longer prominent in the life stories written in the twenty-first century (Jaago 2006). This tendency to ignore family continuity can be confirmed in case of this collection: as a rule, stories of family history remain in the background and the readers do not learn much about the life of the narrators' parents in the prewar Republic, except as secondary accounts. Some writers start their narratives with the beginning of their working life, without making any reference to an earlier family story and thus making no reference to the national story of Estonia's past (so KM EKLA F. 350, 1219, b. 1936; KM EKLA F. 350, 1078, b. 1949, KM EKLA F. 350, 1250, w. b. 1945).

It seems that the inclusion of the topic of parents and grandparents as a theme depends on spatial continuity: if a family continued to live in the same place after the dramatic changes of 1940s and 1950s, we also learn something about the past of the narrator's parents and grandparents. For instance, a narrator born in South Estonia in 1944 talks about the life of her mother and father in the Estonian Republic.

> My mother and father lived in Hellenurme before World War II during the Estonian Republic. There they rented rooms for a shop and lived in a long white house on the bank of Lake Veskijärve. Father ran the Farmers' shop. Mother had young children. (Virve, b. 1944, life story submitted in 2001, KM EKLA F. 350, 1192, 1)

Later on, Virve tells us that both her parents had finished secondary school, and went to live on her maternal grandparents' farm after the war. The deportation of her grandmother in 1949 emerges as a significant and emotional event in the narrator's life story (KM EKLA F. 350, 1192, 3). Major historic events like deportations, which occupy a play a significant role in the national memory, motivate the narrators to spend more time on discussing their ancestors. However, life preceeding the Soviet time is seldom depicted; the occupations of fathers are typically mentioned, but there are no detailed descriptions given.[16]

> Once upon a time, during the Estonian time,[17] my father was an entrepreneur, but when Soviet power came, he had to give all of the shop-floor equipment as a 'gift,' in the true sense of word, to the COOPERATIVE – there was no compensation. However, he was lucky; he was not deported to Siberia. Dreams of a better standard of living and a house of our own went to ruin. (Elle, b. 1944, life story submitted in 2001, KM EKLA F. 350, 1214, 1, grew up in Southern Estonia, and moved to Eastern Estonia as young adult; capitalization by life story narrator)

The same narrator, a teacher, reflected on her 'political consciousness' regarding the issues of the past. Once more, the narrator's dialogue with the public narrative, becomes evident: In the public narrative, the discourse of resistance is very influential: according to this, the 'true history of Estonians' was preserved in private and family circles, and in families resistance to Soviet power persisted, (see also Aarelaid-Tart

2006; Jõesalu 2012; Tulviste 1994), whereas in the public realm the active resistance to Soviet power ended in the mid-1950s, and life in independent Estonia was barely mentioned, if at all, in the historiography. The narrator, however, admits that such issues of the past were not spoken about in her family.

> Our mother and father never talked about politics at home or about how this new world order was brought to us through violence. Until quite recently, I was very naïve.

> As a child, I didn´t have a clue that we were occupied, and the school history prophesized/proclaimed a bright future – COMMUNISM! All the newspapers were writing about advancements. And everything was very well. (Elle, b. in 1944, KM EKLA F. 350, 1214, 4, capitalization by the life story narrator)

It has been noted in earlier research that in the everyday environment the 'Estonian time' continued until the 1960s: if their homes had not been destroyed in the war, people were surrounded by furniture from a previous era and they used prewar commodities (Vahtre 2002; Aarelaid-Tart 2006, 2012a). Women prominent in the field of culture also note the continuation of 'Estonian time' at an everyday level in published memoires. Social scientist Marju Lauristin, born into a family of communists who were imprisoned for political reasons during most of the 'Estonian time,' stresses that her contact with the 'Estonian era' first came about through the material world when living in the house of family friends who had emigrated (*I was brought up by that Merivälja house,* (Lauristin 2010, 27). Valued commodities and pieces of furniture from the Estonian era are mentioned also by another well-known cultural figure Mari Tarand (2008, 31–32, 34).

Aarelaid-Tart posed a direct question to her fellow students at the University of Tartu: 'How much did your parents talk about the "Estonian time" at home?' (Aarelaid-Tart 2012a, 62). In her article, she emphasizes the continuity of the material environment that was surviving in households, as well as a significant awareness of the 'Estonian time':

> To summarize: knowledge about the Estonian time had a place in the consciousness of the post-war generation, since as children they lived in the environment of the previous decades. Furniture and commodities, outfits of family members, etc. – all of this came from previous decades; most families were plagued by poverty and so new items were rare. (Aarelaid-Tart 2012a, 65)

However, in the cases when no special meaning was attached to the objects of previous generations in the written life stories, no connection was made between home environments and the prewar Republic. In the life stories archived at the ECHA, making connections similar to those cited in published memoires is missing, while new rituals introduced by the Soviet system, such as becoming Pioneers or Children of October, appear to be more meaningful for the narrators than mediating the prewar past. Attributing significance to these new rituals follows the narrators' willingness to depart from the official and public interpretation of the Soviet past in these life stories. On the other hand, reminiscing about those rituals has a deeply individual and experiential dimension because such rites of passage organized the social life and the life history of the narrators. Nostalgically recalling of these moments is a way of maintaining autobiographical self-continuity.[18] In a similar way, such rituals are contextualized in the biographical accounts and cultural texts of those born in the 1970s, (e.g. Jõesalu and Nugin 2012; Jõesalu and Kõresaar 2013).

What is characteristic of the life stories of the women of the 'Silent Generation' is that, in comparison with older generations, they relate to the national story in a more fragmentary and critical way. The topic of family history serves as a telling example. On one hand, the experiences of family members connect the life story of the next generation with the story of the nation. On the other hand, family history itself is hardly a central theme in the life stories written at the beginning of twenty-first century: the stories are increasingly more individualistic and are concerned with working life and the importance of managing the everyday life. Moreover, the absence of nationalist ideology and willingness of some of the life storywriters to contest the dominant national discourse makes the life stories of the 'Silent Generation' a site of counter-memory. With the added perspective of the everyday life of the narrators, the retrospective interpretation of the life experience under the Soviet rule becomes diversified. The nostalgic recollections of Soviet everyday life play a double role here: besides securing one's individual self-continuity,[19] they convey political and social criticism.

Managing the everyday: from postwar poverty and a better life in the 1960s to the difficulties in the 1990s

The material poverty during the war and in the postwar years had a strong influence on the childhoods and teenage years of the narrators – this is one of the recurring themes in the post-Soviet narratives. The material improvement of everyday life in the 1960s and 1970s coincides with the period when the narrators began to have their own families. For the narrators, the period of late socialism represented a time of stability, particularly when compared to the economic restructuring of the 1990s, for which not all of them were prepared.

A woman who had been working at a fishing kolkhoz during the Soviet era summarizes the double burden of first suffering poverty during the postwar years and then witnessing another decline in the standard of living as a result of the reforms of the 1990s:

> Why do my generation and I, born during the war, have to suffer such great deprivation the second time around in this one life that's given to us? The sufferers are again the same children raised in poor families: I have an equally great lack of decent food now, in my retirement years, as I had in childhood. Why can no one answer this? (Elve, b. 1943, KM EKLA F. 350, 1241)[20]

The topic of postwar poverty and poor living conditions also emerges in the life stories; in particular, the lack of food and proper clothing is mentioned (see, e.g. EKLA 350, 1274). The scarcity of everyday necessities and commodities is brought up a number of times when writing about studying at secondary school and living away from one's family, either with relatives or in a rented accommodation. The narrators therefore place a high value on practical everyday skills in their adult life and describe how they improved their living conditions during the 1960s and 1970s as a result. For example, they mention their skillful management when there was a shortage of housing; apartments were not freely available and were distributed through housing commissions and work places, thereby creating difficult situations to manage. For example, a family managed to buy and sell three private houses between 1967 and 1987, and, as a result, they gradually improved their living conditions (KM EKLA 350,

1219, w. b. 1936, also in; KM EKLA F. 350, 1250, w. b. 1945). Another example of good management skills is purchasing a car for the family, which is an important theme in the life stories of several women (e.g. in KM EKLA F. 350, 1360, 1314, 1290; see more in; Kõresaar 2003).

The years of late socialism in from the 1960s until the 1980s are described through self-actualization. Struggles on either physical or psychological levels are omitted from these autobiographical accounts. The literary scholar Tiina Kirss associates this with cultural taboos typical of Estonians:

> Yet further, one might speculate on Estonian cultural taboos against revealing weakness, lest one appear to be a 'loser' in life's adversities; hard work, prevailing against all odds, and a stoic, uncomplaining pose are highly valued in Estonian culture; physical and psychological struggles and weaknesses are rendered, if at all, through the texts' silences. (Kirss 2004, 141)

On the other hand, those struggles and weaknesses are represented in the narratives of structural reforms of 1990s that changed the narrators' lives. The following example comes from the story of a woman who gave the section of the life story, describing her life in the Republic of Estonia with the subtitle: 'The Initial Years of the Republic of Estonia broke our normal life – Hard Times are Ahead.' With this subtitle, she notes the struggles of herself and her family in the Estonian society in the 1990s.

> Spending my childhood in the Soviet time, I was never afraid. In fact, I was afraid only once, when they wanted to take us away from home, because our mother was ill [to put the children into an orphanage]. But I was very afraid in the newly re-independent Estonia. Anxieties, being homeless, unemployment, sleepless nights, and hunger deprived us of our will to live. (Helve, b. in 1949, life story submitted in 2001, KM EKLA F. 350, 1188, 5)

Changes in these accounts came about with the transformations of the 1990s, which often also shaped the writing about life during late socialism. There certainly are also successful transformation stories from people born in the 1940s, some of whom belong to the new elite, but these stories have not yet been added to the life-writing project.

The individual narrators' ideas about coping with the changes (as well as how they remember the era of late socialism) are also related to whether their children (mostly born in the 1960s–1970s) were successful in finding their places in the neoliberal society.

The 1960s–1980s are presented as a 'safe haven' in comparison with the recent past; these years are a period of relative stability between the tough postwar years and the turbulent 1990s. The experience of the relative social and economic security of these stable years is seen as a stark contrast to the rapid changes of the 1990s. This is a general tendency in post-socialist countries; many authors have referred to nostalgia for late socialism as a form of critique of contemporary society (Creed 2010; Berdahl and Bunzl 2010; Todorova and Gille 2010). The nostalgia for the years 1960s–1980s works as commentary on many levels: it is a contrast to the insecurity of the 1990s, and sheds light on the disadvantages of the transformation experienced at the individual level. At the same time, the nostalgia for the period of late socialism questions the official narrative about post-Soviet transition. Both inside and outside Estonia, the country's transition in the 1990s has been and is presented as an overwhelming success, which is not compatible with the experiences of the life story narrators. By juxtaposing the experiences of the 1960s–1980s and the 1990s, the life story narrators use late socialist nostalgia as a counter-memory.

Looking for a balance between public life and private life

Devoting themselves to working life is an important topic in many women's life stories in post-socialist times, ranging from the Evenk women in Central Siberia to women in Western Poland (Bloch 2005; Parla 2009; Pine 2002). In this sense, Estonian women are writing into the tradition of valuing the working life of the Soviet time.

During the Soviet period Estonian women, as a rule, worked outside of the home, this was generally so in the case of the postwar generation. The socialist state took over certain functions that used to be privately provided or family based earlier – childcare was provided on the factory's grounds and meals were served at the work-place – which made it easier for women to combine work and childcare. Those born in the 1940s were shaped by the Soviet schooling system; Soviet work collectives and social care system.[21] According to the Soviet public ideology, a child was brought up for the state, not for the family (see e.g. Issioupova 2000; Berdahl and Bunzl 2010; Leinarte 2010, 19–49, Raleigh 2012, 39). Being a housewife was not ideologically endorsed in the Soviet Union (Malysheva and Bertaux 1996, 31) as everybody had to work for the public good and if, for some reason, they did not, this was generally not approved of by the fellow citizens. Thus, a central topic in the life – writing by women in the post-Soviet period is their working life and the balance they tried to establish between their work in the public domain and their work in the private domain, the family.[22]

The narrators wanted to receive retrospective acknowledgment for work that was not done in the public domain or was not officially acknowledged at the time. In the next example, a well-known author of children's books reminisces about how uncomfortable she felt as a 'nonworking' person.

> At first, I was rather bitter [after a forced departure from the newspaper editorial board and staying home with children]. All the more that in those days a housewife was regarded as a do-nothing free-rider, couch adornment and what not. (Leelo, b. in 1947, KM EKLA F. 350, 1369, children's book author)

The narrators set a high value on their work in the public sphere, but in retrospect they also recognize the problems associated with their dedication to working life and acknowledge that combining private and public duties was not easy (see also Sebre 2005, 73 for a comparable study of Latvian women). Questioning one's duties as a mother and a breadwinner does not appear so clearly in the stories of previous generations. In the following two examples, a lifelong teacher refers to this topic in two different stories sent to the Archives in 2001 and 2005:

> Over the years, our family grew and we started living [–] in the teachers' building. For all this time, I believed that work matters most. It was very rare that I missed work due to personal reasons. If sometimes [one of the younger children] was ill, [the older daughter] stayed with them and I kept on working in school. (Elle, b. in 1944, life story submitted in 2001, KM EKLA F. 350, 1214, 9)

> I grew and was brought up at a time when work was most important. Private life, and family life were secondary. Everybody knew what to do at work and how to fulfill societal duties. What your next of kin actually feels or thinks; for that, there was no time. (Elle, b. in 1944, life story submitted in 2005, KM EKLA F. 350, 1826, 1)

During the transformation of society, and during the time of the writing of the life stories, a new meaning was given to gender roles in the post-Soviet space. The public discourse of the 1990s cherished traditional values, among others, and advocated that women should return to the private sphere (Hansson 2003, 145; Jõesalu 2003). As the result of the neoconservative turn in gender relations (Pető 2010), the post-socialist discourse of the 1990s labeled women as 'reproducers' and 'maintainers' of the nation.

In contrast, by putting working life at the center of a life story, presenting one's life as a biography of work is typical of 'Soviet' life stories (see Jõesalu and Kõresaar 2011). This particular focus could be explained by twofold experiences from the Soviet era: on one hand, the meaningful experience of working life itself; and, on the other hand, the ideological importance given to working life in the public sphere, which set it above other spheres of life. With this double experience, the female narrators look for a retrospective acknowledgment for coping with the public and the private during the Soviet era. Putting one's working life at the center of a life story could be read as a critique of the Soviet gender politics and practices, where women's role and efforts in the private sphere were not valued. From a post-socialist perspective, however, these stories could be understood as a social critique of the gender relations in the post-socialist situation as well. Describing one's search for balancing public and private duties also sheds light to the roles of nostalgia as a counter-memory discussed above.

The generation's self-description: 'we wanted to change the world'

A further topic in the narrative unfolding of the nostalgia for late socialism is that of 'idealistic youth.' Having idealist beliefs under Soviet rule is a characteristic that life story narrators attribute to their generation. Using phrases such as *we all, we were, to us it is normal, in our time*, people from different social backgrounds described the 'we-group' as believers in a better world and as people dedicated to their professional working lives. This outlook is tangential with Alexei Yurchak's (2005) account of believing in Soviet ideals during late socialism. Yurchak pointed out that his informants, who were mostly born in the 1950s–1960s, felt proud of having been Soviet citizens. In case of Estonia, however, reminiscing about the ideals held in the past and the belief in a better future for everybody (*making the world a better place*) prevails, which is not directly connected to being a Soviet citizen, but rather gives expression to a more universal belief in the future.[23]

Recalling their childhood and youth in the 1940s and 1950s, the narrators often use language typical of the Soviet period; for example, they use ideological discourse when describing youth activities. It is possible to read this is as irony, but there are no textual resources available now that could 'translate' the experiences of Soviet mass organizations for today's readers (see also Kõresaar 2003; Aarelaid-Tart 2012b):

> We fulfilled the norms of VTK[24] – we were READY FOR THE WORK AND DEFENCE OF OUR HOMES. WE 'CLIMBED' ON THE RANKS OF PIONEERS; the opening of the marching songs 'Always ready' and 'Red Pathfinder' were following us (Elle, b. in 1944, KM EKLA F. 350, 1214, 4, capital letters added by life story narrator).

The ideals are sometimes described as having been naïve from a post-socialist perspective: 'Our generation was idealistic and we were quite unpractical people' (Helja, b. 1947, life story submitted in 2001, KM EKLA F 350, 1343, p. 22, and p. 21 about being a 'Soviet citizen'; for comparable material, see; Sebre 2005).

Another narrator who was active in the *Komsomol* during the 1960s describes herself as a person who still 'believes in life': 'I had rose-tinted glasses, and I still believe in life' (Ene, b. in 1942, life story submitted in 2001, KM EKLA F. 350, 1236,

16–17). She also makes generalizations, bringing out the common features of her own age group:, she sees that her generation has suffered a lot during their lifetime, referring more to the changes of the 1990s than to the hardships of the postwar years, but also stresses that she and her husband believed in the future during their youth.

> The war generations suffered most from changes. The fact that the retirement age was raised was very tough … [–] life is only good for those who have pension. My dream about a nice home and children has been fulfilled. We always had pets at our house. The children come to visit us. Our young folk have often asked whether we with dad really believed in communism so that we had to become party members. This was the way of life; the war had ended, and a new life was being built [–]. Deportations could take place also today; life is also tough nowadays. (Ene, b. in 1942, life story submitted in 2001, KM EKLA F. 350, 1236, 16–17)

Believing in the future and in making the world a better place is not only common for narrators from the eastern side of the Iron Curtain – similar ideals can be found among those who were active in the student movements of the 1960s in the West. 'I was a child of the sixties … [–] In 1968, we completely thought we were going to change the world … we thought we could do anything' (British female activist) (O'Donnell 2010, 375). The same year – 1968 – is also meaningful in the identity building of the Estonian elite of the same generation. Members of Estonian cultural and political elite, especially those who were politically active students at the University of Tartu in the mid-1960s (see e. g. Alatalu 2012; Lauristin and Vihalemm 1998; Veidemann 1996), often stress the importance of the 'golden sixties' in the construction of their identities. The members of this group draw parallels between themselves and their political generation counterpart in Western Europe and the United States.[25] The view of the 1960s as a period of 'tangible' freedom after Stalinism has also prevailed in the public discourse. For those politically and culturally active at that time, the time from 1960s until the end of the Prague Spring represent engagement in the revival of society. It seems that in the context of self-identification through politics, the 'we-group' was defined by a social group rather than gender, for it emerges as topical only in the accounts of prominent intellectuals. In contrast, in the unpublished life stories interpreted in this article, politics remains marginal even for those narrators who studied at universities at that time.

In the following example, the narrator refers to her personal life around 1968 – getting to know her husband, giving birth to her first child, and continuing with her studies while temporarily giving up her child to an orphanage – while politics remains in the background.

> At that time, there were those Czech events and leaflets were being handed out, and there were people who spied on one another. Some of them were very active, but they were known and in their presence no discussion was held. I still have a negative attitude towards them and even now when I hear some of those names [in some context], I will immediately think that he/she was the one who reported about others. But all of this didn´t affect me so directly and was not 'my thing.' My own personal life was more important. (Valli, b. in 1943, life story submitted in 2001, KM EKLA F. 350, 1229, 7)

Political activism does not seem to have been a prerequisite for believing in a better future; such a belief appears to have been cherished irrespective of one's gender or social class. Jaak Allik, an intellectual who was born in 1946 into a family of well-known communists and was an established politician and cultural figure in the late Soviet and post-Soviet eras, has suggested a similar view, describing the essence of his generation as follows:

> But our generation had another attitude towards the prevailing codswallop (as did the successive generation, born in the mid-1950s). We were quite utopian; we wanted to make the world a better place. We hoped that our actions would effect change. (Jaak Allik, interviewed by Jaanika Jaanits, Tallinn, 7 April 2009)

The issue of generational belonging also becomes evident in the reception of published autobiographical texts. Leelo Tungal's (2008) memoir 'Comrade Child and Grownups,' subtitled 'Another story about a happy childhood' has been the most popular among these autobiographical texts. The author's contemporaries receive the book as a story about an ordinary, happy childhood as the title suggests (Läänemets 2008; Reidolv 2008). For example, a lifelong schoolteacher who looks at the book through a generational prism sees in it – as she states in a review in 'Teachers newspaper' – her own and her contemporaries' life experiences that still have not found recognition in public memory discourse:

> Although today it is very common to curse the Soviet time, one should understand that moral virtues and family are valued at all times... [–] This [the book 'Comrade Child'] is the story of this generation. (Urve, b. in 1947, in Läänemets 2008)[26]

In their stories, women born in the 1940s gave expression to their belonging to a certain generational group, although they did not connect the shared belonging with a historical event or action. Generational consciousness is expressed through their common belief in a better future during late socialism, as well as their nostalgic evaluation of the late Soviet everyday life, which thus provides an alternative to the prevailing discourse on the Soviet period. Thus, the themes explored above illustrate the complex role of nostalgia in the life-writing of the 'Silent Generation.' The nostalgic recollection of their idealistic youth strengthens the construction of self-continuity of the life story writers by placing their experience into the collective framework of the generation. The framework of the generation, which is supported by public texts and the transnational perspective promoted by the elite, enables universalization of 'idealistic youth' and detachment of this experience from a specifically Soviet context. At the same time, this picture of 'idealistic youth' deepens the tension between the dominant post-Soviet memory discourse and the discourse represented by those born in the 1940s, thematizing the positive experience of ideology where it is publicly omitted.

Conclusion

In Estonian public memory, the experiences of some generations are more dominant than those of others. In the process of reestablishing independence at the end of 1980s the memoirs of those born in the 1920s were highly valued (Kõresaar 2005) and it is only quite recently that later generations have started to add their meanings to the Soviet past using various cultural tools (Grünberg 2009; Jõesalu and Nugin 2012; Nugin 2010; Jõesalu and Kõresaar 2013). This article examined autobiographical accounts of women born in the 1940s through a generational prism.

Relying on the earlier works of Kelly (2007) and Silies (2007, 2009), the article argued that besides the importance of political and public events, experiences from private life also influence the formation of generational consciousness. Until the new millennium, the experiences of those born in the 1940s remained in the background in public discourse. Thus, this generation can be described as a 'Silent Generation.'

By responding to a life-writing initiative at the beginning of the new millennium, narrators born in the 1940s add new facets to the established discourse about the Soviet period. Concentrating on their experiences from the era of late socialism, the respondents do not contribute to the discourse of the 'long rupture,' but rather undermine the dominant historical narrative, such as questioning the role of the partisans as freedom fighters.

The life stories discussed also give a more nuanced perspective to Estonia in the 1990s. The dominant view inside and outside of Estonia has been Estonia's success – the country has primarily been presented to the outside world as an example of successful liberal transformation, which is also the story endorsed by politicians within Estonia. Women born in the 1940s have represented the 1990s as a time of hardship and a period during which everything was turned upside down, asked critical questions about the reforms in process. Retrospective public discourse has mostly been critical of Soviet work experiences, yet the narrators set a high value on their work contributions during the Soviet era. When recounting their life during late socialism, they want to claim recognition for their experiences that have not been praised publicly. As one of the respondents ironically states: 'Many "talents" of my generation and the previous generation have lived their lives in unfortunate ways' (Helja, b. in 1947, KM EKLA F. 350, 1343, 33).

The narrators offer a counter-memory of the Soviet time that is manifest in their accounts via nostalgia. For example, nostalgia is expressed in the stories through the value attributed to the experience of work. It is this nostalgia that creates an *esprit de corps*, which is a phenomenon also observable in other contexts (e.g. Janelle Wilson, cit. Kõresaar 2008, 762).

As shown, some features are common in the women's stories, such as seeking a balance between the public and the private spheres, and managing the everyday. Through these topics, the narrators present their coping skills in the everyday atmosphere of Soviet reality, referring to values that have not received proper recognition in the public discourse, giving expression to the collective memory culture of the Soviet time.

Generational consciousness also becomes apparent in the stories, which is expressed through a belief in a better future and through the self-evaluation of the women as good workers. These life stories, sent from one age group to the ECHA at the beginning of the new millennium, represent the tendency of being more inclusive in recognizing the memories about the Soviet past. Opening up the narrated experiences of this age group may broaden and diversify the memories about the Soviet past in Estonian post-Soviet memory culture in general, bringing into focus the experiences of those whose voices have not received a hearing until recently.

Notes

1. This is a quote from Romain Rolland's novel *Colas Breugnon* that has actually been used by other groups of life storywriters (e.g. by Siberian survivors, see Kirss 2005, 34). I would like to thank Aigi Rahi-Tamm, who directed me to this source.
2. On the discourse of the long rupture, see Kõresaar (2005).
3. We have analyzed the dynamic of the meaning of the 'mature or late socialism: in Estonian post-Soviet memory culture, within which we also looked at generational differences and where the 1940s served as an example (see Jõesalu and Kõresaar 2013). Here, I will broaden my argument, giving a detailed overview of women born in the 1940s.

4. On nostalgia in an Estonian context, see Grünberg (2008), Kõresaar (2008), Jõesalu and Kõresaar (2013), Jõesalu and Nugin (2012).
5. I am relying here on the observations made by Daphne Berdahl, who described nostalgia, which began to appear in East Germany in the first half of the 1990s, as a kind of counter-memory to the hegemonic western discourse about the communist past (Berdahl and Bunzl 2010, 55–56).
6. He relies here on the broad research in generational studies, especially that conducted in Germany, for example, Bude (1987, 1995), Reulecke and Müller-Luckner (2003). Mannheim's initial work was published in 1923 in the essay 'The Problem of Generations,' which gained recognition after World War II, and has been very influential in the research on generations ever since.
7. Silies analyzed the 'Silent Generation' through the example of the use of the pill by women born in the 1940s (Silies 2007, 2009). It should be stressed here that the everyday (bodily) – experiences of women in Western Europe and those from the same cohort in Soviet Estonia were different. In this context, see a very interesting collection of articles on the topic of gender and generation edited by Sokolová and Kolářová (2007).
8. In the example of East Germany for those who were born in 1949 – the founding year of the German Democratic Republic (GDR) – no generational consciousness has formed in the political sense, although the possibility for that through a political event – the building of the Berlin Wall – was present. (Weisbrod 2007; Wierling 2002).
9. Mary Fulbrook noticed that those who were 'born into' and grew up in East Germany had not questioned the East German reality (Fulbrook 2011, 358).
10. Aside from the collection of Cultural History Archives at the Literary Museum, another collection, consisting of thematic written narratives, is stored at the Estonian National Museum.
11. One example, however, is Jaago (2008).
12. I have also read other life stories that have been sent to the Cultural History Archives since the beginning of the twenty-first century by women born in the 1940s. The campaigns organized during the first decade of this century were more focused on one topic. Also, responses sent to the Archives concentrate more on remediating memories (sometimes remediating other people's experiences) about this narrower topic, while life history remains in the background (e.g. life-writing campaigns such as 'The Impact of War in My Life and in Our Family Life' (Sõja mõjud minu ja meie pere elus), 'Life during the German Time' (Elu Saksa ajal), 'My Life and the Life of My Next of Kin in a Changed Landscape' (Minu ja minu lähedaste elu keset muutunud ümbrust) 'Societies in My Life' (Seltsid minu elus)). Some narrators have sent their stories repeatedly, in response to various campaigns.
13. While unemployment benefit was 400 Estonian Kroons (approximately €25) per month in 1999, the average pension was approximately 1550 Kroons (99€).
14. Partisans, known in Estonia and in other Baltic States as Forest Brothers, fought against Soviet power in the woods and villages after World War II. In the historiography of the 1990s they have been attributed a special place as freedom fighters.
15. Aarelaid-Tart (b. 1947) starts her article with two recollections from her childhood, where she reminiscences about her fear of the partisans, and her understanding of what 'kulak' meant. She has provocatively titled this part of her article 'of my memory and historical truth' (Aarelaid-Tart 2012a).
16. It is also true that many women worked in the domestic sphere in Estonia during the 1930s; being a working mother is more the experience of the narrators themselves. According to the law from 1932, it was forbidden for women to work for the state or local government, or in schools, if their husband was employed by the state (Pihlamägi 2006, 134). I do not have any statistics about the employment rate of women before the Soviet era (which is not my purpose here), but the topic of public–private relationship does comes up in the narratives, especially in the stories of those born in the 1940s.
17. Eesti ajal – During the Estonian Time – refers here to the Estonian Republic before World War II, 1918–1940.
18. On nostalgia as a mode of facilitating continuity see Sedikides, et al. (2008), Wilson (2005).
19. Life-continuity is a notion used in life story and biographical research, 'One crucial process is autobiographical memory: I remember being me. A central function of autobiographical memory is to help individuals to maintain self-continuity' (see more in Bluck and Alea 2008).

20. In a similar way, a man born in 1947 generalizes his own postwar experience of poor living conditions into an experience common for the whole generation: 'There is nothing special to remember from my childhood. It was the postwar era, and this definitely left its mark'. I have sometimes joked with my peers that since the war veterans during the Russian time were made into a nice privileged class, with all kinds of special benefits, then why shouldn't we, the postwar generation, raise our heads now and demand some preferences and benefits for ourselves, because we grew up in such difficult circumstances, which left their mark (Koit, b. in 1947, ERE III, 240).
21. In many stories, it is stressed that the majority of the teachers at primary school level were from the previous system.
22. On the 'double burden' of Soviet women, see for example, Lapidus (1978).
23. Aleida Assmann underlined in a lecture that until the 1980s, the time regime was focused on the future in Western societies; since then, the time regime shifted toward the past (Aleida Assmann in public lecture Theories of Cultural Memory and the Concept of 'Afterlife,' 2 November 2012, at Tallinn University, see also Huyssen 2000).
24. VTK here means compulsory norms in physical education in Soviet society. The abbreviation VTK stands for 'Ready for Work and Defence!' ('Valmis tööks ja kaitseks!').
25. On the '1968' generation and oral history, see Hajek (2013); on 1968 in the German space, see for example, Bude (1995).
26. In the cultural sphere, texts dealing with the 'hard' past are not entirely absent (e.g. novels by Ene Mihkelson, b. in 1944, see on 'Duty of Remembering' in Sakova 2010).

Acknowledgments

This research was supported, in its various stages, by the Estonian Science Foundation (Grant 8190 and 9130), by the institutional research funding IUT34-32 of the Estonian Ministry of Education and Research, and by the European Union through its European Regional Development Fund (Centre of Excellence of Cultural Theory). I want to thank the two anonymous reviewers for their helpful comments and suggestions on earlier drafts of this article and Ene Kõresaar and Ene-Reet Soovik for their suggestions at the final stage of writing.

Disclosure statement

No potential conflict of interest was reported by the author.

References

Aarelaid-Tart, A. 2006. *Cultural Trauma and Life Stories*. Helsinki: Kikimora Publishers.
Aarelaid-Tart, A. 2012a. "Sõjajärgselt sündinute elude metamorfoosid. Ühe kursuse lugu [Metamorphoses of the Lives of Post-war Generation. The Story of a Class]." In *Nullindate kultuur II: Põlvkondlikud pihtimused* [The Culture of 2000s II: Generational Confessions], edited by A. Aarelaid-Tart, and A. Kannike, 56–79. Tartu: Tartu University Press.
Aarelaid-Tart, A. 2012b. "Nõukogude aeg nähtuna erinevate mälu-kogukondade silmade läbi [Soviet Past Through the Lenses of Different Communities of Memory]." *Acta Historica Tallinnensia* 18 (1): 142–158. doi:10.3176/hist.2012.1.06.

Alatalu, T. 2012. "Mälestused. Tartu Ülikooli esimesed üliõpilaspäevad said alguse Käärikult ja KVNi abil [Memoirs. The First Student Days of University of Tartu had their Beginning in Kääriku with Help of KVN]." *Tartu Ülikooli ajaloo küsimusi* XXXX: 216–231.

Anderson, B. A., and R. Võõrmann. 1996. "Women and Equality of the Sexes in Estonia." *International Journal of Sociology* 26 (3): 76–95.

Bela, B. 2009. "Elulood läti ühiskonna uurimise allikana [Life Stories in the Research of Latvian Society]." *Mäetagused* 43: 159–180. doi:10.7592/MT.

Berdahl, D., and M. Bunzl. 2010. *On the Social Life of Postsocialism: Memory, Consumption, Germany.* Bloomington: Indiana University Press.

Bloch, A. 2005. "Longing for the Kollektiv: Gender, Power, and Residential Schools in Central Siberia." *Cultural Anthropology* 20 (4): 534–569. doi:10.1525/can.2005.20.issue-4.

Bluck, S., and N. Alea. 2008. "Remembering Being Me: The Self-Continuity Function of Autobiographical Memory in Younger and Older Adults." In *Self-continuity: Individual and Collective Perspectives*, edited by F. Sani, 55–70. New York: Psychology Press.

Boyer, D. 2010. "From Algos to Autonomos: Nostalgic Eastern Europe as Postimperial Mania." In *Post-Communist Nostalgia*, edited by M. Todorova, and Z. Gille, 17–28. New York: Berghahn.

Bude, H. 1987. *Deutsche Karrieren: Lebenskonstruktionen sozialer Aufsteiger aus der Flakhelfer-Generation* [German Careers: Life Construction of Social Upward-Climbers from Flakhelfer Generation.]. Frankfurt am Main: Suhrkamp.

Bude, H. 1995. *Das Altern einer Generation. Die Jahrgänge 1938 bis 1948* [Aging of One Generation. The Cohorts of 1938–1948]. Frankfurt am Main: Suhrkamp.

Corsten, M. 1999. "The Time of Generations." *Time & Society* 8 (2–3): 249–272. doi:10.1177/0961463X99008002003.

Creed, G. W. 2010. "Strange Bedfellows: Socialist Nostalgia and Neoliberalism in Bulgaria." In *Post-Communist Nostalgia*, edited by M. Todorova, and Z. Gille, 29–45. New York: Berghahn.

Davoliūtė, V. 2005. "Deportee Memoirs and Lithuanian History: The Double Testimony of Dalia Grinkevičiūtė." *Journal of Baltic Studies* 36 (1): 51–68. doi:10.1080/01629770400000241.

Elksnis Geisler, I. 2011. "The Gendered Plight of Terror: Annexation and Exile in Latvia 1940—1950." Dissertation, Michigan State University.

Fulbrook, M. 2011. *Dissonant Lives. Generations and Violence through the German Dictatorships.* Oxford: Oxford University Press.

Grünberg, K. 2008. "Andrus Kivirähki/Taago Tubina lavastus 'Helesinine vagun' (2003) – sissevaade vene multikate põlvkonna hinge? [The Andrus Kivirähk/Taago Tubin Production of the Play 'Light Blue Wagon' (2003). A Look Into the Soul of the Generation that Grew up With Russian Cartoons]" *Eesti Rahva Muuseumi Aastaraamat* 51: 13–46.

Grünberg, K. 2009. "Remembering the Soviet Past in Estonia. The Case of the Nostalgic Comedy 'The Light Blue Wagon'." *Atslēgvārdi/Keywords* 1: 1–16.

Hajek, A., ed. 2013. *Memory Studies. Special Issue. Challenging Dominant Discourses of the Past: 1968 and the Value of Oral History.* Vol. 6(1). London: Sage.

Hansson, L. 2003. "Women on the Estonian Labour Market: Continuity and Change." In *Gender Equality in Central and Eastern European Countries*, edited by M. E. Domsch, D. H. Ladwig, and E. Tenten, 133–150. Frankfurt am Main: Peter Lang.

Helemäe, J., and E. Saar. 2006. "Women's Employment in Estonia." In *Globalization, Uncertainty and Women's Careers: An International Comparison*, edited by H.-P. Blossfeld, and H. Hofmeister, 199–233. Northampton: Edward Elgar Publishing.

Hinrikus, R., and E. Kõresaar. 2004. "A Brief Overview of Life History Collection and Research in Estonia." In *She Who Remembers, Survives. Interpreting Estonian Women's Post-Soviet Life Stories*, edited by T. Kirss, E. Kõresaar, and M. Lauristin, 19–34. Tartu: Tartu University Press.

Huyssen, A. 2000. "Present Pasts: Media, Politics, Amnesia." *Public Culture* 12 (1): 21–38. doi:10.1215/08992363-12-1-21.

Issioupova, O. 2000. "From Duty to Pleasure? Motherhood in Soviet and post-Soviet Russia." In *Gender, State and Society in Soviet and Post-Soviet Russia*, edited by S. Ashwin, 30–55. London: Routledge.

Jaago, T. 2006. "What Happened in Fact? Narratives about the 20th Century Events from the Viewpoint of Oral History." *E-Lore* 13 (1): 1–23.

Jaago, T. 2008. "Ruumi kujutamine eluloos: küsimus tõsielujutustuse žanris [Depiction of Space in Life Writing: the Problem of Genre]." In *Ruumi loomine. Artikleid keskkonna kujutamisest tekstides*

[Creating Space: Articles On the depiction of the Environment in Texts], edited by T. Jaago, 99–199. Tartu: Tartu University Press.

Jõesalu, K. 2003. "Elitaarne kogemus rahvuslikust liikumisest 1980. aastatel." In *Mälu kui kultuuritegur: Etnoloogilisi perspektiive* [Memory as Culture Factor: Ethnological Perspectives], edited by E. Kõresaar, and T. Anepaio, 179–205. Tartu: Tartu University Press.

Jõesalu, K. 2012. "The Role of the Soviet Past in Post-Soviet Memory Politics through Examples of Speeches from Estonian Presidents." *Europe-Asia Studies* 64 (6): 1007–1032. doi:10.1080/09668136.2012.691723.

Jõesalu, K., and E. Kõresaar. 2011. "Working through Mature Socialism: Private and Public in the Estonians' Meaning-making of the Soviet Past." In *Baltic Biographies at Historical Crossroads*, edited by L. Bennich-Björkman, and A. Aarelaid-Tart, 68–85. London: Routledge.

Jõesalu, K., and E. Kõresaar. 2013. "Continuity or Discontinuity: On the Dynamics of Remembering 'Mature Socialism' in Estonian Post-Soviet Remembrance Culture." *Journal of Baltic Studies* 44 (2): 177–203. doi:10.1080/01629778.2013.775849.

Jõesalu, K., and R. Nugin. 2012. "Reproducing Identity through Remembering: Cultural Texts on the Late Soviet Period." *Folklore. Electronic Journal of Folklore* 51: 15–48. doi:10.7592/FEJF2012.51.joesalu-nugin.

Katus, K., A. Puur, and L. Sakkeus. 2005. "Transition to Adulthood in Estonia: Evidence from the FFS." In *The Transition to Adulthood in a Globalizing World: A Comparison of Fourteen Countries*, edited by H.-P. Blossfeld, and E. Klijzing, 215–248. London: Routlede.

Kelly, C. 2007. "'Good Night, Little Ones': Childhood in the 'Last Soviet Generation'." In *Generations in Twentieth-Century Europe*, edited by S. Lovell, 165–189. New York: Palgrave Macmillan.

Kirss, T. 2004. "Three Generations of Estonian Women: Selves, Lives, Texts." In *She Who Remembers Survives. Interpreting Estonian Women's Post-Soviet Life Stories*, edited by T. Kirss, E. Kõresaar, and M. Lauristin, 122–133. Tartu: Tartu University Press.

Kirss, T. 2005. "Survivorship and the Eastern Exile: Estonian Women's Life Narratives of the 1941 and 1949 Siberian Deportations." *Journal of Baltic Studies* 36 (1): 13–38. doi:10.1080/01629770400000221.

Kirss, T., ed. 2009. *Estonian Life Stories*. Budapest: Central European University Press.

Kirss, T., E. Kõresaar, and M. Lauristin, eds. 2004. *She Who Remembers Survives. Interpreting Estonian Women's Post-Soviet Life Stories*. Tartu: Tartu University Press.

KM EKLA F. 350. *The Estonian Life Stories Association's Collection of Written Life Stories Since 1989*. Tartu. Estonian Cultural History Archives in the Estonian Literary Museum. Unpublished materials.

Kõresaar, E. 2003. "Die Normativität des 'guten Lebens'. Autobiographische Erinnerungen an die sowjetische Periode in Estland [The Normativity of 'Good Life'. Autobiographical Memories of Soviet Period in Estonia]." *BIOS: Zeitschrift für Biographieforschung und Oral History* 16: 111–134.

Kõresaar, E. 2004. "Towards a Social Memory of Work. Politics and Being a Good Teacher in Soviet Teachers' Biographies." In *Arbeit im Sozialismus - Arbeit im Postsozialismus. Erkundungen der Arbeitswelt im östlichen Europa*, edited by K. Roth, 290–310. Münster: Lit-Verlag.

Kõresaar, E. 2005. *Elu ideoloogiad. Kollektiivne mälu ja autobiograafiline minevikutõlgendus eestlaste elulugudes* [Ideologies of Life. Collective Memory and Autobiographical Meaning-Making of the Past in Estonian Post-Soviet Life Stories]. Tartu: Estonian National Museum.

Kõresaar, E. 2008. "Nostalgia ja selle puudumine eestlaste mälukultuuris: Eluloouurija vaatepunkt [Nostalgia and its Absence in Estonian Culture of Remembrance: a Gaze of a Life Story Researcher]." *Keel ja Kirjandus* 10: 760–771.

Kõresaar, E. 2011. "Boris Takk – The Ambiguity of War in a Post-Soviet Life Story." In *Soldiers of Memory: World War II and Its Aftermath in Estonian post-Soviet Life Stories*, edited by E. Kõresaar, 343–363. New York: Rodopi.

Kõresaar, E., and K. Jõesalu (2016). "Post-Soviet Memories and 'Memory Shifts' in Estonia", *Oral History* 44 (2): 47-58, *Theme Number "Oral History on the Move"*, edited by A. Heimo, A.-K. Kuusisto-Arponen, and U. Savolainen.

Läänemets, U. 2008. "Krutskitega raamat [A Book with Bag of Tricks]." *Õpetajate Leht* 12: 28. March: 21.

Laar, M. 1993. *Metsavennad* [Forest Brothers]. Tallinn: Helmet Raja.

Laar, M. 2007. *The Forgotten War: Armed Resistance Movement in Estonia in 1944–1956*. Tallinn: Grenader.

Lapidus, G. W. 1978. *Women in Soviet Society. Equality, Development and Social Change*. Berkeley: University of California Press.

Lauristin, M. 2004. "Lives and Ideologies: A Sociologist's View on the Life Stories of Two Female Tractor-Drivers." In *She Who Remembers Survives: Interpreting Estonian Women's Post-Soviet Life Stories*, edited by T. Kirss, E. Kõresaar, and M. Lauristin, 178–202. Tartu: Tartu University Press.

Lauristin, M. 2010. *Punane ja sinine. Peatükke kirjutamata elulooraamatust* [Red and Blue. Chapters from Unwritten Autobiography]. Tallinn: Eesti Ajalehed.

Lauristin, M., and P. Vihalemm. 1998. "Tartu 1968. Kolmkümmend aastat hiljem [Tartu 1968. Thirty Years Later]." *Looming* 9: 1386–1398.

Lauristin, M., and P. Vihalemm. 2009. "Internal and External Factors Influencing Estonian Public Agenda during Two Decades of Post-Communist Transformation." *Journal of Baltic Studies* 40 (1): 1–29. doi:10.1080/01629770902722237.

Lazda, M. 2005. "Women, Nation, and Survival: Latvian Women in Siberia 1941–1957." *Journal of Baltic Studies* 36 (1): 1–12. doi:10.1080/01629770400000211.

Leinarte, D. 2010. *Adopting and Remembering Soviet Reality. Life Stories of Lithuanian Women, 1945–1970.* Amsterdam: Rodopi.

Lember, U. 2007. "Domesticating the Soviet Regime. Autobiographic Experiences of the "Post-War" Generation in Estonia." MA Thesis, submitted to Central European University, History Department.

Malysheva, M., and D. Bertaux. 1996. "The Social Experiences of a Countrywoman in Soviet Russia." In *Gender and Memory, International Yearbook of Oral History and Life Stories,* edited by S. Leydersdorff, L. Passerini, and P. Thompson, 31–43. Vol. IV. Oxford: Oxford University Press.

Niethammer, L. 2005. "Die letzte Gemeinschaft. Über die Konstruierbarkeit von Generationen und ihre Grenzen [The Last Community. On the Construction of Generations and its Borders]." Vortrag bei der Eröffnungsveranstaltung des Göttinger Graduiertenkollegs *Generationengeschichte – Generationelle Dynamik und historischer Wandel im 19. und 20. Jahrhundert,* November 11. Accessed February 12, 2016 http://www.generationengeschichte.uni-goettingen.de/alt/niethammer.pdf.

Nugin, R. 2010. "Social Time as the Basis of Generational Consciousness." *Trames. Journal of the Humanities and Social Sciences* 14 (4): 342–366. doi:10.3176/tr.2010.4.04.

Nugin, R. 2015. *The 1970s: Portrait of a Generation at the Doorstep.* Tartu: University of Tartu Press.

O'Donnell, M. 2010. "Generation and Utopia: Using Mannheim's Concepts to Understand 1960s Radicalism." *Young* 18 (4): 367–383. doi:10.1177/110330881001800401.

Parla, A. 2009. "Remembering Across the Border: Postsocialist Nostalgia among Turkish Immigrants from Bulgaria." *American Ethnologist* 36 (4): 750–767. doi:10.1111/j.1548-1425.2009.01208.x.

Pető, A. 2010. "Anti-Modernist Political Thoughts on Motherhood in Europe in a Historical Perspective." In *Reframing Demographic Change in Europe: Perspectives on Gender and Welfare State Transformations,* edited by H. Kahlert, and E. Waltraud, 189–201. Münster: Lit Verlag.

Petrovic, T. 2010. *Nostalgia for the JNA? Remembering the Army in the former Yugoslavia.* New York: Berghahn.

Pihlamägi, M. 2006. "Tööpuudusest Eesti Vabariigis aastail 1918–1940 [On Unemployment in Estonian Republic, 1918-1940]." *Acta Historica Tallinnensia* 10: 121–141.

Pine, F. 2002. "Retreat to the Household? Gendered Domains in Post-Socialist Poland." In *Postsocialism: Ideals, Ideologies and Practices in Eurasia,* edited by C. Hann, 95–113. London: Routledge.

Raleigh, D. J. 2012. *Soviet Baby Boomers. An Oral History of Russia's Cold War Generation.* Oxford: Oxford University Press.

Reidolv, M. 2008. "Ühe põlvkonna lapsepõlve lugu [The Childhood Story of One Generation]." *Õpetajate leht* 16: 25. April: 15.

Reulecke, J., and E. Müller-Luckner, eds. 2003. *Generationalität und Lebensgeschichte im 20. Jahrhundert* [Generationality and Life History in 20. Century]. München: Oldenbourg Wissenschaften.

Roth, K., ed. 2004. *Arbeit im Sozialismus – Arbeit im Postsozialismus. Erkundungen zum Arbeitsleben im östlichen Europa.* Münster: Lit-Verlag.

Sakova, A. 2010. "Kohustus kannatada, et näha ja mõista. Ene Mihkelsoni ja Ingeborg Bachmanni kirjanikunägemus [The Writer's Duty to Suffer in Order to See and Understand: The Literary Vision of Ene Mihkelson and Ingeborg Bachmann]." *Methis. Studia humaniora Estonica* 5/6: 111–121.

Sebre, S. 2005. "Political and Relational: Autobiographical Narrations of Latvian Women across Three Generations." *Journal of Baltic Studies* 36 (1): 69–82. doi:10.1080/01629770400000251.

Sedikides, C., T. Wildschut, L. Gaertner, C. Routledge, and J. Arndt. 2008. "Nostalgia as Enabler of Self-continuity." In *Self-continuity: Individual and Collective Perspectives,* edited by F. Sani, 227–239. New York: Psychology Press.

Silies, E.-M. 2007. "'Love is all around'. The Pill as a Female Generational Experience in 1960s and 1970s West Germany." In *Gender and Generation: Interdisciplinary Intersections and Perspectives,* edited by K. Kolářová, and V. Sokolová, 21–38. Prague: Litteraria Pragensia.

Silies, E.-M. 2009. "Die stille Generation mit der Pille. Verhütung als weibliche Generationserfahrung in England und der Bundesrepublik (1960–1975) [The Silent Generation with the Pill. Contraception as

Female Generational Experience in England and in Federal Republic of Germany]." In *Historische Beiträge zur Generationsforschung*, edited by B. Weisbrod, 77–116. Göttingen: Wallstein.

Sokolová, V., and K. Kolářová. 2007. "Gender and Generation in Mutual Perspective." In *Gender and Generation: Interdisciplinary Intersections and Perspectives*, edited by K. Kolářová, and V. Sokolová, 1–20. Prague: Litteraria Pragensia.

Sotsiaalministeerium. 2016. "Sotsiaalministeeriumi Soolise Võrdõiguslikkuse Büroo." *Tööhõives osalemine.*

Tarand, M. 2008. *Ajapildi sees. Lapsepõlv Juhaniga* [Inside a picture-story. Childhood with Juhan]. Tartu: Greif.

Todorova, M. 2010. "Introduction. From Utopia to Propaganda and Back." In *Post-Communist Nostalgia*, edited by M. Todorova, and Z. Gille, 1–13. New York: Berghahn.

Todorova, M., and Z. Gille, eds. 2010. *Post-Communist Nostalgia*. Oxford: Berghahn.

Tulviste, P. 1994. "History Taught at School Versus History Discovered at Home: The Case of Estonia." *European Journal of Psychology of Education* 9 (2): 121–126. doi:10.1007/BF03173547.

Tungal, L. 2008. *Seltsimees Laps* [Comrade Child]. Tallinn: Tänapäev.

Tungal, L. 2009. *Samet ja saepuru. Ehk Seltsimees laps ja kirjatähed* [Velvet and Sawdust Or Comrade Child and the ABC]. Tallinn: Tänapäev.

Vahtre, L. 2002. *Elu-olu viimasel vene ajal. Riietus ja mööbel, toit ja tarberiistad, sõiduvahendid, eluase ja muu* [Everyday Life during the Last Russian Time. Clothing and Furniture, Food and Household Utensils, Vehicles, Dwellings and Other]. Tartu: Kirjastuskeskus.

Veidemann, R. 1996. *Ajavahe* [Timespan]. Pärnu: Trükk.

Velikonja, M. 2008. *Titonostalgia. A Study of Nostalgia for Josip Broz*. Ljubljana: Peace Institute.

Weisbrod, B. 2007. "Cultures of Change: Generations in the Politics and Memory of Modern Germany." In *Generations in Twentieth-Century Europe*, edited by S. Lovell, 19–35. New York: Palgrave Macmillan.

Wierling, D. 2002. *Geboren im Jahr Eins. Der Geburtsjahrgang 1949 – Versuch einer Kollektivbiographie* [Born in Year One. The Cohort of 1949 – An Attempt of Collective Biography]. Berlin: Ch. Links Verlag.

Wilson, J. 2005. *Nostalgia. Sanctuary of Meaning*. Lewisburg: Bucknell University Press.

Yurchak, A. 2005. *Everything Was Forever, Until It Was No More. The Last Soviet Generation*. Princeton: Princeton University Press.

Index